CANADA'S GREATEST MURDER CASE:
THE 1895 PROSECUTION OF THE HYAMS TWINS

BY

GEORGE R. DEKLE SR.

www.bobdeklebooks.com

TABLE OF CONTENTS

A NOTE ON SPELLING

The sources have given a multitude of spellings for the names of the various witnesses. Throughout the manuscript I have standardized the spellings to conform with the spelling used by the presiding judge, Justice William Street, in the notes he took on the trial.

The sources are in conflict as to the spelling of the word "defense." Some spell it with an "s," others with a "c." I have standardized the spelling by replacing "defence" with "defense" everywhere except in titles.

ACKNOWLEDGEMENTS

I would like to thank the following people and institutions for their assistance in the preparation of this book. Jennifer Grant, Archivist for the Clara Thomas Archives and Special Collections at the York University Library helped me obtain a copy of Edwin Guillet's manuscript, *Insurance Murderers.* Blythe Koreen, Archivist, of the Archives of Ontario, assisted me in obtaining a copy of Justice Street's Bench Book on the trial. Amber Lee and Patrick Foran, of the Nonfiction Writers Pod of the Gainesville Writers Alliance, read and critiqued portions of the manuscript. Mike Kane read and critiqued the entire manuscript. I am especially thankful to Dr. Martin Friedland, C.C., K.C, James M. Tory Professor of Law Emeritus at the Faculty of Law, University of Toronto Law School, for his gracious agreement to read and critique the full manuscript.

Were it not for the assistance of these individuals, this book would not have been possible.

INTRODUCTION

Were Harry and Dallas Hyams criminal masterminds who orchestrated one of Toronto's most bizarre murders? Or were they nincompoops whose bungling attempts to repair a rickety elevator created a perfect storm of circumstances leading to the accidental death of their employee?

The prominent journalist, Hector Charlesworth, pronounced them guilty. The eminent legal scholar, Albert Hassard, said they were innocent. And the respected historian, Edwin Guillet, sided with Charlesworth. Of the three juries that considered the case, the grand jury said guilty, the first petit jury hung despite unanimously agreeing that they were probably guilty, and the second petit jury said not guilty. Of course, "not guilty" does not mean "innocent;" it simply means that the jury had a what they believed to be a reasonable doubt about guilt.

Everyone can agree that the Hyams brothers were scoundrels, but did their treachery extend to murder? Did a botched investigation doom a legitimate prosecution? Did malicious prosecutors victimize innocent fall guys? Or did the unlimited funds of the brothers' wealthy relatives buy a not guilty verdict?

Whatever else is true about the case, it is true that the case was the most massive, most complex, most hotly contested murder trial in the history of Victorian Era Canada. Britton Bath Osler, Canada's greatest prosecutor, was lead counsel for the Crown. Francis L. Wellman, New York's greatest cross-examiner, oversaw the defense. Both men were supported by the most stellar teams of lawyers who had ever confronted each other in a Canadian courtroom.

We will attempt to answer the question of the Hyams brothers' guilt or innocence as we describe how Willie Wells was killed, how the brothers profited from his death, and how the

Crown decided to pursue charges two years after the death. We will describe the defense's pretrial jockeying for position, the Crown's presentation of the case, and the defense tactics which eventually got the brothers acquitted. We will discuss what the lawyers did right, what they did wrong, and how the actions and attitudes of the presiding judges influenced the eventual verdict. And finally, we will discuss whether justice was served in the case of *Queen v. Dallas and Harry Hyams*.

Erle Stanley Gardner, with his immortal character Perry Mason, created the mystery subgenre known as the "courtroom procedural." *Canada's Greatest Murder Case* is a courtroom procedural in the genre of true crime.

In describing the court proceedings, I frequently critique the performance of the lawyers involved. This does not mean that I think I could have done a better job of presenting the case than was done by these most talented men. I can recognize their mistakes because I made them all myself during my 42-year career as a criminal trial lawyer. I do think that I can shed some light on the trial with the aid of my experience, the leisure of not being in the pressure cooker of actually trying the case, and the benefit of 20/20 hindsight.

CHAPTER ONE:
LAWYER WELLMAN BREAKS A VOW

On February 26, 1895, Francis Wellman did something he vowed he would never do. The chain of events that led him to make his vow began in September of 1893 when District Attorney De Lancey Nicoll announced he would not run for reelection. Wellman wanted to succeed Nicoll in the office of Manhattan District Attorney. During his two years as Nicoll's Assistant District Attorney, Wellman had distinguished himself, winning many significant, hard-fought murder trials and gaining a reputation as a brilliant, incorruptible prosecutor. Becoming the District Attorney would be the next logical step in his legal career; but Richard Croker, the leader of the Tammany Hall political machine, didn't like him, and in Gilded Age New York City nobody could aspire to public office with any hope of success unless he had the blessing of Tammany Hall.

Nicoll did his best to lobby Croker on Wellman's behalf. Nicoll met Croker for supper on Friday, October 13, 1893, at the Windsor Hotel on Fifth Avenue, and there he made his case for Wellman. Croker told Nicoll in no uncertain terms that Wellman could not be Tammany's nominee, nor could Wellman continue as an Assistant under the new District Attorney.[1] It seemed that Wellman was far too unrelenting and vigorous a prosecutor to suit Croker.[2]

Croker ordained that the new District Attorney would be Colonel John R. Fellows, a good Tammany man. Fellows disappointed Croker not only by keeping Wellman but by keeping Nicoll's entire staff.[3] Under Fellows' leadership, Wellman continued to be a thorn in Tammany Hall's side and was able to exact some small vengeance. He helped bring about Tammany

---

[1] "Loew or Fitch?" *Evening World*, 4th ed., Oct. 17, 1893.
[2] "The District-Attorneyship," *Evening World*, 1st ed., Sept. 30, 1893.
[3] "Will Keep Mr. Nicoll's Staff," *Tribune*, December 16, 1893.

Hall's temporary fall from power in the next election by prosecuting corruption cases against high-ranking police officers. Wellman eventually tired of his political enemies' continued sniping at him, and he went into private practice in 1894.

Wellman had been a dedicated prosecutor, and he shuddered at the thought of defending criminal cases. He wrote in his memoirs, "After what I am pleased to call my graduation from the criminal courts and my entrance into private practice, I made up my mind I never again wanted to be connected directly or indirectly with any such heartrending dramas as are there enacted, with all the elemental passions of love, hatred, jealousy, greed, and revenge as their daily theme."[4] Although Wellman was an accomplished jury lawyer, he vowed never to defend a criminal case; he would try only civil cases.

The chain of events that caused Wellman to break his vow not to defend criminal cases began with a death in Toronto on January 16, 1893. It ended on the afternoon of February 26, 1895, when Wellman returned to his office after a hard day in court. On this February afternoon, he wanted to do what many trial lawyers do after the stress of trying a case—sit behind his desk and vegetate. It was not to be. Solomon Hyams, the eccentric recluse known as the "Hermit of the Gilsey House Hotel, had repeatedly telephoned for him while at court. Hyams' messages stated that he urgently needed to Wellman to see him at the hotel. The elderly man was so crippled with arthritis that he found it difficult to leave the confines of the luxury hotel.

---

[4] Wellman, *Gentlemen of the Jury,* 117.

FRANCIS L. WELLMAN[5]

Wellman debated what to do: Put Hyams off until tomorrow morning or pry his weary body from the comforts of his office chair and go to the hotel? As he mulled over the question, he recalled a story told him by the legendary trial advocate, Elihu Root, who later served as Secretary of War and Secretary of State, and won the Nobel Peace Prize for his service in negotiating over 20 international treaties.

Root told Wellman he was luxuriating after hours in the comfort of his office chair when he heard a knocking on the private entrance door that led directly into his office. He initially ignored the knocking. But it continued. Root contemplated answering it and saying, "You blockhead! Can't you read? Can't you see the word 'private' on the door?" Deciding that a soft answer turns away wrath, Root kept his personal thoughts to himself, answered the door, and treated his persistent caller politely. Had Root followed his first instincts to turn the caller away, he might have missed out on a very lucrative case.

---

[5] *Toronto World*, February 28, 1895.

The recollection of Root's story persuaded Wellman that he should go to the hotel to meet Hyams. When he arrived at the hotel and inquired after Hyams, the front desk directed him to a luxurious private suite. If a man could afford to live in such a suite, he had to have a lot of money. Hyams sat in a plush easy chair, drinking expensive bourbon from a bottle on a side table. Wellman could tell from the man's nervousness that he was fretting over a monumental problem. Hyams fidgeted a moment, and then abruptly began to tell his story:

He and his brother, Chapman Hyams, a prominent New Orleans banker, had two wayward relatives, twin brothers, who were arrested in Toronto, Canada, and charged with dropping a 200-pound elevator weight on the head of one of their employees. Hyams was a prominent name in Louisiana politics; one of their ancestors had been Lieutenant Governor during the Civil War. The family's honor could not be stained by the conviction of two family members for murder.

Wellman asked, "When should I leave for Canada?"

"I want you to start tonight." Hyams was emphatic.

"That's a little sudden," Wellman objected. "It's already six o'clock. Also, you do realize it will be rather expensive if you send me to Canada on such short notice?"

"Blankety blank your soul to Hell!" Hyams shouted as he levered himself from his chair, "Did I say anything about expense? I said I want you to go to Canada *tonight*!"[6]

Wellman smiled. There was money in this case. Enough money to break his vow and defend a criminal case. "If you talk like that," he said, "you can send me to China if you want to."

Wellman, his wife, the famous opera singer Emma Juch, and his law partner, W.W. Gooch, boarded a train for Toronto that very night. Wellman's decision to forswear his oath proved to be

---

[6] Wellman, *Luck and Opportunity*, 91.

a profitable one. He received US$40,000 for his work on the case.[7] Adjusted for inflation, that sum equals US$1,448,223.81 in 2023 currency.[8]

This account varies from the account Wellman gave in his memoir *Luck and Opportunity*. He took pains to try to conceal the identities of his clients by not mentioning their names and by fudging the facts of his engagement on the case. He pretended that the man he met at the hotel had just arrived in New York and was unknown to him. In truth, Solomon Hyams was a well-known resident of New York City. Despite Wellman's attempts at concealment, it was an easy task to identify the case he was talking about by going to online archives of Canadian newspapers and searching for "Wellman," "murder," and "elevator." My search led to discovering the most sensational, most complex, longest murder case ever to be tried in Victorian-Era Toronto. The newspapers of the time called it Canada's Greatest Trial.

---

[7] Bostwick, et. al, ed., *The Brief*, 2:372

[8] "Millions in Fees," *Dallas Morning News*, October 5, 1899); CPI Inflation Calculator, https://www.officialdata.org/us/inflation/1895?amount=40000.

CHAPTER TWO:
JOURNALIST CHARLESWORTH BREAKS A STORY

One evening in the last week of January 1895, *Toronto World* journalist Hector Charlesworth trudged down the streets towards his newsroom. He would eventually become one of the most respected Canadian journalists of the early twentieth century,[1] but on this night he was merely a dejected young reporter. Weary from a fruitless day of chasing a story, he dreaded the prospect of reporting to his editor that his efforts had yielded nothing newsworthy. As he neared the *World's* office building, he chanced to meet his old friend Samuel Smoke, a young lawyer whom he had known since childhood. They greeted each other and stood on the street corner exchanging pleasantries for a while, until Charlesworth said, "Look here, can you give me an item? I haven't struck anything for days and will be losing my job soon."[2]

"I know a big story," Smoke said. "Insurance conspiracy. Come and see me tomorrow."

Charlesworth promised to go to Smoke's office the next day and walked on to the newsroom with a spring in his step. When he met with news editor Walter Wilkinson, he gave a full report of his conversation with Smoke. Wilkinson warned Charlesworth to "stick on the trail" and say nothing to anyone, not even another member of the staff, about the story he was working on.

---

[1] Charlesworth edited the 1919 edition of *A Cyclopaedia of Canadian Biography.*
[2] The following narrative comes from Charlesworth, *Candid Chronicles,* 217-222.

The next day, when Charlesworth appeared in Smoke's office, Smoke disappointed him. He had had second thoughts about sharing the details of the case. Apparently, Smoke intended to use the threat of media exposure to extort a settlement in the insurance case but had no intention of seeing the story published. Crestfallen, Charlesworth reported his failure to Wilkinson. Wilkinson urged him to stay on the case and visit Smoke daily to wheedle details from him.

Charlesworth persisted, but talking to Smoke was like talking to a stone wall. Finally, Charlesworth had a stroke of luck. On his second or third visit to Smoke's chambers, he saw the well-known private detective John Hodgins in the anteroom of Smoke's office. Charlesworth knew Hodgins well from the fact that Hodgins had done work tracing debtors for the accounting firm where Charlesworth had been employed.

HECTOR CHARLESWORTH[3]

Charlesworth approached Hodgins and, in a conspiratorial tone, whispered: "I guess we're both on this insurance case." Hodgins acted surprised and immediately changed the subject. That was enough for Charlesworth. Hodgins knew something about the case, but he was as unwilling as Smoke to share the details. When Charlesworth reported this fact to Wilkinson, the editor stepped into the case. Wilkinson, who lived quite close to Hodgins, was friendly with the detective and he was sure he could get Hodgins to talk where Charlesworth failed.

---

[3] *Candid Chronicles.*

The very next Sunday Wilkinson took his young son for a walk. As they passed Hodgins's house, Wilkinson asked Hodgins, who was a pigeon fancier, to show off his birds to the younger Wilkinson. Hodgins happily agreed. As the three were examining the pigeon coop, Wilkinson nonchalantly said, "By the way, Charlesworth tells me you are on that insurance conspiracy case he is working up. He thinks he's got a big story, but it all looks crazy to me. I told him to do his assignments and not bother me with junk like that." This subtle challenge to the importance of Hodgins's case pricked his ego, and he had to answer it.

"It's not such a fake as you think."

"Well," said Wilkinson, "who are the fellows anyway? Charlesworth wrote it up, but I didn't pay much attention."

"Dallas T. and Harry P. Hyams," Hodgins said. Then, realizing that he had said too much, Hodgins turned the conversation back to pigeons. He had said enough, though. These names provided the key which would unlock the story.

Wilkinson and Charlesworth took their information to W.F. Maclean, the publisher of the *World*. Maclean, a mover and shaker in Toronto politics, had connections everywhere. He called on his old friend, J.B. Carlile, an insurance executive who knew all the ins and outs of the insurance business in Toronto. Maclean swore Carlile to secrecy; then Charlesworth and Wilkinson briefed him on what they knew and suspected. Would it be possible for Carlile to ferret out the details of the case without rousing suspicion in anyone? Carlile assured them he could.

Within three days Carlile had the details. Dallas and Harry Hyams had tried to take out life insurance from several companies on Harry's stay-at-home wife, Martha Wells Hyams. About the same time as the negotiations were under way, Harry and Dallas tried to talk Martha into sleeping in a new-fangled bed they had bought. There was a lever on the bed which, when pressed, would cause the bed to quickly fold up against the wall. This style of bed would later become known as the Murphy Bed in honor of William Lawrence Murphy, founder of the Murphy Bed Company, which is still in business today despite several deaths caused when the beds accidentally folded up on sleepers.[4]

When Martha learned the amount of insurance being sought—$250,000—she became terrified. Not only was the amount of insurance obscene, but she also knew that Harry and Dallas, who were always short of money, could not possibly maintain the payments on the policies. It did not take much of an imagination to think that the twins intended to kill her by trapping her in the folding bed and passing her death off as an accident.

An incident just a few years before added to Martha's fears. Her brother Willie Wells had worked for the Hyamses, and they had talked him into taking out some $30,000 in life insurance with the understanding that they would pay the premiums. Willie named Martha as his beneficiary, and he died in a suspicious elevator accident before the second premium was paid on the policy. Martha, who had not yet married Harry, got the money, but Harry had almost

---

[4] "History of the Murphy Bed," Smart Spaces Web Page, https://smartspaces.com/history-of-the-murphy-bed/#:~:text=A%20Murphy%20bed%20(in%20North,of%20a%20closet%20or%20cabinet.

hypnotic powers of persuasion. It was not long before he had wheedled nearly every penny out of her.

Charlesworth and Wilkinson had their story, but there was the minor issue of proof. They needed more than hearsay, and they began to pursue evidence with a vengeance. Wilkinson called in a second reporter, E. Norman Smith, swore him to secrecy, and assigned him to assist Charlesworth in his quest for hard evidence. In his memoirs, Charlesworth vividly recalled one late-night interview he and Smith conducted at the residence of an expressman (delivery man) named Joseph Fox. After they knocked vigorously on his door, Fox appeared to them from a second-story window. As he spoke to them from his upper window it became apparent that he intended to be none-too-cooperative. They negotiated with him until he agreed to come downstairs. Fox disappeared from the window, and Charlesworth wondered if the expressman would ever come to the door. After an eternity, the door swung open, and they stood face-to-face with an angry giant. Fox covered the newsmen with a huge revolver, which Charlesworth found utterly unnecessary. "He was so colossal," Charlesworth wrote, "that he could easily have knocked our heads together, for we were both young and slender." They allayed Fox's suspicions, and Fox put down his gun, invited them in, and gave a full interview. It was highly informative. "This was but one of many incidents [in the investigation]," Charlesworth wrote, but he did not share the others.

Slowly, laboriously, they put the story together, and they were about ready to publish when disaster struck. One night, the police reporter, George Peart, sent a chill down the spines of Charlesworth and Wilkinson when he came into the office and announced, "Say, I was down on Sunday to see my mother at Pickering. There's been some strangers down there talking to the undertaker about a boy named Will Wells whom I went to school with. His folks always thought he was murdered." When the two men disentangled from Peart, Wilkinson called Charlesworth into his office.

"Dammit! You've been talking!" Wilkinson accused, and Charlesworth denied it.

"Well, how did Peart get next?" The two then discussed the situation and decided it was a coincidence. They had to get Peart out of the way. He was a gossip and could never keep the investigation secret. Then Wilkinson had a brainstorm. Why not send Peart to Pickering to get a story at that end? From Pickering, he could not gossip with other reporters, and anything he could learn at that end would add interest to the story, which they planned to run in a day or two.

Charlesworth made an appointment to see Smoke on the evening before the publication. Courtesy dictated that Smoke should hear of the story before he read it in the pages of the *World*. Charlesworth was in the process of telling Smoke about the story when, by the oddest coincidence, Dallas Hyams walked in. Smoke had become friendly with the Hyams brothers, and he had strongly suspected Charlesworth's purpose for making the appointment. Dallas was there to talk Charlesworth out of publishing the story.

After a few preliminaries, Dallas came to the point. Would Charlesworth please convey to Publisher Maclean that it was worth $5,000 to the Hyamses to see the story killed. Charlesworth did not fret long over what to do about the bribe offer. He conveyed the message to Maclean, but not so quickly. In his memoirs, Charlesworth explained, "I kept it to myself until the story appeared in print, because there is a divine mandate against leading anybody into temptation." When the story finally broke on February 7, it covered over half of the front page of the *World*, and to say that it stirred up a hornet's nest would be an understatement.

Charlesworth began his story by discussing a recent rash of insurance fraud cases, one involving the murder of William Henry Hendershott by the beneficiary of his life insurance policy. Charlesworth wrote that unless insurance companies "use the utmost prudence in issuing policies for large amounts the growth of this insurance mania and destruction of human life will be alarming."[5] He then gave a somewhat garbled account of an attempt by Harry P. Hyams to insure his wife's life for $300,000, the equivalent of at least $7,000,000 in today's dollars.[6] Charlesworth reported that when Mrs. Hyams became aware of the amount of insurance her husband was attempting to obtain, she immediately took a series of actions to protect herself. She left her husband and moved in with her sister and brother-in-law. She retained attorney Smoke to file for divorce and alimony. She tried to cancel all policies on her life. And she hired a private investigator as a bodyguard to protect her until the policies were canceled.

---

[5] The narrative in this chapter is taken from the following articles printed in the *Toronto World* on February 7, 1895: "The Insurance Mania" and "Barrister Horn's Statement."
[6] Inflation Calculator — Bank of Canada, https://www.bankofcanada.ca/rates/related/inflation-calculator/.

HARRY P. HYAMS[7]

Attorney Thomas W. Horn, speaking on behalf of Harry Hyams, gave the *World* an interview in which he painted a picture of unscrupulous insurance agents taking advantage of his gullible client.

My client, H.P. Hyams, has only a limited experience in insurance business, and on being pressed to take out some policies by a Montreal insurance agent he discussed it with his wife, as he was already carrying on his own life an endowment policy for $10,000. Their intention was to take out endowment policies for about the amount they could carry. Hyams had done business with insurance companies here in Toronto, and he arranged with his wife to come here [from their home in Montreal] for the purpose of getting her insured.

---

[7] *Philadelphia Inquirer*, February 14, 1895.

In the meantime, the Montreal insurance agent had come to Toronto and had been busy among the agents here, with the result that, instead of getting a reasonable policy within their reach, Hyams found that applications for insurance to the amount of $300,000 had been signed. Before the applications were completed Hyams was called back to Montreal to deal with his newly opened business, a manufactory of printers' ink, glues, and other articles, and the applications were allowed to go in.

Mrs. Hyams, who signed all the applications, had no idea that she was signing for the amount, and when it came to her knowledge that she was being insured for such a large amount she became alarmed and had a telegram sent for her husband to come to Toronto at once.

Mrs. Hyams is of a very nervous temperament and was visiting with her sister at 151 Close Avenue, where she became hysterical. Some stranger called at the house and asked her to go and see a doctor for the purpose of further examination on the evening of last Thursday. She did not understand this and sent a telephone message to her husband's solicitor.

DALLAS T. HYAMS[8]

He went to Parkdale and found her prostrated, and Mr. Aylesworth, her brother-in-law, with whom she was staying, not being able to remain at the house, procured the services of a detective to stay on the premises to frustrate any attempt to complete medical examination. The husband, on being telegraphed for, came at once to Toronto, and on ascertaining the amount of insurance that had been applied for instructed his solicitor to have all the applications cancelled.

All the companies, except for the Mutual Life Insurance Company of New York, agreed to cancel the applications. An action was commenced at once at the instigation of Mrs. H.P. Hyams against the Mutual Life

---

[8] *Philadelphia Inquirer*, February 14,1895.

Insurance Company to have their policy of $50,000 canceled, and to have a promissory note of Mrs. Hyams for one quarter's premium also delivered up and canceled. The writ in this action was issued on Saturday, February 2, and served on the company,

Both Mrs. Hyams and her husband come from very respectable families and feel very keenly the fact that they were inveigled into signing applications for policies that they never intended to take out, and they feel that they have been made the victims of a system of obtaining business adopted by the insurance companies, who are far too eager to make a big showing without regard to the means through which they obtain business. The interested parties regret the publicity which this matter has obtained and feel the injustice that may result to them through it. They complain of the manner in which the insurance companies have made the matter public and threaten action against several of the companies for the wrong they have sustained through their actions.

Mr. Smoke of the firm of Watson, Smoke & Masten has been retained as solicitor for Mrs. Hyams, and prompt action will be taken on her behalf, as well as on behalf of her husband, against the parties who were instrumental in putting up the insurance job.

There is no truth in the claim of an attempt to personate Mrs. Hyams on the medical examination. She has been examined and passed as a first-class risk, and is quite able, and fully intended to carry an endowment policy for some amount in the neighborhood of $5,000, but never intended to apply for any further insurance. One of the arrangements to deceive Mrs. Hyams in connection with her applications was a number of doctors meeting at one house, where she, thinking she was examined for one policy, was in fact examined for four.[9]

Attorney Horne's explanation did nothing to prevent the authorities from launching a criminal investigation.

---

[9] "Barrister Horn's Statement," *Toronto World*, Feb. 7, 1895.

CHAPTER THREE: AN ELEVATOR WEIGHT BREAKS A SKULL

Martha Wells Hyams was one of four siblings whose parents migrated to Canada from England. Not long after coming to Canada, the parents died, and the four children were placed in the care of their aunt and uncle, Mr. and Mrs. Uriah Jones of Pickering. Mrs. Jones mistreated the children so cruelly that the authorities removed them from her custody and placed them under the guardianship of a farmer named Knowles. Mrs. Jones eventually persuaded the older sister, Annie, to come back to live with her, but Annie's second sojourn with Mrs. Jones was not happy. Mrs. Jones then went to Rev. Ockley, her pastor at the Euclid Avenue Methodist Church, and asked him if he could find other arrangements for Annie. Ockley readily agreed to hire Annie as a live-in servant. She worked for him for several years until marrying William Aylesworth.

Martha's life was filled with tragedy. In addition to the death of her parents and her childhood placement in the custody of the abusive Mrs. Jones, her fiancé Headly Aylesworth fell sick of consumption, and she quit her job as a schoolteacher to nurse him. His illness increased in severity until at last, he died in 1887. The next tragedy came in 1891 when her brother Harold sailed back across the Atlantic to tend to a parcel of property in England which gave the siblings a small income. When Harold returned, he was severely ill. He languished under Martha's care and eventually died of pneumonia. During Harold's illness, the Wells family met the Hyams twins, who rented an apartment from them at their residence on 640 Spadina Avenue.[1]

---

[1] "Sensational Developments," *Toronto World*, Feb. 15, 1895.

MARTHA WELLS HYAMS[2]

Martha had just lost a fiancé; Harry Hyams had just lost his wife. In 1888, shortly after coming to Canada, Hyams wooed and won the daughter of a wealthy businessman named Williams. Not long after Hyams married his daughter, Mr. Williams died suddenly, leaving a substantial portion of his estate to his daughter. The heiress wife soon followed her father in death, leaving her fortune to Harry Hyams.[3] Hyams squandered his inheritance and began to look for another woman of financial means.

Although Martha had but a small income from the property in England, the cash flow was enough to interest Harry. He began to court her. It was not long before Martha was engaged to marry Hyams, but there was a catch. Hyams said he could not marry until his mother, who was living with him, died. Harry and his brother Dallas seemed most

---

[2] *Toronto World*, February 16, 1895.
[3] "The Toronto Mystery," *Middletown (NY) Daily Argus*, Feb. 16, 1895.

interested in separating the Wells siblings from their modest income. By February 13, 1892, the Hyams twins had persuaded Martha, her brother Willie, and her brother-in-law Ebenezer Aylesworth to lend them $2,700 for a term of six months. Each put up a third of the total, and each of them later upped their loan by $100, bringing the total to $3,000. In consideration of the loan, the Hyams twins hired Aylesworth and Willie as employees in their business. They did not repay the loans on time, and this failure became a bone of contention between the Hyams twins and their two male creditors. Still, Wells and Aylesworth continued to work for the Hyamses.

After obtaining the $3,000 loan, Harry and Dallas began to talk to Willie about taking out a twenty-year-endowment life insurance policy in the amount of $31,000. When Willie said he couldn't afford to pay the premiums on such a large policy, Harry volunteered to make the payments. Harry explained it as an investment. If Willie lived the twenty years necessary for the endowment to mature, Harry would receive the money. If he died before the policy matured, the insurance benefit would go to Martha. Why didn't Harry just take out an endowment policy on himself and cut out Willie as a middleman? Harry explained that he was in such poor health that his premiums would be too great, and the only way he could realize a profit on an endowment policy would be to insure someone else. With that understanding, Willie was insured in August of 1892.[4]

In consideration of getting the endowment, Harry agreed to pay Willie $2,500 after the policy had been in effect for five years. If Willie lived until the policy matured Hyams was to get the $31,000; but if he died, the proceeds

---

[4] Street, *Bench Book*, 13:330; Guillet, *Insurance Murderers*, 5.

would go to Harry's fiancé, Martha. A little math will show what a poor investment this would be for Harry. The premiums were $384 per quarter, meaning that when the endowment matured, Harry would have paid $30,720 in premiums and would get a $31,000 endowment. Few financiers would call this an adequate return on the investment. If you add in the $2,500 payment to Willie that Harry was to make at the end of five years, when the policy matured Harry would have spent $32,220 on the policy. In other words, Harry stood to lose $1,220 on the deal. There was an odor of decay in a Scandinavian country, and Willie should have smelled it. The only way Harry could possibly make any money on the deal would be to kill Willie and leach the insurance proceeds out of Martha. The Hyamses gave a promissory note for the first premium and failed to pay the second. The policy was ten days into the thirty-day grace period for late payments when Willie died.[5]

After insuring Wells, the brothers opened a warehouse business on Colborne Street. They moved Wells' and Aylesworth's place of employment to the warehouse and set them to busy work while the brothers spent an inordinate amount of time tinkering with the elevator in the multistory warehouse.

The elevator was a simple counterweight affair with two shafts, one for the elevator cage and one for the counterweight. The whole affair was relatively new, having been installed by the previous owners in 1888 after the building that housed it was damaged by fire. After the fire, a new hoist, with counterweight and rope was installed, and the shaft for the counterweight was completely boxed in with horizontal boards. There was approximately three

---

[5] Guillet, Insurance Murderers, 6

inches of space in the shaft. This gave the counterweight enough room to glide easily up and down the shaft, but not enough room to tilt over and come off the hook securing it to the rope. One of the first things the twins did was to have part of the boxing around the counterweight's shaft removed.[6]

They hired Samuel Kidd to do the alterations, Kidd put two openings in the boxing around the shaft. One opening was made on the first story, about four feet above the floor. Kidd put a shelf at the bottom of this opening. The twins told him this shelf would be used to put the counterweight on so they could remove it and replace it with a lighter counterweight. The second opening was made in the basement. This Rube Goldberg arrangement gave the counterweight room to sway out, catch on the shelf, and tip over. If this happened, anyone unlucky enough to have entered the shaft through the opening in the basement was in danger of being crushed when the counterweight came off the hook.

Later, on December 1, 1892, they again had work done on the elevator. They said that the elevator cage was sticking in its shaft, and Charles Lee came in to repair the cage guides. After adjusting the guides, Lee tested the elevator and made sure the cage could travel freely up and down its shaft. One of the twins called his attention to the shelf on the first story, explained its purpose, and asked Lee to get them a lighter counterweight to exchange with the one on the hook. Lee did so.[7]

---

[6] "Tell-Tale Evidences." *Ottawa Evening Journal*, Feb. 16, 1895.
[7] "The Strongest Yet," *Toronto World*, Mar. 20, 1895.

While the repairs were being made on the elevator, Wells decided that he no longer wanted to work for the twins. He visited his uncle, Uriah Jones, in Pickering and negotiated the purchase of a thirty-two-acre farm from Jones. Willie agreed to come back to Pickering on January 6 to finalize the deal. During his visit, Willie told his aunt and uncle that he had almost $40,000 in life insurance, but he was paying only a small share of the premiums. The large policy for $30,000 in New York Life had been taken out as a speculative investment, and the profits of the investment would go to Harry Hyams. Wells said that he was carrying all the insurance he could afford, when Hyams offered at the end of five years to pay him $2500 if he would allow a Harry to purchase a $30,000 endowment policy on his life in the New York Life Insurance Company, with the endowment being paid to Harry when it came due. In addition to the $2500 to be paid to Wells in five years, Hyams agreed pay all the premiums on the policy. Hyams convinced Wells that he was doing this merely as a sure-fire business investment which would make a lot of money. To seal the deal Hyams gave Wells a promissory note for the $2,500 payable at the end of five years. Wells said Harry gave him a $500 bill to make the first payment at the office of New York Life. Wells made the $384 payment and returned the balance of $116, to Hyams. Uriah became distressed at this news. He did not think that the deal was quite as good as Willie did.[8]

The only way that Willie could make the down payment on the farm was to get back the money he had loaned the Hyams twins. Willie had asked for this money several times before and had been put off. Now he became more

---

[8] "Sensational Developments, *Toronto World*, Feb. 15, 1895.

insistent, asking daily for the return of his money.[9] Meanwhile, the days of the grace period for his $30,000 policy were passing. If the second premium were not paid before January 29, 1893, the policy would expire.[10]

True to his word, Willie came back to Pickering to finalize the deal. Willie said he was able to get some money out of Harry when Harry offered to buy back the $2,500 note. "And how much do you suppose I got for it?" Willie asked.

"Twelve hundred dollars," Jones replied.

"No, not so much as that," was the reply. "I received $800 cash in my hands for it." This was not enough for the down payment. Willie explained that Harry told him the warehouse business was failing, and he might not have anything to pay on the $2,500 note when it came due. Wells said he would have the money by January 11, and they set that date to close the sale at the offices of Jones's lawyers. On January 10, Willie sent a telegram saying he would be in Pickering on the afternoon of January 11. Jones spent a fruitless afternoon at his lawyers' offices waiting on Willie. He never showed up.[11]

The continual putting-off of the return of Willie's money became more and more frustrating as Dallas kept giving Willie dates when the money would be paid and then failing to deliver. On Saturday, January 14, another deadline came and went, and Willie lost his patience. Harry assured Willie

---

[9] "The Twins on Trial," *Toronto World*, Feb. 28, 1895.
[10] "A Conspiracy to Kill the Crown Charges," *Toronto World*, May 16, 1895.
[11] "Sensational Developments, *Toronto World*, Feb. 15, 1895.

that he would pay him his money on Monday. Harry promised to immediately telegraph Jones with the good news that both he and Willie would be in Pickering that afternoon to close the land deal. Harry never sent that telegram.[12]

The next day, a Sunday, Dallas came to the Aylesworth home to deliver the message that Aylesworth was to make a trip to Toronto Junction on Monday morning before coming to work at the warehouse. He told Wells, who lived with the Aylesworths, to come in to work early the next morning. Dallas said Wells needed to be at the warehouse by 8:00 o'clock sharp to take inventory with Harry. After delivering those messages, Dallas went to the home of another employee at the warehouse, Miss Mabel Latimer, an attractive young typist. In the short period of time that she had worked at the warehouse she had begun a romance with Willie Wells. Dallas told Miss Latimer that he wanted her to personally deliver two letters to two businesses in two different parts of the city before coming to work the next morning.[13]

On the morning of Monday, January 16, 1893, Willie Wells awoke at the home where he lived with his two sisters and brother-in-law. His sister Martha called him from his bed to help her eat the hearty breakfast she had prepared. After breakfast she helped him on with his coat and he left for work at 8:45 a.m. Brother-in-law Aylesworth left just a few minutes before Willie.

---

[12] "A Conspiracy to Kill the Crown Charges," *Toronto World*, May 16, 1895.
[13] "Mrs. Harry P. Hyams' Story," *Toronto World*, Feb. 16, 1895.

Willie had big plans for that day. After weeks of pressuring the Hyams brothers for the repayment of his $1,000 loan to them, he was finally going to get the money, and that $1,000 was going to be the down payment on Uriah Jones' farm. Willie was going to get the money from Harry that day, and he and Harry were going to take the noon train to Pickering to finalize the purchase.

Upon his arrival at the warehouse, Willie unlocked the door and went in to begin his duties. What happened to Willie in the warehouse that morning? The details are shrouded in mystery. It is no mystery, however, that Willie was soon dead with a smashed skull.

The chronology of the events of January 16 is challenging to establish. Multiple witnesses made multiple conflicting claims about the times that things happened. In the nineteenth century, when clocks and watches were wound manually and unconnected to an internet, they had a proverb that said, "A man with one watch always knows what time it is. A man with two watches is never sure." What follows is a reconstruction of the chronology, placing the events in the most logical order.

Aside from Dallas and Harry, the first person to become aware of Willie's death was Sam Grandage, a money lender who charged exorbitant interest rates. The brothers owed him $150 on a promissory note that was three to four months overdue, and Grandage presented himself at the warehouse early that morning to see if he could corkscrew the money out of them. When he entered the office, he found the ground floor unoccupied. Presently Harry came running up from the basement. Grandage would later recall, "He was very much agitated, and I noticed his hands were covered in blood. There were also blood spots on his shirt front and on the collar of his coat."

Upon seeing Grandage, Harry exclaimed, "We have had a fearful accident! Our young man is killed!" Grandage asked no questions but beat a hasty retreat. He never got a penny from the Hyams brothers, and he eventually had to sell the note at a discount to a third party.[14]

After Grandage left, Harry left the warehouse and boarded the one-horse rail streetcar driven by Jeremiah Riordan. Riordan noticed the blood on Harry's hands as Harry told him to "hustle up," that he was searching for a doctor. Riordan let Harry off in front of the office of Dr. Edmund King, Harry charged into King's his office announcing, "For God's sake, hurry up! There has been a terrible accident!" King rushed to the warehouse with Harry, where he found Dallas, who was apparently in a state of shock. Harry led Dr. King into the basement, where King found Willie Wells lying on the floor near the elevator shaft with his head crushed almost flat. He did not need a medical degree to determine that Willie was dead. How did it happen? Dallas told him, "The weight caught in the boxing and fell and hit Wells. After lifting the weight off, Harry went for you." Dr. King accepted the story of accident without question, but said he still had to go and notify the coroner. Harry sent Dallas home in a hansom cab driven by James Lavelle, and then he locked the doors to the warehouse and waited for the arrival of the coroner.[15]

---

[14] "The Skull in Court, *Toronto World,* Mar. 4, 1895.
[15] Guillet, *Insurance Murderers*, 9; "Mrs. Harry P. Hyams' Story," *Toronto World*, Feb. 16, 1895.

Lavelle noticed that Dallas' trousers below the knees were spotted with dark red stains which looked like paint.[16] When Dallas arrived at his home he was met by Lizzie Pengilley, his maid. He was obviously very excited, pacing up and down. Miss Pengilley asked him what was the matter. Dallas told her Willie Wells had been injured in an accident, but he said nothing further. Dallas then retreated to his bedroom, where he stayed the rest of the day and refused to see anyone.[17]

Miss Latimer was the next to arrive at the warehouse, having delivered the letters as instructed. When she got there, she found Harry pacing up and down in the office and wringing his hands.

"What is the matter?" she asked.

"Willie's killed. He is in the cellar," said Hyams.

"How did it occur?" asked Miss Latimer.

"Oh," Harry replied, "Dallas let the weight slip," then he hesitated a moment and said, "I don't know how it occurred."[18] Harry unlocked the door and let Latimer in. He then told her, "There's been an accident. Poor Willie was killed with the weight from the elevator." Harry said that his brother Dallas was upstairs fixing the weight and it slipped. Harry said that he was not present when the accident occurred, and when he came into the warehouse, he found Dallas running around like a crazy man. He said he sent Dallas home in a cab. Harry also showed her his bloody

---

[16] *Bench Book*, 13:366, 367; "The Wells Insurances," *Ottawa Evening Journal*, May 14, 1895.
[17] "Case for the Crown," *Toronto World*, Mar. 1, 1895.
[18] "Fractured Like Glass," *Ottawa Evening Journal*, Feb. 20, 1895.

hands and said that he injured them lifting the weight off of Willie. Harry then sent Latimer to lunch. When she returned to the warehouse after lunch, Undertaker Humphrey would not let her into the warehouse. She went home and didn't return to work until Thursday, January 19.[19]

Having no work lined up for the morning of January 16, 1895, Expressman Joseph Fox decided to stop by the Colborne Street warehouse to see if he could drum up some business. Fox recalled that he got there around 10:00 am and found the place locked. He tried both entry doors, and then gave up. As he was walking back across the street to his horse and wagon, one of the doors to the warehouse opened and Harry stuck his head out. "Hello, Fox," Harry called out. Fox went back to the warehouse, where he saw that Harry's hands were bleeding. Fox asked what happened, and Harry told him there had been a terrible accident and Willie was killed. Harry said that Willie was doing something with the elevator and the weight broke loose. Fox asked where Willie was, and Harry said, "In the cellar." Fox said, "I'll go down." Harry said to wait until the coroner arrived. "The coroner can't hurt me for looking at him," Fox replied, and he went downstairs to the basement.

When Fox went down to the cellar, he found Willie was lying on the floor with his hands outstretched. His head was on the left side with the right side of the face turned up. The body lay with the head pointing to the northwest and feet to the southeast. His right leg was drawn up a little and his left leg stretched out resting on the concrete. On the hands were a pair of old gloves that Willie used to wear when carrying coal upstairs. Fox removed them. Willie had his coat and vest on. His head was about two feet from the

---

[19] "Avoided His Glance," New-York Herald, May 15, 1895.

weight shaft. The head was lying in a pool of blood. Except for some blood spatters on the elevator casing, that was all the blood Fox noticed. The weight was standing up against the casing of the elevator at the southeast corner of the shaft. It may have been tilted against the shaft about two feet to the east of the block on which it should rest. The cage of the elevator was down as far as it would go. The rope for the counterweight was not in sight in the cellar.

Fox saw that Willie was wearing the glasses he customarily wore. He took them off and gave them to Harry after the coroner had given the order to the undertaker to remove the body. The body was untouched and unmoved from the time that Fox arrived until 12:00 noon when the undertaker removed it. Coroner Aikins arrived and performed a cursory inspection which lasted only 20 to 30 minutes. He did not move the body. This fact calls into question the thoroughness of Aikins' examination. For all Aikins knew, there could have been a bullet hole in Willie's chest.

While they were waiting for the coroner Fox asked how the accident happened. Harry said, "Willie and Dallas were doing something to the hoist and the weight broke loose." He said he found Dallas fainted over Willie's body and sent him home in a cab. When the coroner finished his examination, Harry turned the key to the warehouse over to Fox and told him to lock up after the undertaker had removed the body. After Harry left and before the undertaker got the body removed, a number of gawkers came into the warehouse to look at Willie's body. Fox got them all out of the warehouse before he locked it.[20]

---

[20] Street, *Bench Book*, 13:350-362.

Around noon Harry came to the Aylesworth home. He was very excited, and his hands were bleeding. Aylesworth, who had returned home after running his errands, greeted him at the door. Harry told Aylesworth that Willie had been involved in an accident with the elevator and he was badly injured. Harry nearly fainted, and Aylesworth gave him some liquor to steady his nerves. He then helped Harry upstairs to Harry's bedroom. Harry was complaining about having hurt his back lifting the elevator weight off Willie.

After helping Harry upstairs to bed, Aylesworth left to investigate the matter. His first stop was the office of Dr. King. Next, he went to the undertaker's. He got no satisfaction from either of them. His third stop was at the warehouse. Then he returned to his house to break the news to his wife and Martha that Willie was dead. [21]

When Martha saw Harry being helped to his bed, she went upstairs and found him lying. She asked him about his hands. She got no sense from him because "He was very much excited, almost in tears, very much distressed." Martha went downstairs and found her sister Annie crying and saying that Willie was hurt. Martha went up again and asked Harry if Willie was hurt.

He said, "Yes, on the shoulder." I asked him if Willie was hurt badly.

"No, you needn't be frightened. He is at Dr. King's," came the reply. Martha went back downstairs, where she and Annie prepared a bed to receive Willie back from the doctor. Then Aylesworth arrived back at the house and told

---

[21] Street, *Bench Book*, 13:285, 287.

them Willie was dead. Martha went back upstairs and asked Harry how it happened.

"Mina," he said, "I assure you; I wasn't there." She asked where he was, and he said in the barbershop. He also said that when he found the body his brother Dallas was lying across it in a faint. He said the weight fell on Willie and that he and Expressman Fox lifted it off.

After breaking the news to the sisters, Aylesworth went back to the undertakers and examined Willie's body.[22] Then he went to the warehouse and found it locked and empty. He unlocked the warehouse and examined each floor of the building, paying close attention to the condition of the elevator. The first thing that he found was that the elevator rope had come off the big wheel atop the cage shaft. There was supposed to be a guard on the wheel to keep the rope from coming off, but this guard had either been removed or fallen off. The wheel was in a space which had holes in the floor to accommodate the rope as it went up and down the cage shaft and the counterweight shaft. The rope had fallen from the wheel to the floor of the space, where it had caught and become stuck. The wedging of the rope had prevented the cage from falling all the way to the bottom. Its fall had stopped approximately three feet from the floor of the cage shaft. Aylesworth then went downstairs to the basement, where he found the counterweight leaning against the boxing encasing the cage shaft. It was about a foot distant from the counterweight shaft. One to two feet in front of the counterweight Aylesworth saw two pools of blood. The pools were about six inches apart. He saw no blood between the counterweight and the pools, but he did see blood on the bottom of the counterweight. The leaning

---

[22] Street, *Bench Book*, 13:285, 287.

of the counterweight allowed him to see the blood without moving it. He found two bloody tools in the basement: a chisel and a hammer. Going back to the ground floor, Aylesworth saw a bloody coat that looked as though it had been cut off Wells and thrown onto some packing cases.[23] Aylesworth then went back home. Harry was still there in bed. He asked Harry how the death occurred. Harry said that he didn't know how it happened. Was Dallas there when it happened? No, he was not.[24]

The next morning Fox went to the warehouse and opened it up. Harry came in with a boy to help him clean up the mess in the cellar. He asked Fox to clean off the weight and rehang it. Fox used a broom to get the blood off the bottom and sides of the weight, and then went looking for the rope to hang it. He inspected the elevator shaft and weight shaft looking for the rope to hang it. Going upstairs he found that the rope had twisted off the wheel and that the hook end of the rope had gone down the elevator shaft. Going back downstairs, he found the hook end of the rope inside the elevator cage. He got the rope out of the cage, replaced it on the wheel, and dropped it down the weight shaft. He then hoisted the cage to the top floor so that he could hook the weight to the rope in the basement. From his description, the cage was hoisted up and down by a muscle-powered capstan.[25]

---

[23] Street, *Bench Book*, 13:285-288.
[24] Street, *Bench Book*, 13:287.
[25] Street, *Bench Book*, 13:350-362

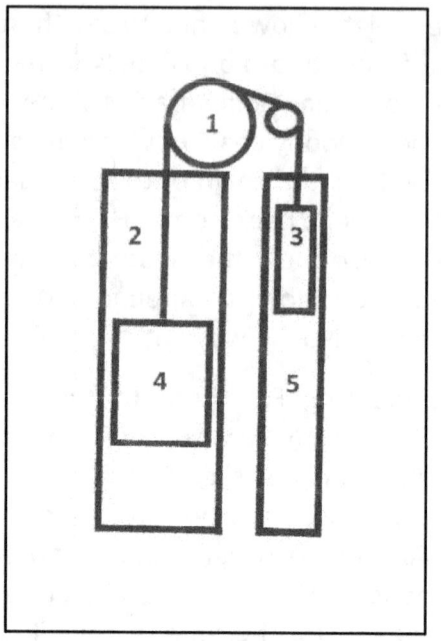

A TYPICAL COUNTERWEIGHT ELEVATOR[26]
[1] Wheel; [2] Cage Shaft;
[3] Counterweight; [4] Cage;
[5] Counterweight Shaft

The day after Willie's funeral Aylesworth asked Harry to explain how the accident happened. He said he came into the warehouse to work, entered the cellar, and found Dallas fainted across Willie's body. Other than that, he assumed that the weight struck and killed Willie while Willie was trying to fix it. Aylesworth next talked to both brothers at their office on King Street. Dallas said he had gone into the warehouse to write a letter to his wife and heard a great crashing sound in the cellar. He went to the cellar and found

---

[26] Drawing by the author.

Willie lying there with the weight on his head. Dallas said he then fainted.[27]

After Martha collected the insurance proceeds, Harry lost his reticence about marrying her before his mother died. As he urged her to marry him immediately, he convinced her to turn more and more of the insurance proceeds over to him. On February 23, 1893, Martha received the first $2,000 in proceeds from the policies. She paid Willie's funeral expenses, and Harry pressured her into giving him the remaining $1,700 so that he could "invest it for her." On March 8, she received the remaining money from the insurance company and deposited it in the bank. Hyams pressured her for more money, but she was reluctant. She thought it best for him to wait until they were married before making any more raids on the insurance money. Between the death of her brother and the constant demands for money by Harry, Martha reached a low ebb in her mental well-being.

On March 22, Attorney Samuel Smoke received a letter from Martha describing her financial connection with Harry and asking for his help. Smoke met with her three days later and agreed to take her case. When Harry learned that Smoke was advising Martha on her money matters, Harry and his lawyer T.W. Horn went to Smoke's office.

Horn proposed to Smoke that the $30,000 insurance proceeds in Martha's possession be turned over to Harry for investment purposes. Horn assured Smoke that Martha had agreed to give the money to Harry. Smoke replied, "I don't understand that Miss Wells has made any such agreement; and I refuse to consent to hand over the money." Horn continued to pressure Smoke to agree, and later that day

---

[27] Street, *Bench Book*, 13:289, 290.

he sent Smoke a draft agreement to hand over the money and requested his signature on it. Smoke did not sign it. After consulting with Martha, Smoke wrote Horn a letter dated April 7 refusing to allow the money to be turned over to Hyams.[28]

While Horn negotiated with Smoke, Harry continued to pressure Martha directly. Over a period of approximately two weeks, he pressured her into giving him a series of "loans" totaling $6,100. The last two of these loans were for $1,900 and $2,500, which she gave to Harry in two checks dated April 18.[29]

Horn having failed to get Smoke to turn over Martha's money, Harry made another attempt. On April 22, Harry went to Smoke's office. During their interview on that day Harry told Smoke that Martha had turned between $8000 and $9000 over to him and that he had securities for the amount that he could hand over to Smoke. Smoke urged him to turn over the securities or return Martha's money. The securities never materialized, but Harry did return $600 cash and gave Smoke a promissory note for an additional $616. This was all that Smoke ever saw of the $9,000 that Hyams had gotten from Martha.[30]

Then Martha heard a rumor that the furniture in Hyams' home was mortgaged. She asked him about it, and he told her yes, he had a mortgage on the furniture, but it was not a "real" mortgage. He had mortgaged the property for a dollar to keep creditors from levying on his furniture, and

---

[28] "The Hook Could Not Come off the Weight," *Toronto World*, May 17, 1895.

[29] "Martha Wells Hyams in the Box," Toronto World, May 13, 1895.

[30] "The Hook Could Not Come off the Weight," *Toronto World*, May 17, 1895.

he could pay the dollar off at any time. Given the circumstances of Willie's death, Harry's relentless pursuit of the insurance proceeds, and his disingenuous explanation of his mortgaged furniture, Martha's suspicions reached a critical mass. She wrote a letter to the Hyamses saying she never wanted to see either of them again.

WILLIE WELLS[31]

Dallas came to see her at the Aylesworths', and she gave in to his relentless requests for an interview. Dallas talked to Martha from 3:00 in the afternoon until 9:00 in the evening. Dallas reassured Martha of Harry's love for her and insisted that unless she saw Harry and promised to marry him, Harry would "go to ruin." Martha asked Dallas how they could keep up the premiums on Willie's life. Dallas replied that he had proved to both Aylesworth and Smoke that he and Harry received an income of $200 per month, and as the premiums were only $384 every three months, they could easily pay. He did not explain to her why they had had not paid the second premium on the policy, and

---

[31] *Toronto World*, February 14, 1895.

the company had deducted that premium from the payment they made to Martha.[32]

After the interview with Dallas, Martha went into hiding at the Bishop Strachan School, a girl's boarding school which was founded in 1867. It is still in operation today.[33] Despite the fact that she did not want to see or hear from Harry Hyams, she wrote him letters with no return address. Harry finally gave Martha's sister a letter to deliver to her. The letter read:

Toronto, May 3rd, 1893.

My Dear Mina, —I received your letter this morning. It has taken a load off my heart in one way, and it has made me sad in another. I never meant to deceive you in any way, but there are things which I should have told you after we were man and wife which I could not do as a lover.

Now, dear Mina, I must have an interview with you in order to explain my position, as the strain and suspense is killing me. You have heard all sides except mine, and I know if you knew what suffering and all I have gone through you would pity me and grant me my request. I will go any time and any place you appoint. I know we both love one another dearly, and if you will only see me I know much suffering can be saved. God knows I have had my share, and I know you have had yours. I send this to Annie and she can forward It to you. Hope you will be able to make it out. I can scarcely hold my pen. So for God's sake. Mina, give me an interview.

---

[32] "Martha Wells Hyams in the Box," *Toronto World*, May 13, 1895.
[33] Bishop Strachan School, https://www.bss.on.ca/.

UNHAPPY HARRY.

That did it. Martha agreed to meet Harry at the school, and Harry managed to talk her into marrying him. They married on May 9, and on May 10 Smoke received a telegraph from Martha telling him that he was no longer authorized to act in her behalf. [34]

Martha wrote a letter to her aunt, Mrs. Uriah Jones, describing her grief and explaining her sudden decision to marry Hyams:

> Oh, auntie, it just seems as though he must walk in! This is 5 o'clock Monday morning. I never can sleep when I once awaken on Monday. I am always so glad when the day is over. Every night of my life when I awake poor Willie is on my mind.
>
> Dr. Strange says I must go to the water and keep away from any kind of trouble. So Harry insisted on my marrying him, so that he could go with me. Annie couldn't, on account of the children. So we quietly drove to the Methodist minister's and were married. It seemed so quiet and sad, but I was not strong enough to stand any fuss. Some friends who heard of my marriage came to say good-bye Friday evening, and brought me some pretty gifts.
>
> We leave to-night on the 7 o'clock train. Harry has to go to New York on some business, and then we will go to some watering place. Don't think it hard that I did not tell you before I married, for there was not fuss at all. It was just on account of my health and being so low-spirited. I am glad it is over. Don't think I will ever regret

---

[34] "The Hook Could Not Come Off the Weight," *Toronto World*, May 17, 1895.

it. Tell uncle he must fat a calf for his Betty when I return.[35]

In short order, Harry had separated her from every penny she had received in proceeds of her brother's insurance policy, except $4,750 that she gave to Annie and $7,964 that she gave to Dallas. The longer the marriage lasted the more reason Martha had to regret her hasty decision to marry.

Not long after the marriage the Hyams twins closed their warehouse on Colborne Street and Harry took his new bride to Montreal, where he went into business as a maker of printer's ink.[36] Harry and Dallas also opened a moneylending business in Montreal, advertising that they gave loans on salaries, pianos, organs, warehouse receipts, and other articles. They advertised that although their main office was in Toronto loans could be negotiated in Montreal. At first, they did a brisk business, but they soon fell on hard times. Harry was forced to pawn over $1,000 worth of jewelry. At first the pawnbroker refused to take the jewelry in pawn, but Harry brought in a banker who vouched for his character. Based on this voucher, the pawnbroker took the jewelry in pawn. It was not long before agents of Ellis & Co., Toronto, sent word to the Montreal Police Department that Hyams had disposed of jewelry upon which they had a lien. Chief Detective Cullen of the Montreal Police made the rounds of the pawn shops and found where the goods had been pawned. The pawnbroker no longer had the jewelry. Only a few days after Harry had pawned the jewelry, he sold the pawn ticket

---

[35] "Tell-Tale Evidences." *Ottawa Evening Journal*, Feb. 16, 1895.
[36] "Too Heavy Insurance," *New-York Herald*, Feb. 15, 1895.

to a third party who had redeemed it. All efforts by Ellis & Co. to find and retrieve the jewelry failed.[37]

As the twins' financial fortunes ebbed, they began to search for another source of insurance proceeds. Dallas Hyams opened negotiations with Mutual Reserve Fund Life Association for a $26,000 policy on Harry's wife, and Harry began talking to Martha about taking out an insurance policy on her life. Dallas' attempt to insure his sister-in-law failed,[38] but Martha eventually agreed to let her husband procure a policy, and Harry enlisted O. Leger of Sun Life's Montreal office to assist with the insurance. They went to Toronto to procure the insurance based in part on Martha's desire to have her family physician, Dr. Fields, conduct the required physical, and in part on the fact that Harry and Martha were moving back to Toronto to live with Dallas. In Toronto Hyams and Leger made applications to eight different insurance companies for life policies on Martha. Some applications were for a little as $10,000, others were for $20,000 or more, and three were for $50,000 or more. The largest application was to Equitable Life Assurance in the sum of $80,000. It all totaled $300,000—over $7,000,000 in today's dollars.[39] The premiums for such an amount of insurance would have totaled at least $6,000 per year, far beyond Harry's capacity to pay.[40]

After he had gotten everything lined up, Leger met Martha. When she heard the amount of insurance Leger had obtained, she panicked.[41] She had only agreed to taking

---

[37] "The Montreal End," *Montreal Gazette,* Feb. 14, 1895.
[38] "The Deal with Mutual Reserve," *Toronto World*, Feb. 7, 1895.
[39] Canada Inflation Calculator,
https://www.in2013dollars.com/Canada-inflation.
[40] "The Insurance Job," *Toronto World*, Feb. 8, 1895.
[41] "The Insurance Mania," *Toronto World*, Feb. 7, 1895.

out a $5,000 policy. Between the obscene amount of insurance, the death of her brother Willie, and Dallas and Harry's efforts to get her to use that new-fangled folding bed, she decided it was time to leave her husband. Martha took immediate action. She moved in with her sister and brother-in-law. She went back to Attorney Smoke and retained him to get the policies canceled and to commence an action for alimony against Harry. All the insurance companies agreed to cancel the policies except one. On February 2, Smoke filed an action to cancel the $50,000 policy held by the Mutual Life Insurance Company and to have a promissory note for the first premium delivered up and cancelled.[42]

When the news of Harry's insurance shenanigans broke, several things happened. Harry and Dallas returned $8,000 of Martha's $30,000 to her; Chief Coroner Pickering called at the offices of the *World* to assure them that at the time of Willie's death he was not consulted on the case because he was absent in England, and several people who knew Martha personally told the paper that Martha was not the kind of person who would willingly allow herself to become an instrument in the perpetration of a fraud of any kind.

The next day the *World* ran an article under the title "The Insurance Job" in which it asked several questions but provided no answers: "Why then did she become alarmed as soon as she became aware that the insurance on her life was in the hundreds of thousands of dollars? Why did she insist that her husband should ask for the cancellation of the policies? Was it simply because she did not wish to incur the liability? Did she suspect that the object behind the heavy insurance was the perpetration of a swindle by the

---

[42] "Barrister Horn's Statement," *Toronto World*, Feb. 7, 1895.

substitution of a dead body for that of the living policyholder? Is she thankful that it is no worse? Did she suspect that there was blood behind it all?"

The *World* presumed that the Hyams twins had some sort of swindle in mind with the taking out of such an exorbitant sum of insurance. Working from that presumption its questions were framed in such a way as to suggest two motives to the readers. Either the Hyams twins intended to present the insurance companies with the corpse of some other person and claim it was Martha, or they intended to take the less complicated route and simply kill Martha.

The first suggested motive is not as outlandish as it seems. Francis Wellman himself had prosecuted a similar case in New York City where Dr. Henry C.F. Meyer and Brandt Baum concocted a plot to slowly poison Baum as part of an insurance fraud. The plan was to make him very sick but not terminally ill and then steal a corpse from the city morgue to palm off as his dead body. Meyer and Baum would then split the insurance proceeds and live happily ever after. The slow poisoning began, Baum got sicker and sicker, and Meyer pretended to hunt for a suitable body. After a period of illness, Meyer simply gave Baum a lethal dose of poison and then had his wife pose as Baum's widow to collect 100% of the insurance proceeds.[43] Francis Wellman would have been very knowledgeable about the details of the case. After Meyer's first trial resulted in a hung jury, Wellman was called in to prosecute the case and convicted the doctor of second-degree murder.

The *World's* last two questions, "Is she thankful that it is no worse? Did she suspect that there was blood behind it

---

[43] Wellman, *Luck and Opportunity*, 69-75.

all?" clearly show that the motive they preferred was the second, simpler motive. That certainly appears to be the motive that Martha deduced from Harry's "insurance job."

CHAPTER FOUR: THE STORM BEFORE THE STORM

Crown Attorney J. Walter Curry, upon reading Charlesworth's article in the *World*, immediately reopened the case on the Hyamses. There were two avenues he could take with the case. He could work up a case on the Hyams brothers for insurance fraud and conspiracy to murder Martha, or he could pursue a case against the brothers for the murder of Willie Wells. The first route would have given him a more recent case with witnesses who still had the events fresh in their minds. The second route presented much greater obstacles. It was a cold case, having happened years before, and the witnesses would not have the events fresh in their minds. Dr. King and Coroner Aikens both signed off on the death as an accident; and it would be difficult, if not impossible, to either get them to change their opinions or overcome their testimony if they stuck by their original opinions. Motive would be hard to prove because when Willie died Martha was his beneficiary, and Martha was not married to Harry.

Taking the first route did not foreclose later taking the second. Pursuing the conspiracy to murder Martha first gave Curry time to build the case for the murder of Willie. Murder cases are seldom improved by making a quick arrest. If the prosecutor has a substantial lesser charge to bring against the suspect, then there is time to pursue the murder case at leisure and build a much better case.

In the Gainesville Student Murders case, the police almost immediately developed a young man named Edward Lewis Humphrey as a suspect. There was evidence leading to a strong suspicion that he was involved, but then State Attorney Len Register resisted pressure to charge him immediately. Instead, he prosecuted Humphrey for a felony assault on his grandmother while the case was further investigated. As time went by more and more questions arose as to Humphrey's guilt until eventually Danny Rolling was arrested for the murders. Rolling pleaded guilty to the murders and was eventually executed at Florida State Prison. Humphrey was never charged.[1] A hasty charge against Humphrey would have resulted in disaster.

When Ted Bundy was identified as a suspect in Tallahassee's Chi Omega murders and the Lake City murder of a 12-year-old, the prosecution in both jurisdictions moved very slowly on filing charges. Initially multiple charges of theft and forgery were filed, and as the prosecutions for those charges progressed the real cases of murder were worked up at leisure, and the cases were in the best shape possible when murder charges were finally filed.[2]

The Rolling and Bundy cases demonstrate the wisdom of sometimes moving slowly on a murder case, and their example suggests that Curry would have been wise to charge the conspiracy to murder case first and then file the murder case after getting a conviction in the conspiracy case. Curry did not do this. Working with Inspector Stark and Detective Sergeant Reburn, he took the testimony of Coroner Aikens, Expressman Fox, and E.W.H. Aylesworth. Based on this testimony Curry had an arrest warrant issued, and on the evening of February 11, the day that the *World* ran an article calling for a thorough investigation of the

---

[1] Personal recollection of the author.
[2] Personal recollection of the author.

death, Detectives William Davis and Alf Cuddy arrested the brothers for murdering Willie Wells.[3]

Attorney T.W. Horn, who represented the Hyams brothers, rushed to the jail to confer with his clients. They instructed him to engage Britton Bath Osler, Q.C., as lead counsel in their defense. Horn announced to the press that they were retaining Osler. Although the brothers were set for arraignment in Police Court on the following day, Horn said he would ask for a week's delay because Osler had just suffered the shock of being in a train wreck.[4]

T.W. HORN[5]

The Number 4 Chicago Express, carrying Osler and several other lawyers, had become mired in the snow near Weston, Ontario, a town just outside of Toronto. They set out flares and deployed flagmen and a foghorn, but the

---

[3] "Should Be Investigated," *Toronto World*, Feb. 12, 1895; "On a Charge of Murder," *Toronto World*, Feb. 13, 1895.
[4] "On a Charge of Murder," *Toronto World*, Feb. 13, 1895.
[5] *Toronto World*, February 28, 1895.

signals failed to stop the Number 6 Local Mail Train, which was traveling blind in the dense fog. The train plowed into the Express, setting fire to two Pullman cars, two baggage cars, and two passenger cars, all of which were destroyed. One lawyer was burned to death in the fire and two others were fatally injured. Many others suffered less severe injuries. Britton B. Osler was only slightly injured, as was his brother the Right Honorable Justice Featherstone Osler.[6]

Landing Osler as defense counsel would be a coup. He was universally recognized as the foremost trial attorney in Canada. He first rose to national prominence prosecuting Louis Riel, the charismatic leader of the Red River Resistance in 1869-1870 and the North-West Rebellion in 1885. The charge was treason, and the penalty was death. Osler got a conviction, and despite numerous calls for clemency, Riel was hanged. After this conviction Osler put together an incredible string of murder convictions. It was said that if Osler prosecuted someone, that person was going to be hanged. On the other hand, as defense counsel he never failed to achieve an acquittal in a murder case.[7] Americans, who are used to full-time public prosecutors, may find it strange that Osler could prosecute one case and then defend another, but the Canadian system was quite different from the American. In Canada they had a modified form of the solicitor/barrister system. Roughly speaking, in England at that time solicitors were office lawyers and barristers were trial lawyers. Solicitors would "brief" cases and then retain barristers to take the brief and try the case. Not having to do extensive investigation and preparation on a case, a barrister could try far more cases than his American counterpart. In Canada, the solicitor/barrister

---

[6] "Collided in the Storm, *Toronto World*, Feb. 9, 1895.
[7]

relationship had broken down. Any attorney could act as either a solicitor or a barrister. The position of Crown Attorney is an example of a lawyer who would perform both functions. Osler was Crown Attorney when he prosecuted Louis Riel, but for most of his other murder prosecutions, he was strictly a barrister retained by a Crown Attorney, who would serve as his solicitor.

Osler had an understanding with the government of Ontario that he would prosecute all their capital murder cases. Some even suspected that he was under contract to do so.[8] If such a formal agreement existed, there was a proviso that he did not have to prosecute any murder case where he believed the defendant to be innocent. One of Osler's biggest fans was the Canadian hangman, John Radclive, who hanged at least sixty-nine people. Record keeping being spotty in the 1890's, he may have hanged many more.[9] Radclive liked Osler's insistence on knowing that a man was guilty of murder before he would accept the case. "When he's on the case, I know that I won't be given the job of hanging an innocent man."[10]

---

[8] Hassard, "Great Canadian Orators—VII: Britton Bath Osler," 354.
[9] Patrick Cain, "The Agony of the Executioner," *Toronto Star*, May 20, 2007.
[10] Charlesworth, *Candid Chronicles*, 217.

BRITTON BATH OSLER[11]

Radclive began his career as an executioner when he was a merchant seaman in the Orient. Common seamen were often detailed to hang pirates from the yardarm. "I was sorry for the poor blighters, they used to struggle and suffer so, so I figured out how to do it quick and mercifullike." When he settled in Canada he occasionally worked under an assumed name as an executioner because "I figured that it was kinder for me to do the job than to have it bungled by one of them farm hands up there, like lots of cases that used to happen." When his true name was accidentally disclosed, he suddenly found himself unable to get a job doing anything other than acting as a hangman. Prior to his assuming the job full time many hangings were far from humane. Hector Charlesworth called them "gross butcheries." Radclive saw himself as a benefactor because his hangings were as swift and humane as possible. "If there has to be hangings," he said, "the only merciful thing is to

---

[11] *Birchall: The Story of His Life*

do it right."[12] Eventually the strain of his job took its toll. He became an alcoholic and died at age 55 of cirrhosis of the liver. Shortly before his death he told the American psychologist Rachel Nair, "Now at night when I lie down," he said, "I start up with a roar as victim after victim comes up before me. I can see them on the trap, waiting a second before they meet their Maker. They haunt me and taunt me until I am nearly crazy with an unearthly fear."[13]

The Hyams family's world was imploding. Martha, who had almost recovered from her shock at learning the amount of insurance her husband proposed to put on her, suffered a relapse when she learned of his arrest.[14] The authorities issued another warrant for Harry on a forgery charge from Montreal,[15] half a dozen suits were filed against the brothers when they were arrested,[16] and their household furniture and other personal belongings were seized to satisfy debts they had run up. The estimated value of all the seized property was $12,000.[17]

When the seized property was sold at auction, scores of people attended, and the auction ran from 11:00 o'clock to sunset. The *World* wrote, "Never in the history of Toronto has so much valuable furniture and bric-a-brac been

---

[12] Charlesworth, *Candid Chronicles*, 217.

[13] Patrick Cain, "The Agony of the Executioner," *Toronto Star*, May 20, 2007.

[14] "Fugitives from Justice," *Toronto World*, Feb. 14, 1895. Another paper reported that only Willie's bones and skin were found. "The Flesh All Gone," *Ottawa Evening Journal*, Feb. 15, 1895.

[15] "The Montreal End," *Montreal Gazette,* Feb. 14, 1895.

[16] "Fugitives from Justice," *Toronto World*, Feb. 14, 1895.

[17] "Should Be Investigated," *Toronto World*, Feb. 12, 1895.

disposed of at auction."[18] The auction grossed a mere $2,600, a fraction of the property's true value.[19]

When the twins appeared in Police Court on February 13, their attorney, W.G. Murdoch, filling in for an ill T.W. Horn, requested a week's delay in the proceedings. He gave as his reason the fact that he needed to confer with Britton B. Osler, who had been retained by the defense. Police Court Magistrate George T. Denison recessed the arraignment until February 20.

Immediately upon the arrest of the brothers, the prosecution got busy doing things that would have better been done before they made the arrest. On the day the twins appeared in Police Court the authorities raided their brokerage business on 11 King Street, seizing all their books and records.[20]

On January 14, Crown Attorney Curry, Dr. John Caven, Detective Alf Cuddy, and E.W.H. Aylesworth left Toronto for Oshowa to have Willie's body exhumed and autopsied. At the cemetery they opened the tomb, and Aylesworth identified the body as Willie Wells. Finding the corpse well-preserved, they returned to Toronto on the evening train. They arrived at 9:30 and placed the corpse with Benjamin D.. Humphrey & Brothers, Undertakers.[21]

Perhaps the most discouraging news the twins received on that date was the announcement that Britton Bath Osler, who had never failed to send a murder defendant to the gallows, had agreed to represent the Crown in their case.[22]

---

[18] "Sensational Developments, *Toronto World*, Feb. 15, 1895.
[19] "Gathering the Bones," *Ottawa Evening Journal*, Feb. 18, 1895.
[20] "Sensational Developments, *Toronto World*, Feb. 15, 1895.
[21] "Sensational Developments, Toronto World, Feb. 15, 1895.
[22] "The Hyamses Plead Not Guilty" *New York World*, Feb. 15, 1895.

It was then that Solomon Hyams, the Hermit of the Gilsey House," decided to recruit Francis L. Wellman. If the brothers couldn't have the best criminal trial lawyer in Canada, then at least they could have the best one in New York City.

On January 15, the police went to the Colborne Street address and ransacked the cellar. They found that the elevator's counterweight had been replaced, and they also found the bloody chisel and hammer which Aylesworth had seen two years before on the day of Willie's death.[23] They also searched the entire building, finding bloodstains on the second floor which suggested that Willie had been killed there.[24] The also found the counterweight which had crushed Willie's skull. Expressman Fox identified it as the counterweight he saw in the cellar the morning of Willie's death.[25]

On the same day that the police ransacked the Colborne Street warehouse, Drs. John Caven and Arthur Jukes Johnson commenced a post-mortem examination of Willie's body.[26] A preliminary examination revealed that the skull had suffered fractures in several places, much like a shattered pane of glass. The skin, however held the bones together, making it look as though the skull was intact. When the skin was removed the bones fell apart, and the doctors quickly adjourned the examination.[27] On February 19, Dr. Caven returned to the autopsy. He spent most of his time piecing the parts of the skull back together, much like a 3-D jigsaw puzzle. This consumed most of his time, but by

---

[23] "The Toronto Mystery," *Middletown Daily Argus*, Feb. 16, 1895.

[24] "Tell-Tale Evidences." *Ottawa Evening Journal*, Feb. 16, 1895.

[25] "Gathering the Bones," *Ottawa Evening Journal*, Feb. 18, 1895.

[26] "Gathering the Bones," *Ottawa Evening Journal*, Feb. 18, 1895.

[27] "Fractured Like Glass," *Ottawa Evening Journal*, Feb. 20, 1895.

the end of the day he had the skull reassembled and was prepared to state some provisional conclusions pending completion of the autopsy. He announced that he felt satisfied about whether the counterweight had hit Willie's head. He did not think it had because he believed so great a weight would have smashed the skull to even smaller smithereens than it was in when he examined it. He was not yet ready to state what had ruined Willie's skull, and that held up his final report.[28]

The defense meanwhile had not been idle. Attorney Horn announced that if he could not retain Osler, he would brief E.F.B. Johnston to defend the case.[29] Little did he know that in a few days Francis L. Wellman, New York City's deadliest prosecutor, would arrive like the cavalry to take on Canada's deadliest prosecutor. It was rumored that the war chest of the defense was bolstered by a check for US$5,000 from the twins' American relatives, and that two ace Pinkerton detectives had been dispatched to Toronto to investigate the case for the Hyamses.[30] News of the arrival of the Pinkertons set the Toronto police in a tizzy. "In the States," said inspector Stark, "this practice is a growing evil, and sometimes leads to a frustration of justice. If any American detectives come here and attempt to interfere or tamper with crown witnesses, they may find themselves in jail."[31]

Attorney Horn had been out of commission for a few days with an illness, but when he returned to work, he was

---

[28] "Fractured Like Glass," *Ottawa Evening Journal*, Feb. 20, 1895.
[29] "Fugitives from Justice," *Toronto World*, Feb. 14, 1895.
[30] "Check for the Hyams' Defense," *Buffalo Evening News*, Feb. 19, 1895; "Money to Aid the Hyams Twins," *New York World,* Feb. 20, 1895; "The Hyams Disclosures," *Ottawa Daily Citizen*, Feb. 21, 1895.
[31] "Fractured Like Glass," *Ottawa Evening Journal*, Feb. 20, 1895.

immediately buttonholed by a reporter seeking a statement about the rumors swirling around the defense case. He told the reporter "Chapman Hyams, of New Orleans, the millionaire brother of the two prisoners, has not come to Toronto. No; nor do I expect him to come. In fact, I believe he will not. All the money that is needed for the defense is forthcoming, however. There will be no lack of it. The crown officers need not profess any fears of their witnesses being tampered with. We know better than the crown what their witnesses will say, and our defense will be completed."[32]

On February 20, the morning of the preliminary hearing, Crown Attorney Curry asked for a week's continuance. Why? Dr. Caven had not completed his autopsy report.[33] Murdoch, still filling in for Horn, opposed any continuance and demanded that the preliminary hearing proceed as scheduled.[34] Murdoch was making a pro forma objection. The defense would not be ready until the A team in the form of E.F.B. Johnston, QC, arrived. It is a standard ploy in criminal cases, when one side professes itself unprepared, that the equally unprepared other side objects to any continuance and demands that the case proceed. Magistrate Denison recessed the case until February 27.

When the preliminary hearing came on to be heard on February 27 before Police Court Magistrate George T. Denison, Britton B. Osler was notable by his absence. Three things could account for his failure to appear at the preliminary hearing. First, he was still recovering from the injuries he sustained in the train wreck. Second, his father, the Rev. Featherstone Osler, had just passed away at the

---

[32] "The Hyams Murder," *Ottawa Daily Citizen*, Feb. 22, 1895.
[33] "Hyams Murder Case," *Buffalo Evening News*, Feb. 20, 1895.
[34] "The Hyams Disclosures," *Ottawa Daily Citizen*, Feb. 21, 1895.

age of ninety.[35] Third, he had a very heavy trial calendar, and was constantly on the road between courthouses going to and from one serious trial after another. In fact, he was due to be engaged in the Hendershott murder case in St. Thomas, some 200 kilometers to the Southwest of Toronto. Coincidentally, the Hendershott case involved an allegation of murder for insurance. In Osler's absence the onus of prosecution fell upon Crown Counsel Curry. In his memoirs Judge Denison had this to say about Curry's performance at the preliminary hearing: "J. Walter Curry, K.C., was Crown Attorney for a number of years, and a most energetic and efficient prosecutor. He worked with indomitable perseverance and in many important cases showed remarkable ability. He was in charge of the prosecution of the Hyams brothers for murder, and with four exceedingly able counsel against him handled his case most skillfully."[36]

Denison had aspired to a career as a professional soldier, but his support of the South during the American Civil War ended any prospect of a full-time military career. He nevertheless rose to the rank of Lieutenant Colonel in the militia and served as commander of the Governor General's Bodyguard during the Fenian Raids of 1866. In part because the raids were made by Irish immigrants to the United States, Denison became a staunch anti-American, a position which he maintained the rest of his life. He became Toronto's Police Court Magistrate in 1877, and he ran his court like a well-oiled machine, clearing his docket so fast that city officials thought his salary was too high. He had

---

[35] "Rev. Featherstone Osler Dead," *Toronto World*, Feb. 18, 1895.
[36] Denison, *Recollections of a Police Magistrate*, 19.

little patience for legal technicalities, declaring that he ran "a court of justice, not a court of law."[37]

There was standing room only in the courtroom, as almost every idler in Toronto had tried to gain entry to watch the judicial combat. Huge crowds of people were turned away from the courthouse. Those lucky enough to gain entry were privileged to see a preparatory battle before the first witness was called. Mr. Johnston asked Judge Denison to give permission for Francis L. Wellman and his partner W.W. Gooch to be associated with him on behalf of the twins so that they could examine the prosecution witnesses.[38] Johnston gave as the reason for this extraordinary request an assertion that Wellman was family solicitor for the Hyamses and had become quite familiar with the case. Johnston admitted that it was only by the courteous exercise of judicial discretion that Wellman and Gooch, who were not members of any Canadian Bar, could be permitted to appear in the case. Given the seriousness of the charge, however, Johnston thought Judge Denison ought to be able to see his way clear to grant the request.

"I am afraid I will not be able to do so," Denison ruled, "because it will establish a precedent. If any extraordinary course such as this is to be taken, I would rather it be taken by the judges of the Superior Court, as this is merely a preliminary investigation. We have quite a number of lawyers of our own. I don't think I can consent to allow Mr. Wellman to proceed."[39] Although Judge Denison's ruling was a blow to the defense, it should not have been

---

[37] *Dictionary of Canadian Biography*, biographi.ca/en/bio/denison george taylor _ 1839 _ 1925 _ 15E. html.
[38] "Brighter for the Twins," *New York World*, Mar. 1, 1895.
[39] "The Twins on Trial," *Toronto World*, Feb. 28, 1895.

unexpected. In Victorian Era Canada, neither lawyers licensed to practice in another province nor foreign lawyers could appear in court unless they were fully admitted to the province's bar. Denison did, however, allow Wellman to sit at counsel table with Johnston and advise him.

In America, an out-of-state lawyer may appear in a case *pro hac vice* (for this occasion only) if they associate a licensed lawyer to appear with them,[40] but counsel from other countries can only give advice. They cannot plead cases in court.[41] Today in Canada an out-of-jurisdiction Canadian lawyer can request and receive permission to temporarily practice in the jurisdiction,[42] but foreign lawyers still cannot plead in court. They can, however, apply for a permit to act as a consultant in Canada.[43] Although the *New York World* attributed Denison's ruling to his well-known anti-American sentiments,[44] judging by modern provisions in both Canada and America, Judge Denison ruled correctly.

With the issue of Wellman's participation in the preliminary hearing decided, Curry called his first witness, A.W. Barber of the C.P.R. Telegraph Company. Through Barber he tried to introduce a telegram sent by Mrs. Dallas Hyams the day after the twins' arrest. The telegram was sent to a Mrs. Cozaroun of 100 East 17th Street in New York

---

[40] ABA Model Rule 5.5(c).

[41] ABA Model Rule 5.5(d).

[42] Application for Temporary Practice Permit Under the National Mobility Agreement and Part VII of By-Law 4, https://lawsocietyontario.azureedge.net/media/lso/media/lawyers/temporary-practice-permit-application-en.pdf.

[43] Application for Foreign Legal Consultant, https://lawsocietyontario.azureedge.net/media/lso/media/lawyers/application-for-foreign-legal-consultant-new-permit_en.pdf.

[44] "Brighter for the Twins," *New York World*, Mar. 1, 1895.

City. It instructed her to destroy the letters and papers in a picture box which belonged to Mrs. Hyams and to instruct a person named Vineberg to keep quiet.[45] Curry did not explain the relevance of the telegram, and Judge Denison quite properly ruled it inadmissible because it had not been sent by either Harry or Dallas.[46]

One of Curry's first witnesses was E.W.H. Aylesworth, who gave the history of his employment by the Hyams brothers and told of the events on the day that Willie died. Aylesworth then repeated the stories Harry told about the death. Aylesworth told of his visit to the warehouse and his finding of the bloody chisel. Curry showed him the bloody chisel found by the police after the twins' arrest, and Aylesworth identified it as the same chisel he saw the day of the tragedy.[47] The Toronto World was not impressed with his testimony, saying that "Aylesworth ... has a more exalted idea of his own cleverness than the majority of those who heard him give his testimony."[48]

There was a straining of necks when Curry called Annie Aylesworth, the sister of Willie and Martha, to the stand. Wearing grey tweed, with a black hat trimmed with black feathers, Annie testified as positively as had her husband, but she did not display his vindictiveness. When Mrs. Aylesworth described how she learned of Willie's death, she burst into tears and showed signs of fainting. She was given a drink of water and time to recover, and then the questioning continued.[49]

---

[45] "The Twins on Trial," Toronto World, Feb. 28, 1895.
[46] "Hyams Case in Court," Windsor Evening Record, Feb. 28, 1895.
[47] "The Twins on Trial," Toronto World, Feb. 28, 1895.
[48] "The Twins on Trial," Toronto World, Feb. 28, 1895.
[49] "The Twins on Trial," Toronto World, Feb. 28, 1895.

Dr. E.E. King, the Hyams family physician whom Harry had summoned to the warehouse, testified about being called to the warehouse to examine Willie. Dr. King thought the wounds to the body were quite consistent with Willie looking up the casing and the weight falling on his head. Curry sparred with the doctor over whether the injuries could have been caused by something else, but King remained firm.[50] He gave his unqualified opinion that Willie was killed by the falling weight striking his head a glancing blow.[51]

One may wonder why Curry would call a witness who materially damaged his case, but Wellman explained in his memoirs that at a preliminary hearing "the Dominion had a very proper rule compelling the Crown to produce every witness that had been found … who had any knowledge of the case whatsoever, whether his testimony was favorable to the Crown or to the accused." Wellman thought that "we ought to adopt a similar rule in this country."[52] It took until 1963 for the U.S. to adopt a similar rule in *Brady v. Maryland*,[53] which requires the prosecution to disclose any and all known witnesses and evidence tending to exonerate the defendant.

For five days Curry worked to substantiate the brothers' guilt by calling witnesses who whose testimony can be classified under five main topics:

(1) MURDER: The Crown had to disprove the accident theory advanced by the brother and accepted by Dr. King

---

[50] "Case for the Crown," *Toronto World*, Mar. 1, 1895.
[51] "Brighter for the Twins," *New York World*, Mar. 1, 1895.
[52] Wellman, *Luck and Opportunity*, 91.
[53] 373 U.S. 83, 83 S. Ct. 1194 (1963).

and Coroner Aikins. This proof would be attempted under two subtopics:

a. IMPOSSIBILITY: It was impossible that the death could be an accident.

b. INCONSISTENCY: The wounds to Willie's head were inconsistent with accident.

(2) MOTIVE: The Hyams brothers were in such financial straits that they had to mortgage their furniture and were frequently delinquent in repaying loans.

(3) MANUFACTURING THE MEANS: The brothers fabricated an elaborate scheme to accomplish the murder. The proof of this scheme came under three subtopics:

a. FUNDING THE INSURANCE: First the brothers insured Willie.

b. FAKING THE BUSINESS: The auction business was nothing more than an excuse to hire the building where the killing was done.

c. "FIXING" THE ELEVATOR: Willie couldn't possibly have been killed without the "repairs" the Hyams brothers did to the elevator shaft; and they undid the "repairs" immediately after Willie's death.

(4) MANEUVERING FOR THE OPPORTUNITY: They cleared the way for the murder by sending away any possible witnesses.

(5) MAKING THE PROFIT: Once the deed was done, the brothers immediately started milking Martha for the insurance proceeds. Insuring and killing Willie proved so profitable, they tried it again with Martha.

We will not give a witness-by-witness description of the proceedings for two reasons: (1) Curry gave a disjointed, disorganized, confusing presentation of the evidence, and (2) The evidence will be described fully when we discuss the trial.

An element of humor was introduced when Curry was trying to prove the impossibility of the death occurring by accident. James Rankin, who worked in the building when the Imrie-Graham printing company occupied it, testified that he had used the elevator six days a week for five years and the weight had never fallen off. It couldn't fall off because the shaft was so narrow the weight would not cant enough for the hook to come loose.[54] When asked if there had ever been any injuries caused by the operation of the elevator Rankin admitted to one injury. He said that because rats overran the warehouse, they brought in a cat to control the rodents. The cat wriggled into the casing of the chute and was killed when the weight hit the floor of the basement.

"Did the weight come off the hook?" Curry asked.

"Oh, no," replied Rankin, "It was in its natural position."

"Was the cat badly crushed?"

"As flat as a pancake," Rankin replied.

---

[54] "All Circumstantial," *Toronto World*, Mar. 2, 1895.

Johnston jumped to his feet and interjected: "Was the cat insured?"

"Not that I know of," said Rankin.

"Then there was no motive for doing away with her?" Johnston quipped. The courtroom erupted in laughter.[55]

Dr. John Caven, who conducted the autopsy upon Wells, was the sole witness called to show the inconsistency of Wells' wounds with a claim of accident. Caven testified about his findings on autopsy and described how he put the skull back together. He caused something of a sensation when he pulled the reconstructed skull out of his valise. The skull got the twins' undivided attention. They stared fixedly at it for some time, and then surveyed the courtroom as though to assess how the crowd was reacting to it.[56]

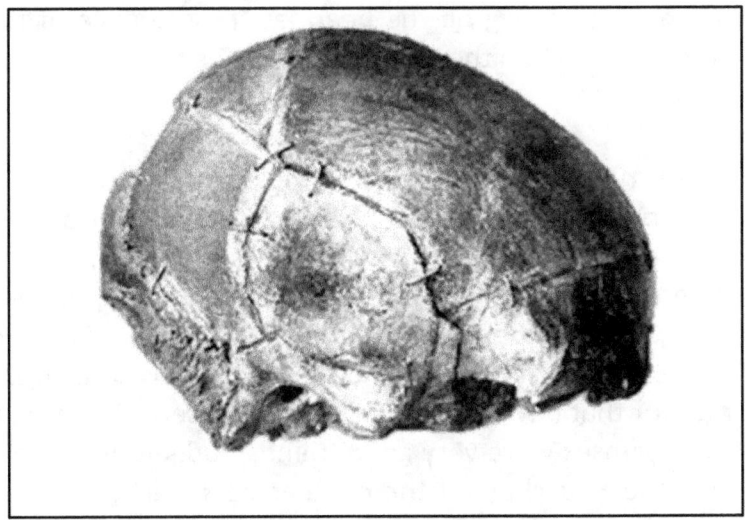

WELLS' SKULL[57]

---

[55] Guillet, *Insurance Murderers*, 19.
[56] "The Skull in Court," *Toronto World*, Mar. 4, 1895.
[57] *The Canadian Practitioner*, June 1895.

After Dr. Caven described the multiple fractures to the skull in detail, he gave the opinion that Willie's injuries could not have occurred as claimed by the Hyamses because: (1) A 200-pound weight falling three floors, as the defense contended, would not have caused the injuries he saw to the skull. (2) Willie was not standing in the shaft looking up when hit by the weight because if it had happened that way, the weight "would have crushed right through the head and must have done some damage to other portions of the body, whereas, so far as I could perceive from my examination, neither the shoulder blade nor any other bones were broken." (3) The skull gave evidence of at least two blows to the head from different directions. (4) If Willie had been in the shaft when struck, Willie's body should have been at the bottom of the shaft and not two feet away with the limbs perfectly straight and the weight resting on the head, as the evidence of those who were first on the scene states it was found."[58]

MOTIVE

Curry called numerous witnesses to testify to the brothers' dire financial straits. Another moment of humor occurred when he called moneylender Richard Lane. Referring to his books, Lane testified that in September of 1892, the brothers owed him a total of $918, bearing interest at from 3 to 5 per cent per month, an exorbitant rate for that day and age. When Lane asserted that he and the Hyamses were very good friends, Judge Denison broke in, "And you charged them 5 per cent per month!" The courtroom broke out laughter at the judge's quip. [59]

---

[58] "The Skull in Court," *Toronto World*, Mar. 4, 1895.
[59] "All Circumstantial," *Toronto World*, Mar. 2, 1895.

MANUFACTURING THE MEANS

Having planted the seed for their future profit by convincing Willie to agree to be insured, they next needed to devise a way of realizing that profit. The warehouse, with its primitive elevator would provide the means quite nicely. They just had to get Willie into the warehouse so they could commit the crime. According to Curry, the way they did this was to put Willie, Aylesworth, and the typist Miss Latimer to work in the warehouse gathering reports that were never read, copying out old directories, and addressing envelopes that were never mailed out.[60]

MANEUVERING FOR THE OPPORTUNITY

Curry contended that the brothers made their opportunity as earlier described, by sending Aylesworth and Latimer away on useless errands on the morning of the tragedy and having Willie come in to work early. As she testified, Miss Latimer, who was quite a beautiful young lady, appealed to Judge Denison to prohibit the newspapers from publishing her picture. Judge Denison gallantly announced, "If this lady requests freedom from notoriety, her wishes must be respected."[61] The *Toronto World* printed an unflattering drawing of her the very next day.[62]

---

[60] Guillet, *Insurance Murderers*, 5, 6.
[61] "Brighter for the Twins," *New York World*, Mar. 1, 1895.
[62] "The Case for the Crown," *Toronto World*, Mar. 1, 1895.

MISS LATIMER[63]

MAKING THE PROFIT

Curry had summoned Martha Hyams to testify about how her husband took all the insurance proceeds for himself, but she sent in a doctor's certificate that she was unable to attend the proceedings due to illness,[64] probably mental prostration caused by the stress of discovering the insurance scheme and the arrest of her husband. In lieu of Martha's testimony, Curry called H.B. Patton of the Imperial Bank to authenticate Martha's bank records and sponsor the introduction of several checks drawn on her account for more than $20,000 which were paid to Dallas and Harry.[65]

---

[63] *Toronto World*, March 1, 1895
[64] "The Skull in Court," *Toronto World*, Mar. 4, 1895.
[65] "All Circumstantial," *Toronto World*, Mar. 2, 1895.

Next, Curry called Attorney T.W. Horn to the stand to testify about his efforts to help Harry corkscrew more money out of Martha. This caused a stir because Horn was sitting at counsel table with Johnston. Of course, Johnston objected. After a vociferous fight over whether Horn should be allowed to testify, Denison reserved his decision until the following Monday, and Mr. Horn stepped down.[66]

The most vociferous fight over admitting evidence came when Curry called Attorney Smoke, Martha's lawyer. Smoke testified that in the spring of 1893 he acted as solicitor for Martha Wells in the transferring of the insurance money to the Hyams brothers. At this point Johnston objected. He made an ingenious argument against Smoke's testimony. Smoke was going to testify about transactions between himself and Martha. Martha had a right to object to their disclosures due to attorney-client privilege. When Martha married Harry, her privilege became his privilege, and his privilege gave him the right to object to Smoke's testimony. Judge Denison said he knew of no authority to support Johnston's contention, and Johnston produced no authority to support his inventive argument. Denison rejected the novel argument: "There's nothing privileged about such evidence."

Johnston reasoned that even if Harry had no privilege, Martha still did, "Martha Hyams has not waived her right of objection to the details being made public."

"She has no right to waive," ruled Denison.[67] Smoke did, in fact, raise the privilege. Denison required him to testify

---

[66] "The Skull in Court," *Toronto World*, Mar. 4, 1895.
[67] Guillet, *Insurance Murderers*, 22, 23.

about actions he took on Martha's behalf, but not confidential communications he had with her.

Smoke testified that he remembered talking to Harry about the insurance proceeds. The conversation occurred in Smoke's office in the presence of Harry's solicitor, Mr. Horn. He could not remember much of the conversation. He thought Horn did most of the talking.

Q: "Was any statement made to you as to the amount of money H.P. Hyams had received from Mrs. Wells?"

A: "An admission was made by either Mr. Horn, speaking for Hyams, or by Hyams himself, that an amount of money had been received by H.P. Hyams from Miss Wells."

Q: "To what extent?"

A: "I have no distinct recollection of the amount, but I have refreshed my memory by perusing the correspondence which I had at that time with Hyams' solicitor." I think that about $9000 was then admitted to be in H.P. Hyams' hands belonging to Miss Wells."

Q: "That would be at what time?"

A: "On the 30th of March 1893."

Q: "Did he give any securities to Miss Wells?"

A: "He said he had securities which he could hand over to her for the whole amount."

Q: "Did you ever get these securities?"

A: "I did not get the whole $9000."

Q: "How much did you get?"

A: "My recollection is that I got less than $1000."

Q: "Did you ever advise your client not to execute a deed or paper containing recitals questioning her ownership of this money and whereby the money would go into the possession of H.P. Hymns?"

At this point, without any objection from Johnston, Judge Denison interjected, "I think that it is a leading question, and I don't think it is a question he can properly answer."

Curry asked another question, "Did you ever receive from Miss Wells such a document?"

"Let that stand until Monday," Denison ruled, when I will decide upon the other point."[68]

And with that, Denison would have recessed court until the next Monday, but the defense had one more motion. Wellman and Gooch had to return to New York City to see after their cases pending in that jurisdiction. Denison accommodated them by adjourning the hearing indefinitely until they could return. The Crown was not disappointed by the indefinite adjournment. Based on how the case had developed, they needed to do some more investigation, and their additional medical experts were going to be testifying in Osler's Hendershott trial the next week. Additionally, they hoped that the extended recess would give Martha Hyams time to recover sufficiently to take the stand when the hearing reconvened.[69]

When the preliminary hearing resumed on March 18, the first order of business was another defense request to

---

[68] "The Skull in Court," *Toronto World*, Mar. 4, 1895.
[69] "The Skull in Court," *Toronto World*, Mar. 4, 1895.

allow Wellman to actively participate in the hearing. Denison summarily denied the request, but his ruling did not prevent Wellman from stage-managing Johnston's cross-examinations of the witnesses.[70] Most trial lawyers would resent such close supervision while they were trying to conduct the examination of witnesses, but the arrangement seemed to work well.

Curry called Sailmaker John Thompson as his first witness. His nautical background made him an expert in the splicing of ropes, and the Hyams brothers called him in on December 28, 1892, to splice a new hook onto the rope attached to the weight. When Johnston attacked Thompson's expertise as a splicer, the witness provoked laughter from the audience by positively saying he was a professional splicer, that he had done a first-class job of splicing the rope, and that nobody could do a better job of splicing than he did. When Johnston tried to suggest that other splicers might do the job differently, Thompson said, "I don't know how other sailors splice ropes, but if they do it right, they would do it my way." Dallas and Harry laughed continuously during Thompson's testimony, and they were particularly amused when Johnston got him to admit that if there was a Know-Nothing party, he might be a member of it.[71]

One important part of Thompson's testimony that Johnston worked hard to undermine was his insistence that the weight could not come off the hook. The replacement hook was too large to go into the hole on the weight, so

---

[70] "Lawyer Wellman's Snub," New York World, Mar. 19, 1895.
[71] The Know-Nothings were a pre-Civil War political party that opposed, among other things, immigration, the Catholic Church, and slavery. Douglas Kierdorf, "Getting to Know the Know-Nothings," The Boston Globe, Jan. 10, 2016.

Thompson chiseled out the hole to make it just large enough to fit the hook. On cross-examination Thompson said he was positive the weight could not come off.

"And any man who said that it did would be a fool?" asked Johnston. This question was, no doubt, asked in a tone of disbelief.

"I don't know anything about any other man," Thompson replied, "I have seen a good many men do a good many foolish things."[72]

The Hyamses appeared to be in good spirits when they arrived in court at 10:30 the next morning, but by the time court recessed they looked haggard and careworn. Curry spent the day presenting more witnesses to prove that the weight could not have come off the hook. Curry had asked John Fensom, a builder of elevators, testified that based on his examination of the elevator, the weight could not come off the hook.[73] Johnston cross-examined vigorously, but Fensom's opinion was firm: "It did not come off, and I don't think it possibly could come off. I have never known one to do so."[74] Charles Lee, who had 14 years' experience as an elevator builder, had never known of a case where a weight fell off a hook. He had heard of accidents to elevators where the rope broke, but never where the weight came off.[75] Donald Craig, an expert elevator builder who had 15 years' experience with elevators of the type in the warehouse, testified next. Curry first established Craig's qualifications and then asked the key question: "Now, from your experience as an elevator man and having seen that

---

[72] "Two Distinct Wounds," *Toronto World*, Mar. 19, 1895.
[73] "The Strongest Yet," *Toronto World*, Mar. 20, 1895.
[74] Guillet, *Insurance Murderers*, 19.
[75] "The Strongest Yet," *Toronto World*, Mar. 20, 1895.

elevator, by pulling on the pull ropes and hoisting the cage, the weight being on the rope and meeting with an obstruction, could the weight fall from the hooks? Craig swore positively that no obstruction in the shaft would cause the weight to fall off. He could not conceive any way how it could occur.[76]

At the request of Judge Denison, Fox, Latimer and Aylesworth were called back to the stand. Denison wanted clarification on was how much business the warehouse had done. The general import of the testimony of the three witnesses was that, although the building had been rented to serve as an auction house, less than one full load of furniture had been brought in. The other merchandise brought into the warehouse consisted of small quantities of sugar, soap, and pearline.[77] If the Hyams twins ever held an auction at the warehouse, none of the three said so.[78]

Curry tried again to call T.W. Horn, who had acted as the Hyams' solicitor in the negotiations over separating Martha from her insurance proceeds. Johnston again objected on the ground that the witness was privileged. Denison decided to defer judgment on the issue until after all the other evidence was introduced.[79]

At the conclusion of the Crown's evidence for the day Johnston asked that permission be granted for Willie's skull to be examined by defense experts without a representative of the Crown being present. Johnston stated

---

[76] "The Strongest Yet," *Toronto World*, Mar. 20, 1895.

[77] Pearline is a type of tinted glassware popular in the Victorian Era. *20th Century Glass Encyclopedia*, https://www.20thcenturyglass.com/glass_encyclopedia/victorian_glass/pearline_glass.htm.

[78] "The Strongest Yet," *Toronto World*, Mar. 20, 1895.

[79] "The Strongest Yet," *Toronto World*, Mar. 20, 1895.

that Dr. Caven, a witness for the Crown, had the skull, and it should be in the possession of some person independent of detectives or Crown officers.

Curry said that he was willing to leave the skull with any court official and have any medical gentlemen examine it for the defense who desired to do so. Johnston saw a problem with that procedure. If his experts examined the skull in the presence of any Crown officers, the comments that they made would be communicated to the Crown. Denison saw no reason the experts could not examine the skull and then go to an adjoining room to make their comments. Denison held that the defense could choose a custodian between Clerk of the Court Morrison and his assistants Webb and Ramsay. Denison said he would order whoever was chosen not to repeat anything he might hear. Denison also gave the defense permission to take the weight to the Colborne Street warehouse and make tests in the presence of a representative of the Crown.[80]

The next day Curry led off with evidence of motive. He called a clerk from the Imperial Bank to show that immediately upon payment of the insurance proceeds to Martha, the Hyams brothers began working to separate her from the money. The clerk produced thirty-seven checks drawn by Martha in favor of either Dallas or Harry, including one $2000 check endorsed by Dallas and one $7964 check endorsed by Harry.[81]

Curry then returned to the injuries on Wells' head. He called numerous medical experts who agreed with Dr.

---

[80] "The Strongest Yet," *Toronto World*, Mar. 20, 1895.
[81] "Wells Was Murdered," *Toronto World*, Mar. 21, 1895.

Craven's opinions on the injury to the skull.[82] Finally, after six days of testimony scattered over three weeks, the Crown rested its case. Johnston moved that Dallas be discharged from prosecution. He began by praising Judge Denison's fairness and urged him to show that same fairness in ruling on his motion to discharge. He argued that no evidence whatsoever had been produced proving that Dallas participated in any murder scheme. There was nothing to show that Dallas had anything to do with placing the insurance on Wells, nor that Dallas had any expectancy of receiving a part of the insurance proceeds. He did not even get the commission for the sale of insurance—the insurance agent gave that money to Aylesworth. There was no blood on Dallas' clothing; the bloody pants found in the Hyams home belonged to Harry. The fact that Dallas was in the warehouse that morning was no more suggestive that he had killed Wells than the fact that Expressman Fox was there suggested that Fox killed him.

"I wish to say," Johnston continued, "and say it strongly, that we have been tried, we have been condemned, we have been hanged, by the newspapers without a particle of evidence. But the press, I am glad to say, have given us fair and impartial reports of the trial. This is the first time we have come to the court, and we ask for justice. We ask the court, despite popular feeling, despite public prejudice and in spite of public comment, to grant us justice. I submit with the greatest confidence that so far as Dallas Hyams is concerned there is not a single thing the Crown can lay its hand upon that will warrant conviction. Suspicion is not enough; there must be something tangible. In conclusion: I

---

[82] "Wells Was Murdered," *Toronto World*, Mar. 21, 1895, "Hyams Held for Trial," *Buffalo Evening News*, Mar. 21, 1895, "The Hyams Committed," *Montreal Gazette*, Mar. 21, 1895.

am not raising a question of accident. No matter whether the defense is accident, willful act on the part of Wells, or a murder committed by somebody else, I claim that there is not a tittle of evidence against Dallas Hyams."[83]

During the argument for his discharge, Dallas became extremely nervous. He squirmed in his seat in the dock and looked like he was extremely excited. Several times he looked like he was about to faint. Harry showed more composure, sitting with his head turned to the right and never removing his gaze from the courtroom wall.[84]

In arguing against the motion, Curry ticked off the factors he believed indicated guilt:

(1) The Hyamses went to Oshawa, where the Wells family lived and persuaded them to come to Toronto and put money into the Hyams' business.

(2) When the Wells family arrived in Toronto, they induced Aylesworth, Willie, and Martha to lend them $3000.

(3) Aylesworth and Willie began to press for their money back.

(4) The brothers, trying to convince Aylesworth and Wells they had plenty of cash, showed them a big pile of money on their desk. When the pile was accidentally knocked over, it was shown that there were only a few large denomination bills on the top, and the rest were one-dollar notes.

(5) They nevertheless persuaded Aylesworth and Wells to leave their money where it was, and then the

---

[83] "Hyams Held for Trial," *Buffalo Evening News*, Mar. 21, 1895.
[84] "Hyams Held for Trial," *Buffalo Evening News*, Mar. 21, 1895.

brothers hired them and put them to doing busywork in the warehouse.

(6) Although the elevator was almost never used, the brothers began to tinker with it.

(7) Dallas oversaw the making of the openings in the shaft for the removal and replacement of the weight.

(8) Meantime Willie was engaged in negotiations to buy a farm in Pickering. He demanded his money back, and the Hyams agreed to give it to him on January 16.

(9) On January 14, the twins arranged that both Aylesworth and Latimer would be away from the warehouse in the morning and that Wells should come in early.

(10) Wells was killed in the warehouse on January 16, and the Hyams brothers were the only other people there.

(11) The brothers were in financial straits when the death occurred. They immediately finagled some of the insurance proceeds from Martha and started paying off debts.

(12) While they owed large sums of money at high interest, they were nevertheless paying huge premiums on Wells' insurance.

(13) In light of the evidence, it must be concluded that the only interest the Hyams had in the Wells family was to see how much money they could fleece them for, and the biggest fleecing was the insurance murder scam.

Denison made his ruling: "I don't wish to review all the evidence and argue the points discussed, but my impression is that, from the evidence adduced there is enough to place the accused on trial. There is no doubt that the evidence is not so strong against Dallas Hyams as against the other prisoner. But the evidence has convinced me that the death of young Wells was not due to accident. There has been ample testimony to show that the weight could not have come off the hook and killed the deceased as alleged. Someone killed him and these two men were the only persons present when he met his death. Anyway, I don't want to argue the case and show the strong points against the prisoners. I will commit both for trial."[85] The *Ottawa Journal* reported that when Dallas heard the judge's ruling, he "broke down completely" and "sobbed bitterly" as he was returned to jail.[86]

Before court closed that last day, Johnston made an accusation of espionage against Curry. He said Curry had interviewed a prospective defense witness. He claimed that the Crown became aware of this witness by eavesdropping on a conversation at the jail between Wellman and the brothers. Curry denied the allegation, saying that the information about the witness had come from another source. He supported his contention with the testimony of Deputy Chief of Police Stuart.[87]

Johnston's effort to put the bloody pants on Harry rather than Dallas revealed a severe problem for the defense team. Dallas and Harry had conflicting defenses. It might very well be in Dallas' best interest to try to shift the blame for the killing completely to Harry. How could Johnston argue that Harry was not guilty out of one side of

---

[85] "Hyams Held for Trial," *Buffalo Evening News*, Mar. 21, 1895.
[86] "He Was All Broken Up," *Ottawa Evening Journal*, Mar. 22, 1891.
[87] "Hyams Held for Trial," *Buffalo Evening News*, Mar. 21, 1895.

his mouth and claim Dallas was innocent because Harry did it out of the other side? The two men needed separate lawyers.

Another issue with the defense was Johnston's tendency to make unsubstantiated claims and then to assure the court that he could back them up with evidence. The most notable instance of this was his claim that the hook had been changed and he could prove it—a claim which Curry refuted with the testimony of Sailmaker Thompson. This tendency did not make much difference before a judge sitting without a jury, but it certainly might have an improper influence on a jury.

Other unsubstantiated claims Johnston made also reveal an unfortunate tendency on his part to engage in unnecessary *ad hominem* attacks on the prosecution witnesses. The attack on Aylesworth as a layabout gambler who squandered his wife's insurance money is one such attack. In another instance, when Uriah Jones was testifying about his arrangements to sell a farm to Willie, Johnston said, "I warn the witness that we propose to show that Jones was attempting to sell a $500 farm to Wells for $2150." This bluster understandably irritated Jones, who emphatically denied that he ever owned a $500 farm.[88] Johnston apparently belonged to the school of lawyering which held that to do an effective cross-examination, one must examine crossly. Sometimes this tactic works, other times it boomerangs. The defense dropped this ridiculous contention that Jones was trying to swindle Willie when the case came up for trial.[89]

---

[88] "The Skull in Court," *Toronto World*, Mar. 4, 1895.
[89] Street, *Bench Book*, 13:273-291, 292-311.

That night Wellman and Gooch dined with Lieutenant Governor George Airy Kirkpatrick.[90] Kirkpatrick held the dinner at the Government House, and twenty-three members of Parliament to attended. During his time in Canada, Wellman was treated as a celebrity. He was constantly invited to dinners and parties, and one time he was the guest of honor at a dinner given by the Toronto Club. Two hundred and fifty attended this meal. The champagne flowed freely at the Toronto Club, and the postprandial hobnobbing lasted until 2:00 in the morning. Wellman was not just after free dinners. His ulterior motive was to disarm some of the public animosity toward his clients. He genuinely felt that this tactic succeeded in helping the prejudice against the brothers to subside.[91]

---

[90] "Bad for the Hyams," *New York World*, Mar. 20, 1895.
[91] Wellman, *Luck and Opportunity*, 1895, 96; *Gentlemen of the Jury*, 119.

CHAPTER FIVE: THE TRIAL BEGINS

Wellman did not immediately go back to New York. He had a few things to do. Seeing that medical testimony would play a decisive role in the upcoming trial, he took steps to deny the Crown of as many expert witnesses as possible. As Wellman described it in his memoirs: "Perceiving early in the course of preparation that the trial would eventually resolve itself into a battle between medical experts, before the Crown was aware of it, I had engaged on my side of the case practically all of the leading surgeons and doctors in that vicinity."[1] Wellman explained his stratagem: "I did not know what they would say, but at least they could not say anything against me. And later, when the Crown began to wake up and look around for doctors to strengthen their side of the case, they had to engage them from Quebec and other outlying cities."[2] Wellman displays faulty memory here. The Crown called many local doctors to testify.

One of Wellman's stratagems miscarried. Crown Counsel Curry learned that Wellman had rented the warehouse where the tragedy occurred, and he took quick action. He went to the Attorney General, and through that officer's influence prevailed upon the landlord to cancel the lease. He then immediately rented the building on behalf of the Crown. He justified his action by telling the press it was necessary to make sure the warehouse remained in the same condition as at present in case the jury wanted to personally view the scene of the crime.[3]

---

[1] Wellman, *Gentlemen of the Jury*, 118.
[2] Wellman, *Luck and Opportunity*, 92, 93.
[3] "Outgeneraled the Defence," *Toronto World*, March 23, 1895

Even though Curry had barred Wellman from renting the warehouse, he willingly allowed the defense to conduct experiments on the elevator—in the presence of representatives of the Crown. The defense conducted its experiments on the morning of March 22. Attorneys for the defense Wellman, Gooch, Johnston, Horn, and Barrett attended. Wellman had retained a group of expert elevator men to conduct the experiments, and representatives of the Toronto Police brought the rope, hook, and weight.

The policemen unlocked the warehouse, and the entire group entered and went directly to the elevator. The experts employed by the defense attached the hook and weight to the elevator, and they ran it up and down the shaft at various speeds. They jerked the weight and did other things to try to make the weight come off, all to no avail. The police detectives stood by to make sure that the hook was not opened wider, the weight stolen, or the elevator turned upside down.

At the conclusion of the experiments a reporter buttonholed E.F.B. Johnston for a comment. He put as good a spin as possible on the defense's failure to corroborate the accident defense, "There was no experiment in the sense that we dropped the weight or tried to drop it. That is not possible on account of the boilers that have been placed below," Johnston said, referring to the fact that extensive alterations had been made to the basement since the Hyams brother had the property, "In fact the changes in the building preclude the possibility by either the Crown or the defense of ascertaining what might or might not happen at the time of the accident."[4]

---

[4] "He Was All Broken Up," *Ottawa Evening Journal*, Mar. 22, 1895.

The rumor mill churned out story after story in the leadup to the trial, some true, some half-true, and some completely false. Unlimited funds were available to the defense, with Wellman receiving US$300 a day himself. A host of experts had examined the skull and were ready to testify that Wells had been struck twice by an axe. The first blow came from the side of the axe as he was standing, and when he fell to the floor he was struck above the eye with the back of the axe. The Crown had uncovered stronger evidence connecting Dallas to the murder, but they declined to say what that evidence was. The defense intended to move for a continuance of the trial when it came up for arraignment.[5] One solid piece of news developed when the Toronto grand jury returned an indictment against the brothers for murder.[6]

On May 1, the day after the indictment was returned, the brothers were arraigned before Chancellor Boyd in the York Assize Court.[7] One of the recent rumors was confirmed when Johnston made a motion for continuance and a motion for a commission to be issued so that they could travel to Cleveland and Philadelphia to take the testimony of foreign witnesses. The defense supported both motions with affidavits. Johnston argued that because the death occurred over two years ago the defense had experienced a great deal of difficulty in obtaining evidence. While the defense team had made every effort to prepare for trial,

---

[5] "The Hyams Defence," *Manitoba Morning Free Press*, Apr. 9, 1895; "Wells Was Killed with an Ax," *Toronto World*, Apr. 13, 1895.

[6] "True Bills," *Manitoba Morning Free Press*, May 1, 1895 "Twin Brothers Charged with Murder," *New York Times*, May 1, 1895.

[7] The narrative of the arraignment and motions is taken from "Hyams' Trial," *Manitoba Morning Free Press*, May 2, 1895; "The Hyams' Trial to Proceed Monday," *Toronto World*, May 2, 1895; "Clara Ford's Motive Still a Mystery," *Toronto World*, May 2, 1895.

they could not hope to be ready for trial in the current session of the court.

Mr. Johnston offered several affidavits of counsel stating that Clara T. Hyams, Dallas' wife, and Clara Hyams, the twins' mother; Chapman H. Hyams of New Orleans; Walter H. Rammage of Philadelphia; John Thomas Bragg of Cleveland; and Samuel Slater were material witnesses for the defense and could not be produced in court. Chapman Hyams was ill at New Orleans and his evidence was absolutely necessary; the Hyams ladies had sailed on a steamer from Savannah, Georgia, going to New York, and could not be reached at present. When Detective Cuddy heard Slater's name mentioned, Cuddy said he had seen the man in the courtroom that very day. Cuddy dashed out of the courtroom and returned in ten minutes with Samuel Slater in tow. At this point Johnston decided that Slater was not a material witness after all and struck his name from the affidavit.

B.B. Osler, fresh from his victory in the Hendershott trial, put in an affidavit that both the Hyams ladies were domiciled in Toronto on the day the brothers were arrested. He also cited cases showing that when postponement is asked in a case the court must be satisfied that the absent witnesses are material, that every effort has been made to get them here, and that there is a probability of them being present at the postponed trial. He argued that the defense had not made out a case. Three of the missing witnesses were close relatives of the accused. What, he asked, can be suggested that the brother in New Orleans knows as to what occurred in Toronto? He opposed postponement and asked for trial to begin on Monday. Osler called T.W. Horn for cross-examination on his affidavit. Under questioning Horn abandoned the claim that the Hyams ladies were material witnesses. He also admitted that he only had hearsay to show that Chapman Hyams was suffering from gout.

Chancellor Boyd held that the materials produced by the defense had entirely failed to make out a reason for postponement. There was no cause for delay whatever, as far as he could see from the affidavits. At Johnston's request his lordship allowed the filing of supplemental affidavits, conditioned on the cross-examination of Horn upon his affidavits.

Both Osler and Johnston were dividing their time between the arraignment of the Hyams brothers and the murder case of Clara Ford, which was being tried in another courtroom. Osler went back to the Ford trial on the following day, but disaster struck that evening. At 8:00 p.m., his wife Caroline died. Crippling arthritis had made her a wheelchair-bound invalid for many years, and she had more recently suffered horrible burns in a house fire. Despite these infirmities, her death was quite unexpected. The following morning the papers speculated that Mrs. Osler's death would cause a postponement of the Ford trial,[8] but it went on as scheduled. So did Osler. He was back in court on May 3, again dividing his time between the Hyams case and the Ford case.

Osler's continuing with the trials despite his wife's death was a result of devotion to duty, not lack of care for his wife. When she was trapped in the burning building, he rushed in and carried her out. This act of heroism cost him dearly. He suffered terrible burns on his hands and face, and he carried permanent scars from the flames. In 1893 he began to build a magnificent stone "summer cottage" for

---

[8] "From the Queen City," *Montreal Gazette*, May 3, 1895.

her on a hill in the middle of a 300-acre tract of land near Blue Mountain in Grey County. Osler hoped that the location would prove beneficial to his wife's health, but she did not enjoy it long. The construction took two years, it was finished in 1894, and Osler held a grand opening in September of that year. He chartered a special train to take family, friends, and business associates to a party at the mansion. Caroline fell in love with the place, and named it Kiontono, a First Nations word meaning "Hilltop," but the giant home came to be known as Osler Castle. Caroline never spent a summer there, dying in Toronto on May 3, 1895. Osler would occasionally visit the mansion over the next five summers, but he never really got much pleasure from the place. After his death in 1901 Osler Castle fell into ruin. Although the stone walls are about the only thing left of the mansion, it has become something of a tourist attraction.[9]

The day after his wife's death saw Osler back before Chancellor Boyd arguing against another motion for continuance. The affidavits in support of this motion alleged that: (1) Chapman Hyams of New Orleans was needed as a witness to prove that for the past nine years he had paid large sums of money to the brothers and their mother. He gave the twins a regular allowance of US$ 200 per month and had made several one-time payments to them, the smallest being US$ 300 and the largest US$ 1900. Chapman

---

[9] Andrew Armitage, "Osler Castle an Enchanting Place Briefly," Ontario Sun Times, August 22, 2008; Sandy McInnis, "Osler Castle ... A Tribute to Love in Bricks, Mortar, and Stone," https://sandymcinnes.blogspot.com/2014/11/osler-castle-tribute-to-love-in-bricks.html; "Osler Castle (Kiontono) – Town of Blue Mountains, Ontario," https://www.waymarking.com/waymarks/WMG1PV_Osler_Castle_Kionontio_Town_of_Blue_Mountains_Ontario.

also gave the mother money from time to time. One time he gave her $3,000 to furnish a house for herself and the brothers. The affidavit did not mention the fact that the brothers repeatedly mortgaged their mother's furniture. (2) John Thomas Bragg of Cleveland was needed to testify to the condition of the cellar where Willie died. (3) Matthew Rammage of Philadelphia could testify that on the morning of the death he, Harry, and Willie walked down from the corner of Victoria and Adelaide Streets between 8 and 9 a.m., and that he and Harry left Wells at the door of the warehouse and walked on to a barber shop in Leader-lane.[10]

Osler answered by saying that money given the twins by Chapman Hyams had nothing to do with the case, that Bragg's proof was available from other witnesses, and that the Crown was willing to admit that Harry might have been in a Leader-lane barber shop between 8 and 9 o'clock the morning of the tragedy.[11]

Chancellor Boyd ruled that the defense had not stated sufficient grounds for a continuance. He did, however, issue a commission for the taking of the testimony of Bragg in Cleveland and Rammage in Philadelphia. He refused to issue a commission for Chapman Hyams. Crown Counsel Curry, T.W. Horn, and a court reporter departed that very afternoon for Cleveland and Philadelphia to take the witnesses' testimony.[12] Curry and Horn made a lightning trip to Cleveland and took Bragg's testimony, but Horn abandoned efforts to take Rammage's testimony. They

---

[10] "Hyams' Trial Next Week," *Toronto World*, May 3, 1895.

[11] "Hyams' Trial Next Week," *Toronto World*, May 3, 1895.

[12] "Hyams' Trial Next Week," *Toronto World*, May 3, 1895.

were back in Toronto by May 6,[13] and the Crown announced they would be ready for trial on Thursday, May 9.[14]

Pressure had been mounting for the Canadian courts to admit Francis L. Wellman for the limited purpose of examining witnesses and speaking in court on behalf of the Hyams brothers. The *Boston Herald* reported that:

> Every effort is being made to prevail upon the authorities to allow Mr. Wellman to appeal for the prisoners. Secretary of State [Walter Q.] Gresham has written to [Ontario] Atty.-Gen. [Sir Oliver] Mowatt, making this quest, and the good office of Atty.-Gen. [Richard] Olney have also been sought.

The *Boston Herald,* after having reported what they believed to be the facts, then repeated some gossip:

> Several of the men who have been active in the prosecution of the American prisoners have long been active in fomenting a feeling hostile to the United States.[15]

The *New-York Tribune* also weighed in on the controversy, severely criticizing the Canadian authorities, and reporting that "The British Minister in Washington was asked to intercede in the matter, but he gave little satisfaction."[16]

The *Toronto World* fired back. "Want Wellman to Plead"[17] accused the U.S. papers of "jingoism and misrepresentation," quoting extensively from an opinion

---

[13] "Hyams Commission Returns," *Toronto World*, May 6, 1895

[14] "The Hyams Case," *Toronto World*, May 7, 1895

[15] "Of International Interest," *Boston Herald*, May 6, 1895.

[16] "Francis L. Wellman Barred Out," *New York Tribune*, May 6, 1895.

[17] May 7, 1895.

article in the *New York Herald*.[18] The following day the *Herald* printed "Cannot Plead in Canada's Courts,"[19] which admitted that the Canadian authorities were within their rights to deny Wellman's appearance. Simultaneous with the *Herald* story, the *Toronto World* published "An International Question," which assumed a more balanced tone, setting forth the reasons that Wellman could not be allowed to appear in a Canadian court.[20] The editorial boards of the two papers apparently had entered into an international peace treaty.

Meanwhile, the pretrial maneuvering continued apace. The Defense asked for a three-day delay of the trial. The Defense argued that a certain case against a man named Dicks was also set to for trial in this term of court, it would take three days to try, and it should be tried before the Hyams case. The Crown replied that it would not be ready to try Dicks until after the conclusion of the Hyams case. Next, the Defense asked for another commission to examine a witness. Mr. J.D. Nesmith had been summoned for the Defense, but prior to receiving his subpoena, he had made arrangements to go to England with his family. Justice William Street, who had been assigned to preside over the trial, promptly denied the application, saying that he lacked the authority to grant a commission. "Otherwise, I should be happy to do so."[21]

Justice Street was an able lawyer and a conscientious judge who "looked neither to the right nor the left in the faithful discharge of his exalted judicial duties." His

---

[18] Diligent search of numerous newspaper archives has failed to unearth this article.

[19] May 8, 1895.

[20] May 8, 1895.

[21] "The Hyams Case Must Go On," *Toronto World*, May 8, 1895.

steadfast devotion to duty made him a humorless man who frowned upon trial counsel's efforts to introduce levity into the proceedings. On the bench he had a calm demeanor which could not be ruffled, nor could any calamity rattle his judgment. A thin man with a closely cropped beard, he was described by his contemporaries as "just, fearless, courteous and fair."[22]

The eve of the trial came, and one more issue arose. A talesman (prospective juror) in the Hyams case went to the office of County Crown Attorney Dewart and reported that someone had attempted to bribe him in connection with the Hyams case. He also said that other talesmen had been approached with bribery offers. Dewart immediately began investigating. He soon discovered that almost all the talesmen had been approached. Dewart had officers dispatched to arrest the culprit, but they had no success.[23]

The investigation revealed that the culprit was a well-dressed gentleman who would approach the talesmen either at home or at their places of business and after a brief conversation would question the talesmen about their religion and whether they believed in capital punishment. Then the gentleman would steer the conversation to the Hyams case. Depending on how that part of the conversation went, the gentleman would slap his pocket and say that there would be lots of money paid to jurors who voted the right way.[24]

The case of John W. Erwood, a talesman whom the defense challenged off the panel, was typical of the approaches. He reported that on the Sunday before the trial

[22] Hassard, *Famous Canadian Trials*, 224, 225.
[23] "Wholesale Attempt at Bribery," *New York Times,* May 9, 1895.
[24] "Wholesale Attempt at Bribery," *New York Times,* May 9, 1895.

was scheduled to begin a well-dressed man who had a decidedly American accent came to his home, introducing himself as a friend of the Hyams brothers. He asked if Erwood were satisfied with his present dwelling and said that if Erwood "did the right thing," there would be a "material consideration" for him. Erwood ordered the gentleman out of his home and immediately reported the matter to Sheriff Mowatt.[25] Thirty-five prospective jurors made similar reports to the sheriff. Erwood was called into the box during jury selection, but the defense promptly challenged him. It seemed that the mysterious stranger, who identified himself as "Mr. Pender," had advised the defense team of the attitudes of all the talesmen he had interviewed. The *Ottowa Journal* reported that the defense lawyers already "knew just about the opinion of every juror, both on capital punishment and the Hyams case."[26]

The stranger was a notorious New Yorker known as Col. Foster, a failed theatrical promoter who had turned to jury-fixing.[27] Foster became involved with the Tammany Hall political machine after the collapse of his Boston Ideal Opera Company, and his gift of gab fitted him perfectly for his new profession. In addition to jury-fixing, he supplemented his income as an expert poker player and pool shark.[28] Jury-fixing in Toronto outside the umbrella of protection provided by the Tammany organization was both more hazardous and less likely to succeed. Toronto had a population just under 200,000 in the 1890's;[29] but

---

[25] "There Was Money in It," *Ottawa Journal*, May 29, 1895.

[26] "There was Money in It," Ottawa Journal, May 29, 1895.

[27] "The Boston Ideals Collapse," *New York Times,* May 11, 1895.

[28] Charlesworth, *Candid Chronicles*, 229, 230.

[29] "Canada City Population History: Montreal, Ottawa, Toronto & Vancouver," http://demographia.com/db-cancityhist.htm.

New York City was in the middle of a population explosion which saw it grow from 1,515,301 in 1890 to 3,437,202 in 1900.[30] Regardless of the identity of the jury-fixer, his efforts failed. The ham-fisted approach taken by the jury-fixer might have worked in the teeming metropolis that was New York City; but it was ill-suited for the less corrupt culture of Toronto.

The press heard the rumors of jury-fixing and went to Dewart for confirmation. Dewart was taken completely by surprise that the story had leaked out. His first reaction was to neither confirm nor deny the story, but eventually he admitted its truth. Dewart said that he had just commenced an investigation into the allegations, that all proper steps were being taken, and that the offender or offenders would be prosecuted. When defense counsel were approached about the reports, they flatly denied knowing anything about such efforts at bribery.[31]

Wellman and Gooch arrived in town that evening amid speculation in the press that the bribery attempts would cause the jury panel to be discharged and a new one drawn, a process which was predicted to take four days.[32] With the arrival of the New York lawyers, all the pieces were in place to begin what the *Toronto World* called the greatest trial in Canadian history.[33]

---

[30] "Population History of New York from 1790 – 1990," http://physics.bu.edu/~redner/projects/population/cities/newyork.ht ml.

[31] "'Doctoring' the Jury," *Manitoba Morning Free Press,* May 9, 1895; "Wholesale Attempt at Bribery," *New York Times,* May 9, 1895.

[32] "Wholesale Attempt at Bribery," *New York Times,* May 9, 1895.

[33] "The Fate of the Twins May Be Known To-Night," Toronto World, May 23, 1895; "Unanimous as to Guilt," Toronto World, May 25, 1895.

Monday, May 9, the trial got underway. The *New-York Herald* described the scene: "In the historic and dingy old building in Court Street, among the fasces and tipstaves. battleaxes and spears, where the Judge is 'My Lord' and where no criminal lawyer may speak for an American citizen, the trial of Harry P. Hyams and Dallas H. Hyams, the remarkable American twins charged with the strangest of murders, was begun at ten o'clock this morning."[34] A huge crowd of spectators filled the courtroom to overflowing. When the officers brought the twins in, they appeared to be in good health, but their pale complexions and their nervous demeanors gave evidence of the stress they were undergoing.

At 10:15 sharp, the court crier called out "Oyez," and Mr. Justice William Street took the bench. As he took his seat, he saw arrayed before him a stellar collection of talented lawyers. Britton Bath Osler, QC, fresh off his defeat in the Clara Ford murder case, led for the Crown, assisted by Deputy Attorney General John R. Cartwright, QC, County Crown Counsel Hartley H. Dewart, and County Crown Counsel James W. Curry. E.F.B. Johnston, QC, fresh off his victory in the Clara Ford murder case, led for Harry Hyams, assisted by T.W. Horn. William Lount, QC, led for Dallas, assisted by W.G. Murdoch. Francis L. Wellman and W.W. Gooch were also at the defense table. The *New-York Herald* called the assembled lawyers "the most imposing array of counsel ever seen in this court."[35] and the first order of business was to determine whether and to what extent Wellman and Gooch could assist the defense.

---

[34] "Hyams Twins' Trial," *New-York Herald*, May 10, 1895.
[35] "Hyams Twins' Trial," *New-York Herald*, May 10, 1895.

The defense had resolved the issue of conflict of interest by splitting their number into two teams, one representing Harry, the other representing Dallas. The division of representation gave the defense a distinct advantage. With one counsel leading for both brothers, there would be only one cross-examination of each witness and one summation when it came time for final arguments. With separate counsel, the defense would be able to "double-team" the witnesses on cross-examination and, at the end of the case, make two final arguments to the prosecution's one.

Mr. Lount made the motion to admit Wellman and allow him to be associated with the defense. He argued that Wellman was a distinguished member of the New York Bar, had been for many years the lawyer for the Hyams family in New York City, and he had been intimately involved in the case from the very beginning. Lount asked that Justice Street "grant the indulgence of allowing him to appear" on behalf of the twins. Many Canadian lawyers, including Lount, had been extended the privilege of appearing in U.S. courts. He asked that Wellman be extended a like courtesy and be allowed to appear on behalf of his American clients. Lount asked especially that Wellman be allowed to conduct cross-examinations.[36]

Lount asked at least for the privilege of allowing Wellman to cross-examine witnesses because Wellman was recognized as one of the best, if not the best, cross-examiners south of the Great Lakes. Wellman first rose to national prominence as a cross-examiner in the Carlyle Harris murder case, where he surgically destroyed the star expert witness for the defense. Wellman's destruction of the witness was so complete that he had the courtroom

---

[36] "The Hyams Twins on Trial," *Toronto World*, May 10, 1895.

roaring with laughter by the time he finished.[37] Wellman would later go on to write the classic *The Art of Cross-Examination*, which is still in print today.

Osler answered: If any foreign lawyer were to be allowed to appear in court in Canada, then Wellman's high standing in the American bar ought to give him the privilege, especially given the seriousness of the charges against the Hyams brothers. Canada's rule, however, excluded Wellman, as well as any member of the British Bar. As Osler understood it, the privilege was extended by U.S. courts to Canadian lawyers, but in Canada no one could plead unless approved by the Law Society.[38]

Justice Street ruled that he had no discretion in the matter; that only lawyers introduced by the Law Society could plead in Canadian courts. If he were to rule otherwise, he would be setting a dangerous precedent which he had no authority to introduce. He ruled, however, that Wellman and Gooch could sit at counsel table with the defense team to advise and assist them, but Mr. Wellman could not cross-examine witnesses.[39]

At the end of the day, as Wellman was leaving the courthouse, a reporter asked him to comment on Justice Street's ruling. Wellman said: "I entirely understand and appreciate the position taken by Mr. Justice Street and Mr. Osler, and do not see, under the circumstances, how they could have acted otherwise. I am entirely satisfied with local counsel conducting the defense and regretted very much that the application had to be made at all, but the

---

[37] See a full description of this legendary cross-examination in Dekle, *Six Capsules: The Gilded Age Murder of Helen Potts*, 115-120.
[38] "The Hyams Twins on Trial," *Toronto World*, May 10, 1895.
[39] "The Hyams Twins on Trial," *Toronto World*, May 10, 1895.

relatives in New York insisted upon it. I am convinced the prisoners will have every opportunity to prove their innocence."[40]

The next order of business was jury selection. Eighty-eight talesmen had been summoned to appear that morning, but only eighty answered the roll call. The first talesman called into the box had served the previous week on the Clara Ford jury. The Crown had him "stand aside," which was the equivalent of a peremptory challenge in U.S. courts. Eleven of the twelve Clara Ford jurors were called into the box, and the Crown had ten of them "stand aside." The eleventh, who had held out for a conviction in the Ford case, was challenged by the defense. The defense had a total of forty peremptory challenges, and they exercised every one of them. The Crown had a total of sixteen talesmen stand aside, and one talesman was excused for cause—he had already made up his mind. The selection process took 90 minutes, at the end of which they had a jury consisting of nine farmers, one pump maker, a carpenter, and a shoe salesman.

The jury being sworn, Britton Bath Osler rose to his feet to make his opening statement. Osler, a huge man over six feet tall and weighing over two hundred pounds, was one of the greatest Canadian orators of the Victorian Era,[41] and his opening statement did nothing to diminish his fame. His opening followed a pattern for forensic speeches which was old when mutineers set Henry Hudson adrift in James Bay. According to the ancient rhetorical texts, a forensic speech should consist of six parts: An **Introduction**, to render the

---

[40] "Wellman is Satisfied," *Toronto World,* May 10, 1895.
[41] Hassard, "Great Canadian Orators," *The Canadian Magazine*. Vol. 54, No. 4, Pages 353-360.

jury attentive, receptive, and well disposed; a brief **Statement of the Case** to give the jury a thumbnail of the facts; a Division, to state the main issues of the case; a **Confirmation**, to persuade the jury to resolve those issues in the orator's favor; a **Refutation**, to answer any arguments that could be made by opposing counsel; and a **Conclusion**, to encourage the jury to return a favorable verdict.[42] Osler's opening statement, which had all the components of the Classical forensic speech, is reproduced in Appendix A.

Osler's speech was much more understated than contemporary prosecution openings made in American courts. For example, in the celebrated case, *People versus George Frank*, in dealing with the issue of circumstantial evidence in a murder case with no eyewitnesses, Wellman said in opening statement: "And altogether the circumstances naturally point to, and satisfy, a reasonable man's mind, that this man was the man who committed the crime in Room 33. But they say, 'You have got no eyewitness to that crime. No one saw it. It is all circumstantial.' It is not so, gentlemen. There was an eyewitness to that crime, and it was the eye of God. And the hand of God has written on the wall the name of this assassin, and science has allowed us to demonstrate it beyond any possible power of contradiction."[43]

The defense made no opening statement, and the taking of testimony began. During the trial Osler called nearly one hundred witnesses, eighteen of them being medical experts. He also called insurance men, telegraphers, elevator manufacturers, carpenters, builders,

---

[42] *Rhetorica ad Herennium*, 1.3.4.
[43] Dekle, *The East River Ripper*, 92.

civil engineers, architects, detectives, university professors, and even one poet. He introduced various models of the elevator shaft, its cage, and the hoist. He introduced photographs and architects plans of the building. He even placed the massive counterweight into evidence, as well as the victim's skull.[44]

The next day the papers were full of superlatives as they described the trial. The *Toronto World* wrote, "The trial which will last at least ten days, will prove in many respects the most remarkable ever heard in Canada;"[45] the *Calgary Daily Herald* said, "It promises to be one of the greatest murder cases ever tried in Canada;"[46] and the *Ottowa Evening Journal* called it "one of the most tragic mysteries Toronto's police have ever been called upon to solve."[47]

---

[44] Hassard, *Famous Canadian Trials*, 230.
[45] "The Hyams Twins on Trial," *Toronto World*, May 10, 1895.
[46] "A Great Trial," *Calgary Daily Herald*, May 10, 1895.
[47] "The Wells Murder Story,"

CHAPTER SIX: THE PROSECUTION CASE, DAYS ONE AND TWO[1]

The Crown began their case with Francis L. Baker, an architect who had drawn floorplans of the warehouse. The plans went into evidence after a brief cross-examination, and then Ebeneezer W.H. Aylesworth took the stand. He cut quite a figure with his gaudy waistcoat and wide-winged collar set off by a bright pink four-in-hand tie. He affected a careless air as he stood nonchalantly in the witness box with his arms outstretched and resting on the rail. The *New-York Herald* observed, "Brother-in-law Aylesworth told his story with an air between ennui and impertinence. As chief witness for the Crown, he feels his importance."[2] Such an attitude could do nothing to enhance Aylesworth's credibility with the jury. Despite the credibility issues, Justice Street thought him an important witness, writing thirty-seven pages of notes on his testimony.[3]

Osler's direct examination of Aylesworth did not follow a strict chronological or topical format. The jumbled, haphazard structure to his first day of direct examination puts one in mind of what is sometimes called "exploratory direct examination." This is the kind of examination that is done when the examiner has only a vague idea of what the witness is going to say. In such an examination the advocate simply starts at the beginning of the witness's testimony and then progresses through, asking questions as they occur to him, frequently getting sidetracked, and sometimes doubling back to previous testimony. Albert

---

[1] Thursday, May 9, 1895 – Friday, May 10, 1895.
[2] "The Hyams Twins on Trial," *Toronto World*, May 10, 1895.
[3] Street, *Bench Book,* 13:273-291, 292-311.

Richard Hassard, who observed the trial, made this same sort of critique of the Crown's entire presentation. Hassard, who that very year received a B.C.L. (Bachelor of Civil Law) with honors from Trinity College, would later write, "The Crown's case did not pursue any particular chronological order very closely, but the facts were so simple, that they required but little of the imagination to piece them satisfactorily together."[4]

Hassard was a man of towering intellect. The B.C.L. was an advanced law degree. Only the best graduates of law school could enter the course of study, and Hassard's receipt of the degree with honors shows that he was the best of the best. His prolific output of books on Canadian law gives further evidence of his genius.[5] That a man of Hassard's ability could sort out the disjointed presentation of the Crown does not mean that the average juror could. The jumbled evidentiary presentation was a weakness.

A coherent order of testimony is important even in a simple one-day trial, but it is of vital significance in a complex, sprawling, multi-week case. It is likely that several factors contributed to the Crown's muddled presentation of evidence:

First, complex cases like the Hyams case were few and far between in the nineteenth century, and only a small minority of lawyers would have sufficient experience with such cases to know how to properly present them.

---

[4] Hassard, *Famous Canadian Trials*, 232.
[5] *Canadian Constitutional History and Law* (Toronto: The Carswell Company, 1900); *Private International Law* (Toronto: The Goodwin Company, 1899); *A New Light on Lord Macaulay* (Toronto: Confederation of Life Building, 1918); *Not Guilty, and Other Trials* (Toronto: Lee Collins Company, 1926).

Second, in the late nineteenth and early twentieth century trial advocacy was not taught as aggressively as it is today, and most lawyers got their training from firsthand experience in trials.

Third, there is a dying philosophy of trial advocacy which looks upon the evidence as the mere raw materials of persuasion. According to this school of thought, the evidence merely serves as a foundation for the persuasion that is to come in final argument. This philosophy has been described as, "Proffer in the evidence; prove up all the elements; pray the jury has good sense." Nowadays the better trial advocates are keenly aware that making a persuasive presentation of evidence is just as important as making a persuasive argument.

Fourth, Britton Bath Osler, the man most experienced with the presentation of complex cases, was so busy trying cases that he had no time to prepare them. As a full-time barrister, he had to depend on lawyers acting in the role of solicitors to marshal the evidence and prepare the case for trial. That task fell to Crown Counsel Curry, who presented the case at the preliminary hearing. As we saw in Chapter Four, Curry was prone to making haphazard evidentiary presentations.

How could the case have been better presented? One way of bringing order to chaos would be to break the case down into "modules" or "mini-trials" of the various components of the larger case. Each module would address one aspect of the case, and all the evidence on that aspect would be presented before moving on to another module. This method was successfully employed in two twentieth century American cases. *State of New Jersey v. Bruno Richard Hauptmann* and *State of Florida v. Theodore Robert*

Bundy. The Hauptmann case consisted of nine modules beginning with the disappearance of the child and ending with the evidence tying Hauptmann to the kidnap ladder.[6] The twelve modules of the Bundy case began with the disappearance of the victim from the school and ended with the evidence tying Bundy to the van in which he murdered her.[7]

What might a modular presentation of the Hyams case look like? In Chapter Four we analyzed the evidence under five topics. Adding a sixth topic for the attempted insurance fraud with Martha, we have:

(1). Murder, not Accident: The impossibility of the death being accidental.

    (a). The Day of the Death.
    (b). The Impossibility of Accident.
    (c). The Inconsistency of Willie's Wounds with Accident.

(2). Motive: The financial straits the Hyams brothers found themselves in.

(3). Manufacturing the Means: This breaks down into three subcategories:

    (a). Funding the Insurance.
    (b). Faking the Business.
    (c). "Fixing" the Elevator.

(4). Maneuvering for the Opportunity: Setting up the ideal situation for killing Willie.

---

[6] Dedman, *The Lindbergh Kidnapping Case: A Critical Analysis*, 46, 47, 97, 101, 102.
[7] Dekle, *The Last Murder*, 142-145.

(5). Making the Profit: Milking Martha of the insurance proceeds.

(6). Menacing Martha: The conspiracy to insure and kill Martha.

The following account of Aylesworth's testimony comes chiefly from the Bench Book of Justice Street. Great care has been taken to unjumble the testimony and put it into some sort of chronological order.

Aylesworth testified that he met the Hyams brothers in 1889 on his marriage to Mary Ann Wells, the sister of Willie and Martha Wells. Both the Wells family and the Hyamses were boarding at 55 Gould Street at the time. The twins had a financial brokerage at 11 W. King Street, and in 1892 they employed both Willie and Aylesworth as clerks in the office. Willie was hired first, and then Aylesworth.[8] He described how they and Martha loaned the Hyamses $3,000, and how the two men tried to get the brothers to repay the loans. The brothers put them off by various ruses. In one ruse the Hyamses brought them into the office, show them a stack of bills topped by a bill of large denomination, and said they could immediately pay the money back, but they would have to let Willie and Aylesworth go as employees if they did so. The two men decided they could wait for their money a little while longer. As they were still gathered in the office with the money on the table, Expressman Fox came in. Seeing the big stack of money on the desk, he playfully grabbed at it and knocked the stack over. This exposed the fact that although the top few bills were large, the lower bills were ones.[9]

---

[8] Street, *Bench Book,* 13:273-275, 278, 279.
[9] Street, *Bench Book,* 13:293.

Another ploy the Hyams brothers used to delay repayment of the loan was to tell Wells and Aylesworth that they were going to open a hotel in Fort Erie, and they wanted the brothers-in-law to manage it for them. They were guaranteed $10 per week salary, a percentage of the profits, and free room and board for themselves and their families. The four men signed an agreement to that effect, but nothing ever came of the purported hotel venture.[10]

The Hyams brothers began to try to talk both Willie and Aylesworth into taking out large life insurance policies in the amount of $25,000 each. In August of 1892 they persuaded Willie to take out polices valued at approximately $36,000, but Aylesworth never took the bait.[11]

As explained in Chapter Three, after the Hyamses paid premiums for 20 years, they would realize no appreciable profit from the deal. As procurers of the insurance, they were entitled to a $36 per month commission on each payment made on the policy, but they agreed to let Aylesworth collect the commission. He got $36 for the one premium paid.[12] The brothers either were idiots or they had some sinister motive for the insurance scheme.

Another red flag about the insurance deal was the fact that the Hyamses did not have the money to pay the first premium. They gave the insurance agent a promissory note. Sometime toward the end of November 1892, Harry made the payment on the first premium by giving Willie $500 cash to retire the note. Willie dutifully went to the insurance

---

[10] "The Wells Murder Story," *Ottowa Evening Journal*, May 10, 1895.
[11] Street, *Bench Book,* 13:273-275, 278, 279.
[12] Street, *Bench Book,* 13:279; "Martha Wells Hyams in the Box," *Toronto World*, May 13, 1895.

agency, paid the premium, and brought the change back to Harry.[13]

It was in September of 1892, one month after Wells agreed to be insured, that the Hyamses opened the Toronto Warehouse Company on Colborne Street and moved both Wells and Aylesworth from the financial brokerage on King Street to the warehouse. The warehouse was a multi-story affair with a counterweight elevator. Almost all the goods brought into the warehouse were stored on the ground floor. Nothing came into the warehouse for the first three weeks, but finally some grocery stock and some barrels of sugar came in. The sugar was stored in the basement. Then they got in about three or four dollars' worth of furniture and six large, empty packing cases. No customers came into the warehouse. Despite this booming trade, the brothers hired another clerk to work at the warehouse, Miss Latimer the typist.[14]

What was there for three clerks to do in an almost-empty warehouse with no customers? Osler wanted to know. They spent their time copying lists of names and addresses and addressing envelopes that were never mailed out. Aylesworth never saw any money come into the warehouse.[15]

Q: What did Wells do in this warehouse?

A: Wrote envelopes.

Q: What for? What was the result of this?

---

[13] Street, *Bench Book,* 13:280, 282.
[14] Street, *Bench Book,* 13:275, 276.
[15] Street, *Bench Book,* 13:277.

A: When we got through writing what had been given us, we would give them to Mr. Hyams.

Q: Were there any customers?

A: Not that I know of.

Q: What practical use was this writing?

A: I never knew.[16]

Osler then had Aylesworth identify Willie's handwriting on one hundred identical handwritten copies of a mercantile report which had been taken from the warehouse. These sheets were introduced into evidence in support of the Crown's contention that the brothers had no need of Willie's services, but simply used the ruse of copying useless reports to keep him at the warehouse until they could kill him.

Shortly after the opening of the warehouse, Willie decided that he would strike out on his own and become a farmer. He needed the $1,000 he had loaned to the brothers so that he could make the down payment. He began to pester the brothers about getting his money back. The brothers repeatedly promised to return the money at a future date which never seemed to come. Finally, Willie's persistence seemed to bear fruit. Harry agreed with him that on Monday, January 16, he would go with Willie to Pickering to give Uncle Uriah Jones the $1,000 down payment on the farm.[17]

On Saturday, January 14, Willie wanted to send a telegram to his uncle to let him know that he would be in Pickering on Monday to deliver the down payment. He

---

[16] "Hyams Twins Trial," *New-York Herald,* May 10, 1895.
[17] Street, *Bench Book,* 13:280.

wrote it out and read it in the presence of Harry, Aylesworth, and Martha. Harry volunteered to send the telegram, and Willie turned it over to him. Harry left, ostensibly to send the telegram, but it never got sent.[18]

When Aylesworth and Willie left church on Sunday evening, January 15, they went to the warehouse to lay on a fire so that the place would not be cold when Willie arrived the next morning at 8:00 a.m. There was nothing in the warehouse requiring the use of the elevator. The few items of merchandise in the warehouse were all in their proper place, and no new merchandise had come in on the previous Saturday. Neither Aylesworth nor Willie did anything to the elevator that evening.[19]

Aylesworth's account of the events of January 16 was substantially the same as the account he gave at the preliminary hearing, but his description of what he found in the basement bears repeating. When he examined the basement after Willie's death, he found the counterweight leaning against the boxing encasing the cage shaft. It was about a foot away from the counterweight shaft. One to two feet in front of the counterweight Aylesworth saw two pools of blood. The pools were about six inches apart. He saw no blood between the counterweight and the pools, but he did see blood on the bottom of the counterweight. The leaning of the counterweight allowed him to see the blood without having to move it. He found two bloody tools in the basement: a chisel and a hammer. Going back to the ground floor, Aylesworth saw a bloody coat which looked

---

[18] Street, *Bench Book,* 13:282.
[19] Street, *Bench Book,* 13:291.

as though it had been cut off Wells and thrown onto some packing cases.[20]

Although Justice Street took extensive notes on the testimony, there are two glaring omissions from his notes of this part of Aylesworth's testimony. Nothing is said about blood being at the bottom of the counterweight shaft, and nothing is said about any streaking of blood on the floor from the counterweight shaft to the two pools of blood. The weight certainly didn't fall to the opening in the basement and then taken a 90 degree turn to hit Willie's head. If it hit Willie's head in the shaft, then Willie would have been found with his head crushed at the bottom of the shaft, and blood would have been at the bottom of the shaft. When the weight was moved and Willie was pulled from the shaft, there would have been bloody drag marks leading to the pools of blood.

There are four possible interpretations of this absence:

(1). Aylesworth mentioned the blood in the shaft and the bloody drag marks, but Street didn't deem it important to make a note of that fact.

(2). The blood was there, and Osler purposely omitted it to make the Hyams brothers look guilty.

(3). The blood was there, but Osler neglected to have Aylesworth mention it.

(4). The blood was not there, and Osler neglected to have Aylesworth make a point of the fact that it wasn't there.

---

[20] Street, *Bench Book,* 13:285-288.

Given Street's diligence in taking notes, the probability of interpretation (1) is remote. Of the four interpretations, interpretation (2) is the least likely. Osler knew that Aylesworth was going to undergo cross-examination by William Lount and Ebenezer F.B. Johnston, two of the foremost cross-examiners in Ontario, and they were being coached by the best cross-examiner in New York. They would surely bring out this exculpatory evidence if it existed. Better to "steal their thunder" and have the witness give the evidence on direct examination. Interpretations (3) and (4) have greater probability given the haphazard structure of Osler's examination. Ill-prepared counsel often overlook important evidence.

It is important to decide which of these last two interpretations is correct. Under interpretation (3), the Hyams brothers can be innocent. The weight fell down the shaft and struck Willie, who was at least partially in the shaft himself. Under interpretation (4), the twins must be guilty. Willie was knocked unconscious in the cellar, and then the weight was dropped on his head one to two feet from the counterweight shaft. To decide between these last two interpretations, we will have to wait until we study the cross-examinations of Lount and Johnston. If there was blood in the shaft, they would surely emphasize it in cross-examination.[21]

Toward the end of the day Osler covered two other topics in his examination. The first topic was the exhumation of Willie's body. For the purposes of the autopsy, Osler had to prove that the body dug up out of the ground at the cemetery was the Willie Wells who had been buried there. He accomplished this with Aylesworth. The

---

[21] Street, *Bench Book,* 13:290.

authorities had Aylesworth accompany them to the cemetery, and he identified the body they exhumed as the body of Willie Wells. He also knew and identified Dr. John Caven, who performed the autopsy, as being present when the body was exhumed. This established the identity of the body which was autopsied as the same Willie Wells who died in the warehouse.[22]

The second topic was the operation of the elevator, which should have been covered when he had Aylesworth describe it. According to Aylesworth, the elevator ran "all right," but the counterweight sometimes got stuck in the shaft when the cage was on the second floor. This was easy to fix. All that needed to be done was to tug on the rope above the elevator cage and jostle the weight loose from where it was caught.[23] And with this last bit of information supportive of the defense theory, Osler ended his examination for the day.

The next day the twins appeared much more cheerful as they assumed their places in the special box behind counsel table reserved for criminal defendants. Such an arrangement would be deemed objectionable in the U.S. because the seating impedes the defendants' ability to communicate with counsel.

Dallas became less cheerful as the morning wore on, and it was determined that he was suffering from a toothache. A dentist came in over the noon recess to pull

---

[22] Street, *Bench Book,* 13:289, 290.
[23] Street, *Bench Book,* 13:290, 291; "The Hyams Twins Trial," *Toronto World,* May 10, 1895.

the infected tooth, and Dallas regained his cheerfulness after lunch.[24]

THE PRISONERS AND THEIR COUNSEL[25]

One thing which contributed to the twins' cheerfulness was the fact that when court opened, Ebeneezer Aylesworth was nowhere to be found. He finally showed up ten minutes late, and Justice Street administered a severe tongue lashing. Thoroughly chastened, Aylesworth took the witness stand to undergo cross-examination by Lount and Johnston.[26] According to the papers, he spent eight hours on the stand undergoing "a most unmerciful cross-examination."[27] At the beginning of the day he was "fresh

---

[24] "Under Fire for Eight Hours," *Toronto World*, May 11, 1895.

[25] *New-York Herald*, May 14, 1895.

[26] "Under Fire for Eight Hours," *Toronto World*, May 11, 1895.

[27] "Eight Hours under Fire," *Ottowa Evening Journal*, May 11, 1895.
The following account of Aylesworth's cross-examination comes from

and rosy, with a confident air," but by 5:00 he was "weary and shaken after hours of damaging cross-examination."[28] The expense of dispatching Pinkerton detectives to Toronto seems to have paid off. They had dug up a lot of dirt on Aylesworth, and the defense team used every bit of it to discredit the man.

Lount was first to cross-examine Aylesworth. He began by getting a brief history of Aylesworth's adult life, and then he began his "most unmerciful cross-examination." He began by getting Aylesworth to admit that he shot pool and bet on the horses, and then asked a series of questions designed to show that Aylesworth was a gambling addict who had wasted his wife's insurance proceeds betting on sporting events. Aylesworth insisted that he was about $200 ahead in his bets on the horses.

If Aylesworth hadn't squandered his wife's money on the horses and in the pool rooms, where was it? Aylesworth refused to answer until Justice Street ordered him to do so. Aylesworth said that the money was invested in chattel mortgages. He couldn't remember the names of the borrowers without reference to his books.

He was asked about several different rooms he had rented at various times and in various places around about Toronto. One room he rented to store furniture that he had taken for the nonpayment of a chattel mortgage. The other rooms were taken for Aylesworth's "own accommodation."

Lount asked, "What accommodation?"

"Under Fire for Eight Hours," *Toronto World*, May 11, 1895, and Street, *Bench Book,* 13:294-310.

[28] "Worried a Witness," *New-York Herald*, May 11, 1895.

Aylesworth replied, "Oh, I don't know, but if its card playing you mean I never played cards in my life."

Lount continued to insist on knowing why Aylesworth rented so many different rooms. Aylesworth continued to insist it was for "My own accommodation."

Lount persisted until Aylesworth finally elaborated his answer, "My own accommodation. I might want to take a friend there."

"Female friend?" Lount asked.

"No, not females, if that's what you are driving at," Aylesworth indignantly replied.

Lount denied that he was attempting to do that.

"Well," replied Aylesworth, "you're insinuating mighty hard."

Lount kept up this line of questioning for an hour and a half, but Justice Street took few notes on this portion of Aylesworth's testimony.

Lount then tried to show that Aylesworth was biased against the Hyams brothers by showing that he always suspected that Willie was murdered, and that he had conducted a private investigation to try to dig up evidence against them. Aylesworth even went as far as to hire a private investigator to shadow Harry after he moved to Montreal. Aylesworth denied bias against the Hyams brothers, but his admission that he had tried to gather evidence of murder against them told another story.

Mixed in with the torrent of questions designed to assassinate Aylesworth's character, the defense did manage to ask a few questions which were relevant to the facts of the case. For one thing, they established that the Hyams brothers had decided to open a warehouse before Willie was insured. Justice Street underlined his notes on this issue and made an annotation in the margin of the page to highlight the importance of this fact.[29] It strongly weighed against the argument that because the brothers had opened the warehouse after Willie was insured, that meant they intended the warehouse solely as a ruse to further a murder-for-insurance scheme. Aylesworth admitted that he had not mentioned the blood on the hammer and chisel when he testified at the preliminary hearing, and he further admitted that he had taken the bloody chisel and given it to a schoolmate of Willie's so that the friend would "have something which to remember the dead man."[30] But the recent search of the warehouse had uncovered a bloody chisel in the basement. Where did it come from?

Lount questioned Aylesworth about the blood in the cellar, and again Aylesworth said that there was blood close to the bottom of the weight shaft, about one or two feet from it. Justice Street, who was in the habit of underlining in his notes portions of the testimony he thought important, did not underline this part. The significance of the fact that there was no blood in the bottom of the weight shaft had escaped everyone except the defense team. Lount wisely avoided directly asking, "Was there blood at the bottom of the shaft?" The value of a positive answer was outweighed by the damage a negative answer would do.

---

[29] Street, *Bench Book,* 13:303.
[30] "Under Fire for Eight Hours," *Toronto World*, May 11, 1895.

Toward the end of Lount's cross-examination, Aylesworth yawned. "Are you tired?" asked Lount.

"Yes, I am," admitted Aylesworth, who had by this time been standing in the witness box for eight hours, "Good and tired."

"Come down here and lift this weight for me, will you?" said Lount, indicating the counterweight which was in evidence.[31]

At first Aylesworth was reluctant to attempt the task. "I am a much larger and stronger man than either of the prisoners and I cannot lift that weight from the ground. I find it hard to lift one end of it," he declared.[32]

Lount then insinuated that Aylesworth was a weakling. His manhood challenged, Aylesworth left the witness stand and attempted the lift. On his third try, he got a good grip on the weight and lifted it two feet from the ground. "It's a heavy weight," Aylesworth said, as perspiration stood out on his face.

"Yes," said Mr. Lount, "and you're about as big as both the prisoners together. Do you believe that either of the prisoners, or even both, could have lifted that weight?" Aylesworth said he thought it would depend on how they caught hold of it.[33]

The counterweight weighed two hundred pounds.[34] This is not too great a weight for a full-grown man to lift

---

[31] "Worried a Witness," *New-York Herald*, May 11, 1895; "Under Fire for Eight Hours," *Toronto World*, May 11, 1895.

[32] Street, *Bench Book,* 13:307.

[33] "Worried a Witness," *New-York Herald*, May 11, 1895; "Under Fire for Eight Hours," *Toronto World*, May 11, 1895.

[34] Street, *Bench Book*, 14:24.

from the ground; the only problem would come in trying to get a grip on it as it lay on the floor. Two men, one on each side of the weight, should easily lift it.

Lount then had Harry Hyams stand beside Aylesworth to demonstrate the size disparity between the two men.

AYLESWORTH AND HARRY HYAMS[35]

Finally, Lount polished Aylesworth off with a prior inconsistent statement. Aylesworth had sworn on direct examination that Harry Hyams said he found Dallas lying across Willie's body. "You said not a word of that at your former examination!" Lount thundered.

"Didn't I?" Aylesworth replied meekly.

"No!" Lount cried, "You've been hunting up evidence ever since the funeral. And when you helped to collect the insurance on Wells you told the agent it was an accident, told him nothing of the blood on the chisel, nothing of the

_____

[35] *New-York Herald*, May 14, 1895.

blood on the weight, nothing of Dallas Hyams lying across the body, and you took some of the money—blood money, if this was murder!"

"I wasn't suspicious then," Aylesworth defended.

"Why man," Lount said triumphantly, "this insurance was collected months after the funeral, and you have sworn your suspicions began at the funeral."

"Well," Aylesworth replied, there are a lot of suspicions."

"And you," Lount continued, "suspecting these men, and already following them, and looking up evidence, countenanced the marriage of your sister-in-law to Harry Hyams! Did you or did you not?"

"She was satisfied," said Aylesworth.

Lount countered, "Were you at the marriage of Harry Hyams and Martha Wells?"

Aylesworth admitted that he was.

"Then, although you had suspicions from the day of the tragedy, you assisted in filling out the claim papers, which purported to show that the affair was an accident; your wife accepted a portion of the insurance money, which if a murder had been committed was blood money, and nothing but blood money; you knew that Harry Hyams was continuing to pay attention to Martha Wells, and yet you never breathed to this young woman the suspicions you had of a crime and permitted her to marry the man who, according to your suspicions, had murdered her brother. That's all I wish to say to you, sir."[36]

Johnston conducted a brief cross-examination,[37] and then Osler asked a few questions on redirect, doing some damage control, but the expressions on the faces of Wellman and Gooch told the story of who had won the encounter between Lount and Aylesworth. Wellman clearly approved of the hatchet job that Lount had done on the witness, but his frustration at not being able to conduct the cross-examination himself was equally plain.[38]

Annie Aylesworth's direct examination concluded the proceedings on this, the second day of testimony. When she took the stand, Lount asked that her husband, who was seated on the front row directly in front of the witness stand, be excluded from the courtroom for her testimony.[39] Osler again conducted a disjointed, non-chronological direct examination. Annie's testimony corroborated her husband's, but she did give some additional details. She described the relentless onslaught of persuasion that Harry unleased against Willie to get him to agree to the insurance scheme. It lasted over several weeks, and Harry assured Willie that the insurance was a sound investment which would make him "quite a wealthy man in a few years."[40]

She remembered Harry coming to her house on the day of the killing about 1 o'clock. He seemed both excited and exhausted. He said his back was strained from lifting the

---

[36] "Worried a Witness," *New-York Herald*, May 11, 1895; "Under Fire for Eight Hours," *Toronto World*, May 11, 1895.

[37] Street, *Bench Book,* 13:309, 310.

[38] "Worried a Witness," *New-York Herald*, May 11, 1895.

[39] "Fainted in Court," *New-York Herald*, May 12, 1895.

[40] Street, *Bench Book,* 13:315.

weight. His fingers were bleeding. He didn't give Annie much detail as to how the tragedy occurred. What he told her was that the weight fell and hit Willie, breaking his collarbone. She specifically asked if Willlie were dead, and Harry said, "No, he is not."[41]

When Dallas came to the house five days later, he said he had gone into the office to write a letter to his wife. He had taken off his coat when he heard a noise, ran down cellar, and found Willie pinned to the ground with a weight. He then fell over the body."

Pressed for details as to what the brothers said about the incident, Annie said, "The Hyams didn't wish to talk about the affair at all."

"Why do you say that?" Osler asked.

"Because our uncle was suspicious and wanted the brothers to go out to the country and explain to him how the tragedy occurred, but they would never go. They said people would talk anyway, and the best thing was to pay no attention to them."[42]

Annie was also able to shed some light on Martha's hiding from Harry at the Bishop Strachan School. She said that Martha "had words" with Harry over Harry's constant dunning her for the insurance proceeds and decided to hide out at the Bishop Strachan School. She enrolled in the school and began boarding there, trying to keep her location a secret. During the time that Martha was in the school, both Harry and Dallas were constant visitors, trying to learn of Martha's whereabouts. They discovered her hideout, and Harry visited her there, persuading her to

---

[41] Street, *Bench Book,* 13:322, 323.
[42] "Under Fire for Eight Hours," *Toronto World*, May 11, 1895.

marry him. She married Harry on May 9, 1893, and then went back to the school to finish the semester. These facts, which Osler should have brought out on direct examination, were uncovered by Lount in his cross-examination on the following day.[43]

The next morning Annie withstood a cross-examination that was not as brutal as the one her husband had undergone, but which severely damaged both her credibility and the credibility of her husband. Lount walked her through several apparent discrepancies between her testimony at the preliminary hearing and her testimony at trial. Most of these discrepancies were the result of her adding detail that she had not mentioned at the preliminary hearing. Oddly enough, these details were details which her husband had omitted from his testimony at the preliminary hearing, but which he remembered for his direct examination.[44] Justice Street, who had recorded these same discrepancies in Mr. Aylesworth's testimony but thought little of them, took copious notes on them when they began to crop up in Mrs. Aylesworth's testimony, cross-referencing them in the margin of his benchbook.[45] The contradictions were:

> (1).   On direct, when she testified about the efforts to convince Willie to be insured, she mentioned the sum of $30,000 as the value of the insurance, but at the preliminary hearing she said nothing about the amount of the insurance.[46]

---

[43] Street, *Bench Book,* 13:319, 320.
[44] "Fainted in Court," *New-York Herald,* May 12, 1895.
[45] Street, *Bench Book,* 13:319-324.
[46] Street, *Bench Book,* 13:315, 320.

(2). At the preliminary hearing she said nothing about the weight falling, and she said she was told Willie had broken his neck.[47]

(3). On cross-examination she testified that Harry had said nothing about the accident after that first day. Justice Street saw this as a contradiction of a statement she made on direct that Harry had said he was in the barbershop.[48]

One particularly damaging thing she said when challenged about the omissions at the preliminary hearing was, "I only answered the questions they asked me." Her husband had given the same explanation in identical words when he was challenged about the omissions at the preliminary hearing. Mrs. Aylesworth denied that she and her husband got together and made sure that their testimony would be the same when they took the stand,[49] but it was obvious that they had. The veracity of these new facts was called into question by the Aylesworth's boneheaded move. Different people remembering the same facts from the distant past naturally remember them differently, and minor discrepancies are to be expected. The song "I Remember it Well" from the movie *Gigi* parodies this all-to-human phenomenon.[50] It wasn't minor discrepancies that sank the credibility of the Aylesworths, it was their too-perfect agreement that did it.

Once Annie had so damaged her credibility, Lount felt free to give her a small dose of the storm and thunder that

---

[47] Street, *Bench Book,* 13:222.

[48] Street, *Bench Book,* 13:316, 323.

[49] "Fainted in Court," *New-York Herald*, May 12, 1895.

[50] I have recited this song many times to jurors to explain minor discrepancies in testimony.

he gave her husband. When she contradicted herself on who left home first on the morning of the death, whether it was Willie or Aylesworth, Lount thundered, "Two men's lives hang upon your answer. You are not playing with dollars and cents now!"[51] This last cut served as a reminder that she had profited from Willie's death to the tune of $4,750.

On redirect Osler did damage control by having Annie explain the discrepancies. She said that at the time of the preliminary hearing she had been ill and bedridden with a pregnancy. Her baby had been born just three weeks prior to the preliminary hearing, and that she was still in delicate health when she testified.[52] And thus ended the second day of testimony. The next day, May 11, would prove to be one of the most remarkable days in the annals of Canadian jurisprudence.

---

[51] "Fainted in Court," *New-York Herald*, May 12, 1895.
[52] Street, *Bench Book,* 13:324; "Fainted in Court," *New-York Herald*, May 12, 1895.

CHAPTER SEVEN: THE PROSECUTION CASE
DAYS THREE AND FOUR[1]

On this, the third day of the trial, the composition of the crowd was quite different. Elegantly attired women filled half the seats in the dingy courtroom, anticipating a scene never before enacted in a Canadian trial—the spectacle of a wife voluntarily taking the witness stand to testify against her husband in a murder trial.[2]

But first, Lount spent an hour demolishing Annie Aylesworth on cross-examination, and then came some yawn-inducing testimony from J.R. Winters, a mercantile agent who had been in the business for seventeen years. Winters explained that in his business he had a list of subscribers who wanted up-to-date information concerning chattel mortgages, bills of sale, mechanic's liens, and other types of commercial paper. He sent his subscribers periodic reports describing these documents. To make up the reports, he had runners who went to all the other mercantile agencies in town and compiled the information. This information was then sent to a printer and mailed out to the subscribers. Given the volatility of the market, it was necessary to update the information regularly. Osler showed Winters 100 hand-copied sheets of his February 12, 1891, issue. Willie had made these copies in the winter of 1892. Osler wanted to know what purpose could be served by one hundred hand copies of an eighteen-month-old mercantile sheet. Winter said such sheets would be perfectly useless.

---

[1] Saturday, May 11, 1895 – Monday, May 13, 1895.
[2] "Fainted in Court," *New-York Herald*, May 12, 1895.

Lount had done a fair imitation of Atilla the Cross-Examiner up to this point, but he adopted an entirely different strategy with Winter. Adopting the demeanor of an adoring student sitting at the feet of an all-knowing guru, he asked a series of questions designed to flatter Winters. After sufficiently stroking Winters' ego by praising his business acumen, financial success, wealth, and honesty; Lount got to the point. Might someone who was planning to go into the mercantile business distribute out-of-date reports to potential customers as samples? They certainly might, although Winters himself would never do such a thing. Wasn't it less expensive to hand write these reports than to have them printed? Yes, it probably was.[3]

Osler then announced Martha Wells Hyams as the next Crown witness. Lount immediately asked that the admissibility of her testimony be argued outside the presence of the jury. Justice Street excused the jury, and the legal argument began. At the common law, an accused could not testify, nor could the spouse of the accused say a word either for or against the accused. This all had changed under the Evidence Act of 1893, and the accused was allowed to testify in his own defense. The wife of the accused could also give voluntary testimony, but she could not be compelled to testify against her husband. Even if she chose to testify, her husband could prevent her from disclosing anything he said to her in private. Before Martha Hyams took the stand, no Canadian wife had ever chosen to testify against her husband in a murder prosecution.

---

[3] "Martha Hyams Wells in the Box," *Toronto World*, May 13, 1895.

MARTHA HYAMS ON THE STAND[4]

Lount expounded on his interpretation of the statute. He argued that although the common law incompetency of a wife had been abolished, the common law still looked upon a husband and wife as one, a presumption which harked back to Genesis 2:24. "Now," Lount continued, "we have this enactment under which a wife, if she chooses, may become a witness, but cannot be forced by the Crown to do so. The same enactment permits an accused person to testify in his own behalf. I hold that the amendment was only passed in order to free the prisoner charged with an offence from restraint, and that the section only goes and was intended to go to the extent of affording freedom of the husband to give evidence and freedom of the wife at his instance, and only at his instance, to give evidence in his behalf. There was no intention to alter the common law, but the measure was passed only for the purpose of providing the prisoner with the opportunity of availing

---

[4] *New-York Herald*, May 17, 1895.

himself of his wife's testimony. Therefore, the wife is not a competent witness and cannot give evidence against her husband. While a competent witness at the request of the person charged, she is not a competent witness against his desire. I submit that this is the construction of the code: The prisoner is competent and may call himself. His wife is competent and may be called by him but is not a competent witness against him. The only judgment I have been able to find bearing on the subject is the People against Wood, New York. There is nothing in our courts, nor can I find an English authority. The question rarely arises of a wife anxious to give evidence against a husband, and therefore no cases are cited."[5]

In the case cited by Lount, the defendant Wood had killed his father-in-law by ambushing him and shooting him in the back. Wood pled not guilty by reason of insanity and called his wife as a defense witness to testify that shortly before the killing the father-in-law had raped her. The trial court had held the testimony inadmissible. The Court of Appeals reversed Wood's conviction, holding that the wife's testimony was relevant to the issue of insanity because it shed light on Wood's state of mind at the time of the killing.[6]

Whereas Lount had argued long and hard against the evidence, Osler's reply was succinct: "The meaning of the amendment is plain, and it is this: Prior to the enactment the wife was not competent; under it she is made competent."

Judge Street ruled, "I have no doubt whatever on the question. If the counsel for the Crown presses the matter, I

---

[5] "Martha Wells Hyams in the Box," *Toronto World*, May 13, 1895.
[6] *People v. Wood*, 126 N.Y. 249 (1891).

see no reason whatever for excluding her testimony. To be sure, the statute before excluded her. Now the statue says she is a competent witness." Lount asked for a reserved case, but Street said the question could be decided at the end of the trial. At that point he saw no reason for reserving a case.[7] In asking for a reserved case, Lount was laying the groundwork for an appeal of the point should his client get convicted. Under Canadian law at the time, an issue could not be appealed to a higher court unless the trial judge had allowed a reserved case on the point. Counsel had to ask for a reserved case before the jury returned with a verdict.[8]

Finally, Prosecutor Osler called Martha to the stand. One might question the "voluntariness" of her appearance. She was a woman who had established a pattern of succumbing to high-pressure tactics. As we have seen, Harry had repeatedly bent her to his will by means of his insistent, persistent pleading, persuasion, and manipulation. It was only after she came to believe that he was preparing to kill her that she was able to escape his clutches. She was a woman whom life had beaten down by constant tragedy—the deaths of her parents, the abuse by her aunt, the deaths of her brothers, the death of her fiancé, the loss of her inheritance, and the betrayal by her husband. She went to the witness stand as a condemned prisoner might go to the death chamber.

She wore a half-mourning dress of black with mauve dots and a black picture hat decorated with ostrich plumes. Projecting an air of fearful sadness and physical exhaustion, she took her place on the witness stand, set a bottle of smelling salts on the rail beside her, and sat there trembling

---

[7] "Martha Wells Hyams in the Box," *Toronto World*, May 13, 1895.
[8] *Canadian Criminal Law Digest*, 1103.

in anticipation. Unlike the male witnesses who had preceded her, she was not required to stand as she testified.[9]

Osler began to ask questions, and she answered in a low, tremulous voice which could hardly be heard at counsel table. Osler moved to within three feet of her so that he could hear, and he repeated each of her answers verbatim for the benefit of counsel, judge, and jury. She sat facing a window on the west wall of the courtroom, and never looked at her husband, whom she called "Mr. Hyams" throughout her testimony.

Martha's testimony was frequently interrupted by the defense, as they opposed almost everything she said, objecting question-by-question as Osler labored to place her story before the jury. According to the *Toronto World*, "There were several lively passages between counsel ..., but the [outbursts] of temper manifest in in similar trials in the United States were lacking, and the Americans present expressed surprise at the decorum with which the proceedings were conducted."[10]

Martha told of how she first met the Hyams brothers when her family was living at 640 Spadina Avenue, and traced her on again, off again love affair with Harry Hyams down to the day she fled for fear he was preparing to kill her.

---

[9] The following account of Martha Hyams' testimony is taken from "Martha Wells Hyams in the Box," *Toronto World*, May 13, 1895; "Fainted in Court," *New-York Herald*, May 12, 1895; "An Exciting Case," *Manitoba Morning News*, May 13, 1895; "The Wells Insurances," *Ottawa Evening Journal*, May 14, 1895; and *Bench Book*, 13:326-344.

[10] "Martha Wells Hyams in the Box," *Toronto World,* May 13, 1895.

Martha continued, "Mr. Hyams always gave me to understand that he would never get married while his mother lived, and, as she was very old and ill, I thought it reasonable, but just before Christmas, 1892, he said he was getting tired of just coming to the house and going out, year after year, and proposed that we get married. My brother Willie objected unless Mr. Hyams would tell his mother. Mr. Hyams wrote to his mother, or said he did, to ask about it, but before he got an answer my brother was killed.

"I saw Mr. Hyams on the day before Willie's death. and he agreed to go to Pickering the next day with Willie. I told Mr. Hyams that he had been promising Willie money for three weeks, and that if he could not return the $1,000 on Monday, which was the next day, he should name a day when he could pay it, no matter if it were three months later. He said he would pay on Monday, and we were all to go to Pickering that day as Willie was to buy a farm with the money. It was on Monday Willie was killed. Mr. Hyams left messages with me to tell Mr. Aylesworth to go to the East End and get some reports, and for Willie to go to the warehouse early. We gave Mr. Hyams a dispatch to send to Jones in Pickering, the man whose farm Willie was to buy, telling him we were coming the following day."

As her testimony inched closer to the day Willie died, Martha became more and more tearful. She then described the morning of Willie's death. One important aspect of her testimony was Harry's appearance when he arrived at the home. "I noticed that his linen was spotted with blood— very fine spots of blood on the front of his shirt—his cuffs were badly spotted." Fine spattering such as Martha described is more consistent with back spatter from being near someone who suffers a massive, skin-breaking blow to the head than it is with lifting a heavy weight off a crushed

129

head. Commenting on this evidence, the *Toronto World* said, "The Crown will lay stress on the minute blood specks which Martha Wells saw on Harry Hyams' shirt front after the death of her brother. Experts claim that a blow on the skull, where the blood vessels are exceedingly small and not numerous, will produce minute spurts of blood, which might leave such specks. During the MacWherrell trial this physical fact was brought out in the medical testimony."[11] No testimony was given concerning this point during the prosecution's case.

Upon learning that Willie was dead, Martha took to her sickbed and remained there for several days. While she was in bed recovering, Dallas came and talked to her. He told her that he had gone to the warehouse to write a letter, and that he heard a terrible crash. He rushed to the basement to investigate and fainted when he saw Willie. After this communication, neither Harry nor Dallas would speak to her about the incident.

Then Osler led Martha through a detailed description of how Harry milked her for the insurance money, describing in detail each time Harry hit her up for money. The first time she gave him money was February 25, when she reluctantly gave him $1,700 of the $2,000 payment she received from Covenant Mutual. On March 8 she deposited to her account the payment of $29,838 she got from New York Life. After this, Harry upped the pressure for money. She succumbed to his persuasion on March 30, when she wrote him a check for $600. Over the next eighteen days she wrote Harry six more checks totaling $5,500. One of these checks was written because Harry told her he wanted to lend Dr. Duncan McPherson $1,900. Martha wrote this check

---

[11] "Martha Wells Hyams in the Box," *Toronto World*, May 13, 1895.

directly to Dr. McPherson.[12] After their marriage the money went even faster.She gave her sister a check for $4,750, Dallas a check for $7,964. The rest of the money went to Harry.

Lount tried hard to keep out evidence of the payments Martha made to Harry after the marriage on the grounds that it fell within the husband-wife confidential communication privilege. Justice Street ruled that he could not see how a check written from a wife to a husband could be twisted into a confidential communication from the husband to the wife. The checks written after the marriage were allowed into evidence.

"Now. Mrs. Hyams, what money have you left?" Osler asked.

"I have none," she replied. She then said that on April 18, the day she gave Harry two checks for $1,900 and $2,500, she told him that she had heard a rumor that all his furniture in both his home and his office was mortgaged. When she asked if the rumor was true, he replied that all brokers to protect their homes paid a dollar and got a mortgage.

After Harry made this admission, Martha went into hiding at the Bishop Strahan School. Osler had Martha testify that she left no forwarding address when she went to the school, but Harry found her there anyway. He reassured her about his honorable intentions and pressed her to "marry him at once lest my friends should prejudice my mind against him. I consulted my sister about it. Mr. Aylesworth was then in Oshawa attending his sick mother. When my sister and I had talked it over I decided that I had

---

[12] "The Wells Insurances," *Ottawa Evening Journal*, May 14, 1895.

wronged Mr. Hyams, and my friends had wronged him, and I consented to marry him. Mr. Hyams really looked bad, and that touched me more than anything. This was on Sunday, and on Tuesday we were married."

"And then you married him?" Osler repeated.

"Yes," she said, "on May 9, 1893."

"And how long did you live with him?" asked Mr. Osler. The paleness of Martha's face intensified, her lips trembled uncontrollably, and she had difficulty speaking her next answer, but she finally got it out.

"Until January of this year," she whispered. Then, for the first time during her testimony, she looked her husband in the face. She then shot up from her chair, let out a plaintive wail of "Oh! Oh! Harry!" and collapsed in a fit of hysterics. Martha fell from the witness stand into the arms of defense attorney W.G. Murdoch, who caught her before she hit the floor; the brothers, white as chalk, leaped from their chairs; Mrs. Aylesworth and several other lady friends rushed to her assistance; and she was carried into the judge's chambers. A doctor who happened to be in the audience was summoned to the judge's chambers to attend Martha. When she had recovered sufficiently, they sent her home in a cab.

The only persons in the courtroom who seemed unaffected by the disturbance were Britton Bath Osler and Mr. Justice William Street. Street simply noted the commotion in his bench book with the entry "Hysterics here. 5.20 p.m." After Martha left the courtroom, Osler seamlessly transitioned to another topic.

"And now, my Lord," Osler said coolly, "I wish to give notice that the Crown will seek to introduce a letter this

132

witness received from her husband." Osler was preparing to offer evidence about the Hyams brothers attempt to insure Martha's life for $200,000. The defense objected to this evidence and asked that the jury be excused while the point of law was argued. Osler said that he failed to see why anything bearing on the case should be heard outside the presence of the jury. Justice Street gave evidence that his vision was better than Osler's by ordering the jury out of the courtroom while the point was discussed.

Osler's offer of proof presented a problem of similar fact evidence. For example, if Dan Defendant is charged with committing an armed robbery while wearing a Santa Claus suit, it might be relevant to prove that he committed a similar armed robbery while wearing a Santa Claus suit. It would not, however, be relevant to prove that he committed a burglary while wearing a ninja suit. The two Santa Claus robberies share similar facts, but the facts of the ninja burglary are too dissimilar to be relevant.

In the case of Willie Wells, the Hyams brothers heavily insured him beyond their ability to keep up the premiums, he was killed in a tragic "accident" with an elevator weight, and they reaped the insurance benefits from his death. In the case of Martha Hyams, the brothers heavily insured Martha beyond their ability to keep up the premiums, and then tried to get her to sleep in an automatic folding bed. If she had done so and died in a tragic "accident" when the bed folded up on her, the brothers would reap the insurance benefits from her death. Were the two cases similar enough to allow evidence of the aborted insurance scheme involving Martha at the trial of the insurance scheme involving Willie?

Osler cited the recent case of *Makin v. Attorney General for New South Wales*[13] as authority for the proposition that the evidence was admissible. In that case John and Sarah Makin were charged with the murder of an infant whose body was found buried in their back yard. The Crown introduced evidence that the bodies of several other infants were found buried in their back yard. In ruling the evidence of the other bodies admissible, Lord High Chancellor Herschell wrote:

> [T]he mere fact that the evidence adduced tends to shew the commission of other crimes does not render it inadmissible if it be relevant to an issue before the jury, and it may be so relevant if it bears upon the question whether the acts alleged to constitute the crime charged in the indictment were designed or accidental, or to rebut a defense which would otherwise be open to the accused.[14]

Osler's most obvious argument in favor of admitting the evidence was the argument that the defense was trying to show that Willie's death was an accident, and the *Makin* case held similar fact evidence admissible to show that the crime wasn't an accident. He also argued that the evidence was admissible to show why Martha left Harry, but he missed his best argument. The evidence was arguably admissible to rebut the defense attack on Martha as a treacherous witch malevolently trying to testify her husband onto the gallows. How could she be faulted for testifying when Harry had tried to kill her, too?

Lord Chancellor Herschell's opinion came with three provisos: First, the Crown can't offer evidence of other

---

[13] [1894] A.C. 57.
[14] [1894] A.C. 57, 65.

crimes just to prove that the defendant is a bad person. Second, even if the evidence of the other crime is relevant, it cannot be admitted if its probative value is outweighed by its prejudicial effect. Third, "The statement of these general principles is easy, but it is obvious that it may often be very difficult to draw the line and to decide whether a particular piece of evidence is on the one side or the other."[15] This third proviso sent a clear message to all trial judges—if you don't want to get reversed on appeal, hold similar fact evidence inadmissible. Justice Street reserved ruling on the argument until further evidence could be proffered on the point.

The spectacle of a wife testifying against her husband captured the imagination of the various newspapers covering the trial, and they were full of comments and speculation on all aspects of her testimony. The *New-York Herald* predicted that there was little prospect that Martha would "prove a satisfactory witness" under cross-examination. The *Herald* explained: "Mrs. Hyams' extraordinary conduct in appearing against her husband, and the sensational denouement, have caused no end of comment. The woman has the appearance of an invalid, and one who could be persuaded to do almost anything. Indeed. She swore that the little man who is her husband persuaded her to do many extraordinary things. Of her appearance to-day, the Crown holds the secret, and the Crown is silent. It will evidently be a task of great difficulty to cross-examine Mrs. Hyams with the harshness necessary in the interest of the prisoners, but it must be done. The trial will be resumed on Monday."[16]

---

[15] [1894] A.C. 57, 65.
[16] "Fainted in Court," *New-York Herald*, May 12, 1895.

Whether she would ever resume the witness stand was another topic of conversation. On the Sunday following her fainting spell, reporters buttonholed Crown Counsel for comment. The spokesman for the Crown held out little hope for her returning to the stand, saying that she was liable to be "nervously prostrated" at any moment. She was bedridden for weeks after the arrest of her husband, and during the preliminary hearing brother-in-law Aylesworth kept her off the stand with daily filings of medical certificates attesting that she was too ill to appear. When they questioned Aylesworth, however, he was confident that she would be able to continue her testimony. Upon being made aware of Aylesworth's comments, defense counsel accused him of playing Svengali to Martha's Trilby.[17]

This remark by defense counsel was an allusion to the 1894 best-selling novel *Trilby* by George Du Maurier, which tells the story of an unfortunate young girl who falls under the influence of Svengali, a sinister hypnotist who bends her to his will, causing her to perform acts which she normally would never have done.

On Monday morning Osler announced that Martha was too ill to resume the stand. He said that Dr. Riordan, her attending physician, had reported that she would be ready to continue her testimony on Tuesday. With that announcement, Osler called employees of the telegraph company to establish that Harry had not lived up to his promise to send the telegram to Uriah Jones. Then Mr. Jones took the stand to testify that he never received any

---

[17] "Say He Is a 'Svengali.'" *Philadelphia Inquirer*, May 13, 1895.

telegram stating that Willie would be in Pickering on January 16 to close the deal for the purchase of the farm.[18]

Osler walked Jones through a series of letters and telegrams that Willie had sent, making and breaking appointments to close the land deal, one for each time Harry had promised to deliver the $1,000 and each time he had reneged on his promise. Despite Jones' illiteracy, Osler was able to sketch the history of negotiations over the farm. The discussion of correspondence opened an avenue for the defense to cross-examine Jones concerning a letter he had gotten from the Toronto Chief of Police Grasett telling him that Willie's death had been determined to be an accident.[19]

URIAH JONES IDENTIFIES HIS MARK[20]

---

[18] "Keep Your Mouth Shut Said Dallas to Fox," *Toronto World*, May 14, 1895.
[19] "Keep Your Mouth Shut Said Dallas to Fox," *Toronto World*, May 14, 1895.
[20] *New-York Herald*, May 18, 1895.

Osler next called Expressman Joseph Fox, who ran a package delivery service out of the Melinda Street hire stand. From that base of operations, he used a horse and wagon to deliver packages, crates, and other bulky items all over Toronto.[21] He was a huge man by Victorian Era standards, standing 6 feet 2 inches in his stocking feet. Years of handling heavy packages had given him both the appearance and the reality of great physical strength. Fox made a good witness. His frank, open demeanor convinced listeners that he was anxious to tell the truth even though his testimony differed in several material respects from what he had said at the preliminary hearing.

Fox had known the Hyams brothers five or six years, and he had done business with them before they opened their warehouse on Colborne Street. Shortly after the warehouse opened, Fox brought in some barrels of sugar, barrels of pearline, and boxes of soap to the warehouse. He next hauled three small loads of furniture to the warehouse. Some of the furniture was placed on the ground floor and some on the second. Fox carried some of the furniture up on the stairway and some on the elevator. The loads consisted of bedsprings, mattresses, washstands, chairs, and two bureaus. The final delivery Fox made to the warehouse was a shipment of empty packing crates. Fox never carried anything away from the warehouse until after Willie's death. Although he made few deliveries to the warehouse, he was a frequent visitor there because he could pick up extra money doing odd jobs around the place.[22]

---

[21] Street, *Bench Book*, 13:350.
[22] The following narrative is based upon Justice Street's *Bench Book*, 13:350-362.

Many of Fox's odd jobs involved helping the Hyams brothers tinker with the elevator. Fox helped Dallas procure a lighter counterweight and helped him put it on. Dallas said he thought it would facilitate lighter loads, but Fox thought it made the elevator more dangerous. To facilitate changing the weights, Dallas had carpenters cut a hole in the weight shaft on an upper floor. Fox thought the shelf useless. He lowered the weight to the bottom of the shaft in the basement and changed the weights there. Dallas experimented with the lighter weight and found it unsuitable. Fox put the heavy weight back onto the rope in the counterweight shaft.

Fox then described his involvement in the events surrounding Willie's death: "When I went down to the cellar," Fox testified, "Willie was lying on the floor with his hands stretched on the floor. His head was on the left side with the right side of the face turned up. The body lay with the head pointing to the northwest and feet to the southeast. His right leg was drawn up a little and his left leg stretched out resting on the concrete. On the hands were a pair of old gloves—I am quite confident about that because I took them off his hands myself. He used to wear them when carrying coal upstairs. He had his coat and vest on. His head was about two feet from the weight shaft—that is from where the weight would come down. It was standing up against the casing of the elevator at the southeast corner of the shaft. It may have been tilted against the shaft about two feet to the east of the block on which it should rest. The cage of the elevator was down as far as it would go. The rope [for the counterweight] was not in sight in the cellar."

Continuing his description, Fox testified, "Willie always wore spectacles. They were on his body—on his face—that morning. I took them off and gave them to Harry after the

139

coroner had given the order to the undertaker to remove the body. The head was lying in a pool of blood—that was all the blood I noticed." The body was untouched and unmoved from 10:00 am when Fox arrived until 12:00 noon when the undertaker removed it.There were two important points in this portion of Fox's testimony. First, he saw no blood at the bottom of the weight shaft. This fact squares with Aylesworth's testimony and militates strongly against any accident theory. Second, Coroner Aikins did not move the body when he inspected it. This fact calls into question the thoroughness of Aikins' examination. For all Aikins knew, there could have been a bullet hole in Willie's chest. Another fact which calls Aikins' examination into question is Fox's estimate that the coroner was on the scene only 20 to 30 minutes.

Fox made one other important observation on the morning after Willie's death, but it had to be brought out on cross-examination by Lount. In the basement Fox saw blood spatters on the boxing enclosing the weight shaft. If the prosecution was aware of this fact, it should have been brought out on direct examination. If, as is often the case, the fact was first disclosed to the prosecution on cross-examination, there should have been follow-up on redirect. Lount's cross put blood spatter on the boxing but did not pinpoint the location of the blood. If the blood spatter was on the outside of the boxing, then Willie was killed in front of the weight shaft and could not have been hit by a weight falling down the shaft. If the blood spatter was inside the weight shaft, then that is consistent with the defense theory of accident. The defense didn't ask for the precise location of the blood spatter and the prosecution didn't follow up on redirect. This one omission could be the difference between conviction and acquittal.

Having overlooked the especially important evidence of the blood spatter on the boxing of the weight shaft, Osler asked about Fox's communications with Undertaker Humphrey after the incident. At the preliminary hearing Curry had been unable to get Fox to admit to any communications, but Osler was more successful. Fox unwillingly admitted that he visited Undertaker Humphrey's establishment on one occasion after Willie's death.

Osler asked, "Was it in consequence of anything that either of the prisoners said that you went there?"

"Dallas told me to go there and tell Humphrey to keep hie mouth shut, that's all," said Fox. Then he went on "Mr. Sullivan, of the Oriental laundry, who had borrowed $1300 or $1400 from the Hyams, came to my house and said that if the Hyams didn't keep their mouths shut about the money Sullivan would 'open up' on them." Sullivan said "they" intended to go to see Undertaker Humphrey. Then Dallas told Fox to see Humphrey.

"What was Humphrey to keep his mouth shut about?" asked Mr. Osler.

"I don't know," said the witness.

"Now, I want you to tell me just what you told Dallas Hyams before he told you to see Humphrey," Osler demanded.

"I told Dallas that Sullivan had been at my place and said that if the Hyams didn't stop suing Wilson, cashier in one of the banks, that they were going to open out on the Hyams; that the best thing the Hyams could do was to keep quiet .... Then Dallas said: 'Well, you just go up and see Humphrey and tell him to keep his mouth shut, and have no conversation with him,' something to that effect."

"What was Humphrey to keep his mouth shut about?"

"I can't tell," replied Fox.

Osler tried to pinpoint the time when Sullivan sent this warning to Dallas, but the best Fox could do was to say that Sullivan gave him the warning at the annual dinner of the Orange Lodge, a club to which they both belonged.[23]

It was then Lount's turn to examine the witness.[24] The first thing he did was to have Fox re-emphasize that he went by the warehouse between 9:00 and 10:00 am every morning. Next, he honed in on Willie's cavalier attitude towards the elevator. Willie used to ride a bicycle around the empty storage space on the ground floor. Dallas warned him that he might fall through the opening for the elevator cage. Willie persisted, and Dallas had Carpenter Kidd install gates to close off the entrances into the elevator shaft. On a couple of occasions Willie entered the elevator cage, pulled himself up to the top floor, and rode the elevator down to the basement. Harry eventually told Willie that no one except Fox was to operate the elevator.

Fox estimated that the weight shaft was about half again the size of the weight, giving it about two inches play from north to south. He also described one incident when he was pulling the elevator cage down from the top floor. The weight, which started its journey resting on the wooden block in the floor of the shaft, caught on the ground floor, which he said projected a little into the weight shaft. One morning shortly after the renting of the warehouse Fox

---

[23] "Avoided His Glance," New-York Herald, May 15, 1895.
[24] Street, Bench Book, 13:363, 364.

heard a rattling and a bang, and upon going into the basement to investigate he found the elevator weight off the hook and lying on the bottom of the shaft. Osler, on redirect, clarified that the incident with the weight catching occurred before the Hyams brothers began making alterations and repairs to the elevator.[25]

Lount then attempted to make a few points which missed the mark. He asked Fox, "Now you have said that when you first saw the body it was lying on its stomach with the right side of the face upward. Now, that would be the position, would it not, in which a person would fall, if he was looking up the shaft and was struck by the weight?"

"It might possibly be so," Fox replied. He was trying to be helpful, but he was unwilling to endorse Lount's point that the positioning of Willie's body was consistent with accident.

Lount tried to weaken Fox's testimony concerning Dallas' message to Undertaker Humphreys concerning Sullivan's threat, but Fox refused to cooperate. "I am instructed by Dallas," he said, that what he told you was to tell Humphrey to pay no attention to them. Is that correct?"

"No," said the witness, "he told me to tell Humphrey to keep his mouth shut. I remember that distinctly."[26]

Lount also emphasized that Fox could not tell the date of the supper. "You have meetings every month, do you not, and often have spreads?"

"Yes," replied Fox.

---

[25] Street, *Bench Book*, 13:365.
[26] "Keep Your Mouth Shut Said Dallas to Fox," Toronto World, May 14, 1895.

"And the boys go home feeling pretty good, eh?"

"No, sir," Fox replied, "Nothing of that kind."

Lount was trying to show that it might have been at any one of these monthly suppers that Sullivan made the threat to open up on the brothers, but Fox was emphatic that it occurred at the annual supper, "And we only have one annual supper a year," he said. The courtroom to burst into laughter.[27] Osler later called William Steen, secretary of the Orange Lodge, to testify that the banquet occurred on March 2, 1894.[28]

Lount ended his cross by having Fox testify that, although he spoke with Harry approximately 15 minutes, he saw no bloodstains on the front of Harry's shirt. Osler's redirect, though brief, went over until Tuesday morning, May 14.

---

[27] "Mrs. Harry Hyams Again a Witness," *Toronto World*, May 15, 1895.
[28] "Defence Scores a Point," *Montreal Gazette*, May 16, 1895.

The first new witness on Tuesday morning was Thomas Chambers, who operated a livery stable out of 103 Mutual Street. He testified that his records show a rental of a coupe to Harry Hyams on January 16, 1893. This would have been the cab in which Harry sent Dallas home. Chambers' driver, James Lavelle, remembered driving Dallas home from the warehouse. He noticed on Dallas' pants, just below the knee, dark red stains, which looked like paint.[2]

Jeremiah Riordan, a streetcar conductor, testified that he was driving a one-horse car down Church Street on the morning January 16, when a man with bloody hands boarded the car. The passenger told Riordan that a man had been killed by a weight. The man told Riordan to hustle up, he was going to find a doctor. Riordan was unable to positively identify his passenger, but he said it could have been one of the Hyams brothers. He couldn't be sure of the time that the man boarded his car.[3] Osler called three employees of the streetcar company to establish that this could not have happened before 10:42 am, when time records showed that Riordan went on duty.

A.J. Gardipey, who ran a barbershop on Leader Lane, took the stand next. Osler had him testify that he shaved Harry Hyams between 8:30 and 9:00 on the morning of Willie's death, and that he heard of Willie's death by 9:10, not more than 20 minutes after Harry left the barbershop.

---

[1] Tuesday, May 14, 1895—Wednesday, May 15, 1895.

[2] Street, *Bench Book*, 13:366, 367; "The Wells Insurances," *Ottawa Evening Journal*, May 14, 1895.

[3] Street, *Bench Book*, 13:368; "Mrs. Harry Hyams Again a Witness," *Toronto World*, May 15, 1895.

Taken with the testimony of Expressman Fox that he saw Harry in the warehouse at 10:00, Gardipey's testimony established that Harry had a one-hour window of opportunity to commit the murder. And during that entire one-hour window of opportunity, Fox could be expected to drop by at any moment. The direct examination did little to advance the Crown's case, and Lount's cross-examination did much to damage it.

"Did he appear as usual?" Lount asked, "He didn't act like a man who had a horrible murder on hand and intended to get shaved and then go down and do the deed, did he?"

"No," replied the witness.

"He didn't act like a man who had something on his mind, who was contemplating the slaying of someone, did he?" Lount asked.

"No, sir."[4]

Mabel Latimer took the stand next. Reporters from both the *Toronto World* and the *New-York Herald* were smitten with her beauty. The *World* reporter wrote "The beauty of Mabel's attractive face was enhanced by a black costume faced with ruby and a natty straw hat trimmed with white flowers and brown ribbon."[5] The *World* reproduced the picture of her which they had published at the time of the preliminary hearing, but the *Herald* published a picture of her testifying at the trial.

---

[4] "Mrs. Harry Hyams Again a Witness," *Toronto World*, May 15, 1895.
[5] "Mrs. Harry Hyams Again a Witness," *Toronto World*, May 15, 1895.

MISS LATIMER ON THE STAND[6]

Latimer testified that she went to work for the Hyams brothers at the Colborne Street warehouse in late November or early December of 1892. Her hours were 9:00 am to 5:00 pm with an hour off for lunch. Willie usually beat both her and Aylesworth to the warehouse in the morning. The Hyams brothers kept no regular hours there.

Her only job at the warehouse was to address envelopes. She would pick out the names from the 1892 Toronto directory and write them on envelopes. She then put the envelopes in boxes labelled with the occupations of the addressees. She never knew of any of these envelopes being mailed. Osler produced several boxes of addressed envelopes which she identified as some of those she had addressed. One of the boxes bore the label, "boarding houses, nurses, machinists." Another box was labeled

---

[6] *New-York Herald*, May 17, 1895.

"fruit, fish and justices of the peace." The courtroom was convulsed with laughter when she read off that label.[7]

On Saturday evening, January 14, Harry Hyams came to her home and gave her three letters to deliver on Monday morning before coming to the warehouse. This was the third time that Miss Latimer had been given such a task while working at the warehouse. That morning she dutifully went to the three locations to deliver the letters, and then returned to the warehouse. When she got there, the east door was locked.

Harry unlocked the door and let Latimer in. He then told her, "There's been an accident. Poor Willie was killed with the weight from the elevator." Harry said that his brother Dallas was upstairs fixing the weight and it slipped. Harry said that he was not present when the accident occurred, and when he came into the warehouse, he found Dallas running around like a crazy man. He said he sent Dallas home in a cab. Harry also showed her his bloody hands and said that he injured them lifting the weight from Willie's head.

Harry then sent Latimer to lunch. When she returned to the warehouse after lunch, Undertaker Humphrey would not let her in. She went home and didn't return to work until Thursday, January 19. Latimer stayed on the job at the warehouse until the middle of May 1893.

Lount scored a key point on cross-examination when he got Latimer to testify that she saw no blood spatters on the front of Harry's shirt. Despite the importance of this testimony, which corroborated Fox's testimony and directly contradicted Martha Hyams, Justice Street made no

---

[7] "Mrs. Harry Hyams Again a Witness," *Toronto World*, May 15, 1895.

mention of it in the extensive notes he took on her testimony.[8]

Osler then called three more witnesses to shore up the time at which Jeremiah Riordan started work at the railway company on the morning of January 16, 1893, and then called Martha Hyams back to the stand.[9] The assembled newsmen expected that Osler would question Martha about the brothers' efforts to insure her for $200,000, but Osler announced that he would test the admissibility of this evidence by calling another witness, and if Justice Street ruled it admissible, he would recall Martha to testify to that aspect of the case.

When Martha took the stand, she was sedated and accompanied by a professional nurse, who sat in a chair beside her. She was agitated, but not as much as on the previous Saturday when she fainted and fell from the witness stand. Despite the anguish apparent on her face, she gave her testimony in a clear voice. Osler conducted a brief direct examination of Martha and then turned her over for cross-examination. He got out one significant fact on his brief direct. Shortly after Harry met Martha, he asked her how much money she and her brothers had.[10]

Lount disappointed the New York reporters with the manner of his cross. They expected a fire-and-brimstone cross-examination, instead they witnessed an examination conducted more in sorrow than in anger. The *Toronto World* praised his gentleness. "Perhaps it was because he thought the spirit of Christian mercy should open its

---

[8] Street, *Bench Book*, 13:370-374; "Avoided His Glance," *New-York Herald*, May 15, 1895.

[9] Street, *Bench Book,* 13:375-378.

[10] "Mrs. Harry Hyams Again a Witness," *Toronto World*, May 15, 1895.

sanctuary of tenderness to a sister in affliction and offer her the tribute of its pity without limit and without blame, or perhaps it was because he feared that a severe badgering would bring about another fit of hysterics."[11] The *New-York Herald* drew a sharp contrast between Lount's conduct and the treatment Martha could have expected in a New York courtroom: "Mr. Lount, who cross-examined Mrs. Hyams, was at once merciful and skillful. In New York this woman would have been questioned into hysterics in fifteen minutes. Mr. Lount was satisfied with softening the points of her evidence which are the most damaging, and thus weakening the circumstantial case of the Crown, and all through it the crown lawyers sat silent. In American courts objections and exceptions would have been interposed frequently."[12]

Lount attempted one tactic of intimidation, but quickly abandoned it at the request of the witness. Osler had been careful to position himself in such a way as to have the brothers out of her line of sight when she looked at him. Lount positioned himself to make her look in the direction of the defendants. Osler asked that he reposition himself so as not to force Martha to look at her husband, but he declined. When she looked at Lount, she could not help but look at her husband, but she avoided making eye contact with him.

Having forced Martha to look in the direction of her husband, he asked, "Do you feel that you are able to undergo cross-examination today, Mrs. Hyams? If not, I shall decline to proceed."

---

[11] "Mrs. Harry Hyams Again a Witness," *Toronto World*, May 15, 1895.
[12] "Avoided His Glance," *New-York Herald*, May 15, 1895.

"If you will come up here beside the witness box, as Mr. Osler did on Saturday, I think I can go on," she whispered. Lount immediately repositioned himself so that she could look at him without seeing her husband, and after that she could talk easily.

Lount traced the course of Martha's on-again-off-again romance with Harry, emphasizing that he had shown a romantic interest in her long before the subject of insuring Willie was broached. Recounting the details of their courtship began to get Martha agitated, and the nurse had her drink a glass containing what the newspapers called a "quieting potion."

Lount then moved to the insuring of Willie's life. "Willie simply regarded the insurance as a business venture," Mrs. Hyams said. "He was twenty-two, and Mr. Hyams was thirty-eight, and the rate offered at Willie's age was more advantageous. It was an endowment policy."

"I suppose you know." Mr. Lount said, "that Harry Hyams could have got an ordinary policy, payable only at death, for a very much smaller premium?"

"Oh, yes," Mrs. Hyams said.[13]

"Did Harry Hyams say anything in furtherance of the obtaining of this policy?"

"Nothing beyond what I have told you."

"Did you not know that Harry Hyams had undergone a surgical operation, and that illness prevented him from getting his own life insured, and that, therefore, he placed the policy on Wills' life in your favor?"

---

[13] "Avoided His Glance," *New-York Herald*, May 15, 1895.

"I knew he was very ill in the spring of 1892."[14] Lount worked hard to get Martha to say that Harry was completely uninsurable due to his illness, but she refused to cooperate. She did not recall Harry ever saying that his illness prevented him from getting any insurance at all. She believed her memory was good enough to say that he never made such a remark—the only thing he said was that Willie being much younger than he, the policy would be less expensive.[15]

"Did you ever ask Harry for the $1,000 owed to 'Willie' except on the day before Willie's death?"

"Never before," She replied, "He assured me then that he would have it next day."

"And you remember the words after two years have elapsed?"

"Oh," Martha answered, "there are things which stick in the mind."[16]

Lount also tried to show that Harry did not send the telegram to Uriah Jones on the Sunday before Willie's death because all the telegraph offices were closed by the time he got it.

"On the night before the tragedy what time did Harry Hyams leave?" he asked.

"It was after 11 o'clock," was the answer.

---

[14] "Avoided His Glance," *New-York Herald*, May 15, 1895.

[15] "Mrs. Harry Hyams Again a Witness," *Toronto World*, May 15, 1895.

[16] "Avoided His Glance," *New-York Herald*, May 15, 1895.

"Yes," said Mr. Lount, "after the telegraph offices were closed?"[17]

With this last exchange, Lount's cross ended for the day, and court recessed with the expectation that the cross-examination would continue into the next day.

The next morning Martha retook the stand and struggled through Lount's cross-examination until she was again near collapse. Lount took the gloves off for this part of the cross-examination, seeking to discredit some of Martha's most damaging testimony against the twins. He zeroed in on three points: (1) What time Willie left for work on the fatal day; (2) whether Harry told her that he and Expressman Fox together lifted the weight from Willie; and (3) whether Dallas said he was in the building when the weight fell.

The first point was important because barber Gardipey had said Harry left his shop at 9:00, and he heard of the death of Wells at 9:10. To fit in the defense timeline, Willie's departure had to be moved earlier than the 8:45 that Martha had testified to on direct examination. Either Gardipey or Martha was wrong, and for the purposes of the defense, it had to be Martha who was mistaken. This was the first point at which Lount abandoned his courteous demeanor.

Martha insisted that she knew Willie left the house that morning at 8:45 because she had looked at his watch. "You don't know whether his watch was right or not, do you?" Lount challenged.

"I presume it was," Martha replied.

---

[17] "Mrs. Harry Hyams Again a Witness," *Toronto World*, May 15, 1895.

"Don't presume, and don't make excuse for your answers," Lount snapped back, "Merely answer my questions."[18]

The *Toronto World* explained the significance of the conflicting times: "The hour at which Willie left the house is important, in view of the statement of the Leader-lane barber that he heard of the tragedy at 9.10. The Crown claims that sufficient time did not elapse between 8.45, when the boy left home, and 9.10 for the boy to have been killed either accidentally or otherwise."[19]

Lount then went to work on trying to discredit Martha's testimony concerning Harry's statement about the discovery of Willie's body. He first had Martha repeat that when Harry came to Aylesworth's house at noon on the fatal day, he appeared distressed and on the verge of tears.

"Like a person who had suffered a great shock or great grief," Lount suggested.

"Yes," said the witness.

Lount then got her to repeat what Harry told her. Martha began to cry, and again said that Harry told her, "I assure you, Mina, I was not there. I was at the barber shop. When I came in with Expressman Fox. I found no one there and Fox and I went downstairs and found Willie. Fox and I lifted the weight off Willie's head."

Lount challenged her: "Is not this what was said? That he went to the basement and found Willie there and lifted

---

[18] "A Conspiracy to Kill the Crown Charges," *Toronto World*, May 16, 1895.
[19] "A Conspiracy to Kill the Crown Charges," *Toronto World*, May 16, 1895.

the weight off, and Expressman Fox came in after he lifted the weight off?"

"No," Martha replied, "that is not what was said. I told you, Mr. Lount, word for word what was said that day. That occasion so impressed the words upon my mind that I have not forgotten one of them." Lount softened his demeanor and asked quietly if, after the passage of two years, she could be sure that is what he said.

"Those words," she said, "will go with me to my dying days."[20]

Nor would she back off her recollection of what Dallas had told her. She was positive that he said he had gone into the office to write a letter, and hearing a terrible noise ran down to the cellar and found Willie. The scene sickened him, and he fainted.

This aggressive line of questioning on such an emotionally charged topic caused Martha to begin trembling violently. She pressed her hand to her head and leaned back in her chair. Her complexion paled to an even ghastlier shade of white, she gasped, and then she looked pleadingly at Justice Street. Street nodded to the nurse, who helped the shattered woman down from the stand and took her into the judge's chambers.[21] The cross-examination was suspended, and it was assumed that Martha would have to take the stand a third time to allow the defense to complete their cross-examination.

After having done a superb job of cross-examining Martha on the previous day, Lount thoroughly botched his

---

[20] "Hyams Twins Gain a Point," New-York Herald, May 16, 1895.
[21] "A Conspiracy to Kill the Crown Charges," Toronto World, May 16, 1895; "Hyams Twins Gain a Point," New-York Herald, May 16, 1895.

second day of cross-examination. His two contrasting performances lend credence to the old maxim that cross-examination can sometimes be suicidal rather than homicidal. The *Toronto World* said of her testimony, "If weeping counts for anything this strange little woman does not wish to hang her husband, yet, when the questions do not refer directly to the killing, she testifies clearly and distinctly, and evidently has no doubt that her brother was a victim of the ingenious plot outlined by the Crown."

The *World* then displayed a profound misunderstanding of the mechanics of trial advocacy by pontificating, "Her examination will be resumed when she is stronger. The defense has yet to ask her why she appeared against her husband when she knew she could not be compelled to testify."[22] Asking this question would violate the time-honored maxim of cross-examination that you should never ask "Why." The cross-examiner takes a huge risk in asking "Why?" The question surrenders control to the witness and gives her an opportunity to say almost anything she wants to harm your case.

Some analysts might say that asking Martha "Why?" would also violate the maxim that you shouldn't ask a question on cross when you don't know what the answer will be. Once again, the cross-examiner takes a significant risk in asking exploratory questions without any inkling of what the witness will say. That is not the case with asking Martha why she was testifying against her husband. The defense *knew* why, and they didn't want the jury to know why. If Lount had asked Martha why she was testifying against her husband, he would have gotten back this answer: "Because he tried to kill me, too."

---

[22] "Hyams Twins Gain a Point," *Toronto World*, May 16, 1895.

As previous quotations from various newspaper articles have shown, Victorian Era men, who were the only people qualified to serve on Victorian Era juries, were completely scandalized by the supposed treachery of a wife who had the temerity to testify against her husband. The defense would later argue to the jury that Martha was unworthy of belief because she was a vindictive harpy betraying her husband. Such an argument could have been stopped cold by the counterargument, "Martha is not the betrayer. She's the betrayed. Her husband set out to kill her, and she's testifying in self-defense." But Justice Street held that evidence inadmissible.

Osler called William Steen to clear up the date of the Orange Lodge's annual supper, and then he called Eliza Pengilly, the Hyams brothers' maid, to testify about the events of January 16. Pengilly had worked as a domestic for the Hyams family for eight years, and at the time of Willie's death she was living with the brothers, their mother, and Dallas' wife and child at 57 Gould Street. On the day of the tragedy the mother and wife were away on a trip, and only the 12-year-old daughter, Clara, was at home when Dallas returned sometime between 10:00 and 11:00. He was troubled, "as if he had a great shock," and was pacing back and forth. She asked him what was wrong, and "He said they had met with a terrible accident at the warehouse and that Mr. Wells was killed." He retreated to his bedroom with instructions that no one was to disturb him. Pengilly turned away numerous would-be visitors that day. Dallas stayed sequestered in the house for several days.[23]

A few days after the funeral Harry gave her a pair of bloody pants and asked her to try to get the bloodstains

---

[23] Street, *Bench Book*, 13:380, 381.

out. There were small blood specks about the size of a pinhead on the pants leg below the knee. Try as she might, she could not wash the bloodstains out. When Mrs. Hyams returned home, she had Pengilly take the pants to a dyer to be dyed.[24]

John Wright, a plumber, took the stand next. He testified that he was a friend of Willie Wells and learned of his death by reading the notice of Willie's funeral in the paper. The day after the funeral, Wright went to the warehouse and spoke with Harry. Harry took him downstairs into the basement and showed him where Willie was found. Hyams told him that Willie's head was about two feet from the weight shaft and his feet were pointed away from the shaft. Harry said the weight was lying on Willie's head when he found him.[25] Upon inspection of the basement, Wright saw that there was no boxing at all around the weight shaft in the basement. The weight swung loose. Nor was there a block at the bottom of the shaft to receive the weight. Someone had removed the boxing from the basement weight shaft and the wooden block placed at the bottom of the shaft to receive the weight. Wright examined the concrete floor to see if any depression had been made in it by the weight in falling. There was a depression in the concrete, of about half an inch wide about the size of the end of the weight. Wright did not report seeing any blood spatter at the bottom of the weight shaft.[26]

Wright testified that he measured the dimensions of the shaft, and found that the weight had ¾ of an inch to one

---

[24] Street, *Bench Book*, 13:381.

[25] Street, *Bench Book,* 13:381, 382.

[26] "A Conspiracy to Kill the Crown Charges," *Toronto World*, May 16, 1895.

inch play in the shaft. He said he then worked to try to take the hook off the weight, but it was difficult to remove. He had to tilt the weight to a significant degree to get the hook to come out. Osler had him demonstrate. The *Ottawa Evening News* described the demonstration: "Mr. Osler, then, in the presence of the jury grasped the rope which held the original weight and Wright was unable to separate the hook and the weight, even when the rope had six inches slack, nor could he remove it while holding the rope loose which joined the hook. The only way that the hook could be removed was by means of turning the hook in a most peculiar and almost impossible position."[27] Given the difficulty of removing the weight from the hook, it is hard to see how the hook could have accidentally worked its way off the weight in the narrow shaft.

Sam Grandage took the stand next to testify about his financial dealings with the Hyams brothers. He began by chronicling the numerous loans he had made to the brothers and described his efforts to collect on those notes. He lent the brothers a total of $1,400, and he had much difficulty in getting them to pay off their debts. By December of 1892 he had gotten most of his money back, but the brothers tried to borrow an additional $500. Given the difficulty Grandage had experienced in getting his money back from the brothers, he refused the loan. The final sum they owed him was $140, and he began to dun them daily to get that money back. When he hit them up for repayment, they would usually give him $1 to $5. On January 16, 1893, he made his twentieth trip to the warehouse to try to collect. Harry Hyams received him into the warehouse and told him there had been a terrible accident. Grandage, who saw the blood on Harry's hands

---

[27] "Insurance and Notes," *Ottawa Evening Journal,* May 16, 1895.

and the blood spatters on the front of his shirt, left without collecting any money. He finally discounted the note to Richard Lane, another moneylender.

On cross-examination by Johnston, Grandage testified that the Hyams brothers were very honorable men. He said that after he discounted the last note they owed him, one of the brothers came to him and asked him how much he had lost on discounting it. Grandage told him $12.50. Hyams pulled a $10 bill from his pocket and gave it to Grandage, asking if that would be satisfactory. Grandage told him it would be most satisfactory. On redirect Osler clarified that this last incident with the $10 bill occurred after the insurance proceeds had been paid out.[28]

Richard Lane took the stand next and testified that in September of 1892 the Hyams brothers owed him $3,700 in promissory notes. He was charging them 5% per month on some of the notes, twice the going rate of 2.5%. Osler started to go into the dates on which repayments were made, and Lount objected. Osler assured the court the timing of the repayments was truly relevant. As it turned out, the date of each of the Hyams brothers' payments coincided with the date of a check from Martha to Harry.

On cross-examination Lount got Lane to testify about one loan that he didn't make to the brothers. On January 13, 1893, they tried to borrow $1,000 from him. He told them that he would give them the money on January 14. When they came to him to get the $1,000 Lane told them he didn't have it at the moment, but they could certainly get it on the following Monday, January 16. They did not

---

[28] Street, *Bench Book*, 13:382-384; "Insurance and Notes," *Ottawa Evening Journal,* May 16, 1895.

come to get the money on the 16th, and the loan never went through.[29]

On redirect Osler got confrontational with Lane, and the tactic boomeranged.

Q: You are particularly friendly to the prisoners, Mr. Lane, are you not?

A: I am only particularly friendly because I am perfectly satisfied of their innocence of this crime.

Q: You had doubts as to their making this warehouse business a success and yet you favored them going into it?"

A: I had strong doubts as to their financial capacity to succeed in anything.

Q: And you advised them to go into it?

A: I did.

Osler ended his direct examination by saying, "And yet you call yourself their particular friend. That will do,"[30] Osler, of course, was saying this for rhetorical effect, not expecting an answer. He got one anyway.

---

[29] "A Conspiracy to Kill the Crown Charges," *Toronto World*, May 16, 1895.
[30] "A Conspiracy to Kill the Crown Charges," *Toronto World*, May 16, 1895.

"I advised them to go into it because I thought they'd do better at it than at the business they were in." And on that defeat, Osler ended his redirect.

Next Osler called Dr. Duncan McPherson. Martha had testified that Harry got $1,900 from her to lend the money to McPherson. McPherson testified that he never borrowed money from the Hyams brothers, that the money from Martha went to pay off a $1,700 chattel mortgage that that he held on the brothers' furniture. A few days after paying off the mortgage, the brothers negotiated another chattel mortgage on their household goods. The note was for $1,000, and it went unpaid for sixteen months, until the brothers redeemed it in August of 1994. [31]

Oglivie Leger, the manager of the Sun Insurance Company, took the stand next. Osler had just begun his questioning when Lount interposed an objection and asked that Leger's testimony be proffered outside the presence of the jury. Osler saw no reason to excuse the jury, but Justice Street sided with Lount. Leger had been called to testify concerning the Hyams brothers' abortive attempt to insure Martha. Street wanted to know what Osler intended to prove by Leger, and Osler replied that he was going to prove by Leger and eleven other witnesses that Harry P. Hyams told Leger that there was a lady in Toronto whom he wanted to insure for $100,000. Harry said that the lady was wealthy, that her wealth would die with her, and she wanted to insure her life in his favor. Leger later learned that the woman was Harry's wife. Osler said he proposed to show that Harry and Dallas tried to purchase $300,000 in life insurance on Martha, and that there was no way the

---

[31] "A Conspiracy to Kill the Crown Charges," *Toronto World*, May 16, 1895.

brothers could keep up the premiums on so large a sum of insurance. He argued that this evidence should go before the jury on the issue that was being tried, because it was evidence as to the intent with which the insurance upon the deceased's life had been placed. and it was evidence within the authority of *Makin v. Attorney General for New South Wales,*[32] which we discussed earlier. He contended that, wherever an equivalent act was surrounded with good or based on evil intentions, the court and jury should have light thereupon, and it was for the purpose of throwing light on the first transaction that evidence as to the second transaction was desired. Osler concluded, "If the Crown's contention is correct that it was with a criminal design that the insurance was placed on Wells' life the jury had a right to hear the evidence."[33]

If Judge Street ruled against the admissibility of this evidence, it would be a near-fatal blow to the prosecution. An old maxim of trial advocacy says that if you're arguing a key point to the judge, you should give the judge three reasons to rule in your favor. By making three arguments you have tripled the chances of getting a favorable ruling. Osler argued only one rationale for admissibility of the evidence. He did not argue two other important points in favor of allowing the evidence. First, the Hyams defense was that the death was accidental; similar fact evidence of the type offered by the Crown is almost universally held admissible to rebut the defense of accident.[34] Second, the

---

[32] [1894] A.C. 57.

[33] "A Conspiracy to Kill the Crown Charges," *Toronto World*, May 16, 1895.

[34] *People v. Vandervleit*, 508 N.W.2d 114, 444 Mich. 52 (1993) *Williams v. State*, 110 So.2d 654 (Fla. 1954).

evidence explained why Martha would be so "treacherous" as to testify against her husband.

Justice Street suppressed the evidence without allowing the defense to say a single word in opposition to the Crown's proffer.[35] Justice Street said that if Martha had been killed under suspicious circumstances, then the evidence would have been receivable, but he had looked over the cases that Osler cited to him on Saturday and had found none that were analogous.[36] He noted in his *Bench Book*, "I rule against the admissibility of evidence of applications for further insurance on the wife's life. Mr. Osler applies for a [reserved] case, which I am willing to grant."[37] What this means is that Osler wanted to be able to appeal the adverse ruling at the conclusion of the trial. At that time in Canada, the prosecution could appeal under two circumstances. First, if the case resulted in a mistrial, the prosecution could appeal the point before the case was retried. Second, if the judge's adverse ruling was egregious, the prosecution could even appeal a not guilty verdict. The appellate courts at that time were comfortable with the prosecution appealing after a mistrial, but they were extremely reluctant to grant a new trial after an acquittal, no matter how badly the trial judge erred.[38]

The Crown released their twelve witnesses, and the jury filed back into the box. The brothers breathed sighs of relief, and spectators in the courtroom easily recognized how great a victory the defense had won without voicing a single word in opposition to the proffer. The *New-York*

---

[35] "Hyams Twins Gain a Point," *New-York Herald,* May 16, 1895.

[36] "A Conspiracy to Kill the Crown Charges," *Toronto World*, May 16, 1895.

[37] Street, *Bench Book*, 13:387.

[38] *King v. Phinney (No. 2)*, 7 Can.Cr.Cas. 280, 1903 CanLII 96 (NS SC).

Herald described the victory as "spiking one of the biggest guns of [the Crown]."[39] The *Manitoba Morning Free Press* said the defense had "scored a great victory for their client, when they succeeded, with the help of the judge, in ruling out all evidence [of the attempt to insure Martha]."[40]

Having had one his biggest guns spiked, Osler then called Dr. Edmund King, who contributed to the downward spiral of the Crown's evidence. King, a practicing physician since 1886, had been personal physician to the Hyams brothers since 1893. According to King, shortly after 9:00 on the morning of January 16,1893, Harry Hyams rushed into King's office on the corner of Queen and Bond Streets. He told King that there had been an accident to a young man in his warehouse and exclaimed "For God's sake, hurry up, as I don't know whether the young man is killed or not!"[41]

King rushed to the scene, where he found both brothers, Harry having beaten him to the warehouse. The front door was unlocked, and Dallas was on the ground floor leaning against the railing that separated the office from the warehouse area. King went down to the cellar, where he saw the hoist on the west side of the cellar floor. He saw the body of Willie Wells lying on its back some eighteen inches from the weight shaft. The head was toward the weight shaft and the body laid with the feet pointed away from the weight shaft. The arms were down to the sides, slightly bent. The legs were nearly straight. King was certain that he saw no glasses on the corpse, and he was almost as positive that there were no gloves on the

---

[39] "Hyams Twins Gain a Point," *New-York Herald,* May 16, 1895.

[40] "Anxiety Relieved Evidence Against the Hyams Brothers Ruled Out," *Manitoba Morning Free Press*, May 16, 1895.

[41] "A Conspiracy to Kill the Crown Charges," *Toronto World*, May 16, 1895.

hands. He recalled trying to get a pulse from the wrist, and that the wrist was bare.[42] The head was mashed to a cone toward the top. King saw a break in the skin over the right eye. The eye sockets bulged, but the lids were closed, and King did not see the eyeballs.[43]

King asked how it happened. The brothers said the weight had fallen and hit Wells on the head. One of the brothers, possibly Harry, said "We took the weight off him to relieve him of further injury." The brothers told him that the hoist was out of order and the weight fell and struck Willie on the head. They said the hoist was frequently out of order.

King saw the weight was resting on its bottom near the weight shaft. King could not see the hook or rope to which the weight had been attached. King examined the weight shaft and found it boarded on three sides, with the front of the shaft open. He saw a wooden block at the foot of the shaft. The elevator cage was in the basement as low as it could go. After determining that there was nothing he could do, King went home and phoned the Coroner's Office. He said he placed the call shortly before 10:00.[44]

Johnston conducted the cross-examination, and it was devastating to the Crown. He started by having King say, "I had no reason at the time from what I saw to believe it was anything but an accident." Then he had King describe the blood. "There was a considerable pool of clotted blood where the head was lying, and another considerable pool where the weight had come down on the slot. I understood that the body had been moved when the weight was moved

---

[42] "Medical Evidence in the Hyams Trial," 454.
[43] Street, *Bench Book*, 13:388, 389.
[44] Street, *Bench Book*, 13:389, 390.

and there was evidence of the trail between the two pools. There was blood spattered above the buffer on the north side of the interior of the weight shaft."[45] King was satisfied that the body had been dragged from the first pool of blood in the weight shaft to the second pool of blood under the head.[46] The defense had worked hard up to this point with the other witnesses to get someone to say that there was blood at the bottom of the weight shaft, but they could not get any cooperation. They finally succeeded with Dr. King, and this success was extremely important to the accident theory.

Johnston then had Dr. King demonstrate how he thought the death occurred. King took a position in the witness box as if leaning over to look up the weight shaft. He said the weight came down, and as he described the weight striking the head, he clapped his hands together. The *Manitoba Morning Free Press* said the clap "resounded through the room and added intensity to his portrayal. The position and description of the doctor made up another sensational feature of this wonderful trial."[47]

Osler on redirect pointed out one or two minor discrepancies between King's present testimony and the testimony he had given at the preliminary hearing, and then he began to ask King about how he thought the death occurred. Lount objected, but Justice Street allowed the questions. Osler outlined a diagram of the elevator shaft and the weight shaft on the door to Justice Street's chambers and suggested to King that Willie was standing in

---

[45] Street, *Bench Book*, 13:391.

[46] "A Conspiracy to Kill the Crown Charges," *Toronto World*, May 16, 1895.

[47] "Anxiety Relieved Evidence Against the Hyams Brothers Ruled Out," *Manitoba Morning Free Press*, May 16, 1895.

a certain position relative to the weight shaft when he was struck. King accepted the outline of the shaft, but he disagreed with Osler as to how the victim was standing when the weight fell.

"Come down here, then, Doctor, and show the jury," Osler directed. Dr. King complied, demonstrating that he thought Wells was standing at the door of the shaft right below the weight and looking up in such a way that the weight, when it fell, struck him in the right temple.[48]

Osler concluded redirect by saying: "Your idea is, doctor, that Wells was looking up the shaft with his back towards the wall, and that in this position he waited for the weight; that the weight struck him, and as he fell the weight followed him; that his head alighted on the buffer and the weight having followed him down lodged on the head. I'll leave you with that, doctor."[49] The net effect of Osler's redirect examination was to bolster the defense case. Sometimes the best thing to say on redirect examination is, "No questions."

The *Toronto World* analyzed the evidence of May 15 by saying: "The defense will be that Willie Wells went down the cellar of the warehouse early on the morning of Jan. 16 to fill the coal scuttle, preparatory to attending to the fires; that he put the scuttle on the elevator, which failed to work properly; that he looked up the weight shaft to see what was the matter, and the weight fell and killed him. It is for this reason that the defense lay so much stress on the evidence of Fox, the expressman, that the boy had on his hands at the time of his death an old pair of gloves, which

---

[48] "Medical Evidence in the Hyams Trial," 454.
[49] "A Conspiracy to Kill the Crown Charges," *Toronto World*, May 16, 1895.

he was in the habit of wearing while doing chores around the warehouse.

"Dr. King, who was the first party in the warehouse after the killing, testified yesterday, however, that he did not see any gloves on the boy's hands. He also flatly contradicted Fox with reference to the spectacles alleged to have been worn by the dead boy. Fox swore that there was a pair of spectacles on the boy when he came into the warehouse, and that he took them off himself and handed them to Harry Hyams. Dr. King, who was there before Fox, swore positively that there were no spectacles, and had there been he must have seen them. The Crown claims that, if Fox is not mistaken, both the gloves and the spectacles had been put on by somebody after Dr. King had left the place."[50]

According to the *World,* "The evidence of the Crown yesterday was in many respects the strongest yet presented against the twins. It was proven by the evidence of several moneylenders that prior to the tragedy the Hyams' had mortgaged their household furniture, their office furniture and the effects in their warehouse. It was also proven that these chattel mortgages were retired subsequent to the death of Wells and after Harry Hyams had been advanced part of the insurance money by the sister of the dead boy— that, in fact, one of the cheques issued by Martha was used to retire the chattel mortgage on the Hyams' furniture."[51]

Wellman was happy with the results of the afternoon in court, but his joy had to have been tempered by a grave

---

[50] "A Conspiracy to Kill the Crown Charges," *Toronto World*, May 16, 1895.
[51] "A Conspiracy to Kill the Crown Charges," *Toronto World*, May 16, 1895.

disappointment. His application for membership in the New York City Bar Association had been rejected. Lawyers did not need to be members of the city bar association to practice law, but it was a prestigious organization. Most of the members of the association were prominent attorneys, and it was a feather in the cap for lawyers who could gain admission. Wellman had practiced for many years in New York City, but always as an employee of either the city government or the District Attorney's Office, where membership in the association was not as important. When he went into private practice, he quite naturally sought to enhance his image by becoming a member. Wellman, however, had made many enemies in the private bar with his aggressive tactics and abrasive personality, and this led to the bar association's membership committee to disapprove his application.[52]

---

[52] "Hyams Twins Gain a Point," *New-York Herald*, May 16, 1895.

CHAPTER NINE: THE PROSECUTION CASE
DAYS SEVEN THROUGH NINE[1]

The day began with Osler announcing that Martha Hyams could not return to the stand due to nervous prostration. Lount announced that he would waive any further cross-examination of Martha so that the case could continue. Absent a waiver by Lount, Judge Street had two remedies at his disposal. First, he could strike Martha's testimony and instruct the jury to disregard it, but this could hardly prove a viable option given the length and significance of her testimony. Second, he could declare a mistrial and the case would have to be completely retried during the next session of the Assizes. Why didn't the defense ask for a mistrial? They probably felt that the case had gone well for them, and they were confident of a not guilty verdict. They took a huge risk when they did not ask for a mistrial, and it almost resulted in disaster.

During her direct examination, Martha had identified several love letters written by Harry to her, and they had been received into evidence. Osler published portions of the letters to the jury by reading them into evidence. The *Toronto World* reported that Osler declined to read the full letters "in deference to the feelings of Harry Hyams." The defense, however, much to Harry's embarrassment, insisted that the letters be published in their entirety. Throughout the reading of the letters Harry blushed beet red, and his eyes darted about the courtroom seeking to see if anyone was laughing at what the *World* called his "epistolatory effusions."

---

[1] Thursday, May 16, 1895 – Saturday, May 18, 1895.

A letter dated June 12, 1891, written while Martha was visiting in Detroit, Michigan, read: "Tuesday came and no letter from my little girl, dearest Mina; I am afraid you are sick; you are not careful of your health, and you work too hard; you scold me for working too hard and do it yourself. Send me a small picture of your dear self so I can see how you look. I wish I could see you, Mina, dear, if only for a day. Write to me, darling, if only a few lines. Do I write too often? Mina, dear, I close, with lots of love and kisses. —Harry."

A week later he wrote: "I want you to be careful of your health; write me as often as you can, and be careful not to make a mash on some handsome young man and forget your Harry." This statement did not sit well with Martha, and she wrote him back addressing him as "Dear Friend." He shot a letter back protesting, "It seems cold to head your letters 'Dear Friend.' I send you lots of love—something you never send me. I send you a great, big kiss, from your own little boy, Harry."

Then on August 7, 1891, he wrote: "You are the only girl I care for, though you think I do not care for you. How I long to see you Mina, Dear, and have a long talk about matters, business and otherwise. I advise Annie [Mrs. Aylesworth] to do as her husband desires. Write to your Harry; he never tires of Mina. Dallas says he thinks we're in love, but don't mind him; he's an old married man."

Many more letters followed in a similar vein. The last letter read into evidence was the one he sent to her after discovering that she was hiding from him at the Bishop Strachan School. The letters may have influenced the jurors, but Justice Street demonstrated his disregard for their contents by not taking a single note on them in his *Bench Book*.[2]

Samuel Smoke then took the stand. He testified that Martha had retained him as her financial advisor after she received the proceeds of Willie's life insurance. He then began to relate the circumstances of a meeting he had with Harry and his attorney, T.W. Horn, on April 7, 1893.

"What was the subject matter of that interview?" Osler asked. Lount sprang to his feet objecting to the question on the grounds of attorney-client privilege. Smoke volunteered that Martha had authorized him to divulge anything the Crown wanted to know.

"What was the subject matter of that interview?" Osler asked again.

"A certain proposition was made," replied Smoke.

"What was the proposition?" Lount was again on his feet objecting, this time on the grounds of the best evidence rule.

"Was the proposition reduced to writing?" he asked.

"I don't propose to ask questions to suit my learned friend," retorted Osler, "I have asked a question. It is either regular or irregular, and I wait for the ruling upon it before I ask another."

Justice Street ruled the question proper, and Smoke testified that Hyams and Horn were trying to get possession of all Martha's insurance proceeds. They said that Martha had agreed to turn the money over to them. Smoke told them he did not understand that from his client, and he

---

[2] Street, *Bench Book*, 13:392

would have to consult with her before he could agree to turning the money over to them. On the same day, Horn sent him a draft agreement to turn over the money, but after consultation with Martha, he refused to allow Harry to have the money.

In a second interview two weeks later, Harry admitted that he already had between $8,000 and $9,000 of Martha's insurance money. Smoke pressed him to refund the money, but all he ever got from Harry was $600 in cash and a $616 promissory note. On May 10, 1893, the day after Martha's marriage to Harry, Smoke received a letter from her terminating his employment as her solicitor.

"Have you since acted for her?" Osler asked.

"Yes sir," Smoke replied, "in January last."

"Did you have any communication with Mr. Horn at that time?"

"Yes."

"What was the purport of that communication?"

Lount objected on the grounds of relevance. Osler was obviously trying a back door approach to get at Harry's attempt to over-insure Martha. Street saw through the ploy and sustained the objection.[3] The defense conducted very little cross-examination.

William H. Richie took the stand next to testify that a few days after Willie's death he bought several items from the Colborne Street warehouse: two barrels of sugar, four barrels of salt, five boxes of pearline, three boxes of Sapolio

---

[3] "The Hook Could Not Come Off the Weight," *Toronto World*, May 17, 1895.

soap, and a case of corn. It was a small load, but it almost completely cleaned out the warehouse. Some of the items had blood on them, but these spots could be attributed to Fox cutting off Willie's bloody coat and placing it on the boxes.[4]

Undertaker Benjamin D. Humphrey testified that he received a telephone call from Expressman Fox to come to the Colborne Street warehouse and arrived there shortly after noon. When he got to the warehouse, he was met by Expressman Fox. He went into the office and saw Harry Hyams coming up from the basement on the stairs. Hyams' hands were bleeding. Humphrey went downstairs and found the body lying on its back with the head approximately two feet from the weight shaft. From Humphrey's description of the basement, Justice Street drew a diagram in the margin of page 397 of his *Bench Book*.

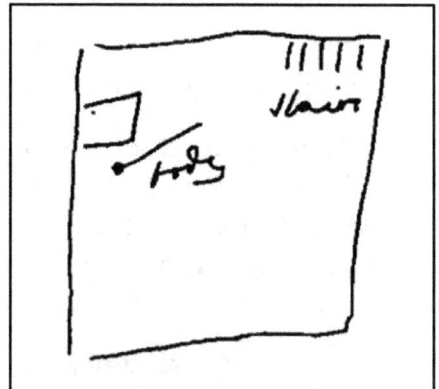

Justice Street's Diagram of the Scene[5]

---

[4] Street, *Bench Book*, 13:394, 395.
[5] Street, *Bench Book*, 13:397

Humphrey saw neither glasses nor gloves on the body. He didn't recall anyone taking off Willie's coat. He saw a pool of blood underneath Willie's head, but he saw no indication that the body had been moved before he got there. This statement starkly contrasted with Dr. King's assertion that there was a pool of blood at the bottom of the shaft and bloody drag marks from there to the pool of blood that was under the body.

Was there a blood trail from the bottom of the weight shaft to the resting place of the body? Nobody other than Dr. King reported seeing such a trail; and Humphrey said the body appeared unmoved, meaning that there was no blood trail. Unless Willie was killed in the shaft, his death could not have been an accident. Did King's friendship with the Hyams brothers cause him to imagine that he had seen a blood trail that wasn't there?

Humphrey did not touch the body until after Coroner Aikins had come and completed his inspection. Humphrey recalled that Aikins stayed in the basement no more than ten minutes and left without turning the body over. Humphrey heard Harry explaining to the Coroner what had happened. Harry said that the weight fell three stories.

Humphrey got assistance in removing the body from the cellar and took it to his mortuary to prepare it for burial. The head was split, and it leaked blood as the body was being moved. Humphrey stopped and wrapped the head with bandages to keep from leaving a blood trail up the stairs and out of the building.

In preparing the body for burial, Humphrey had an excellent opportunity to assess the damage to Willie's body. Humphrey observed no injuries, not even bruising, below the neck. The head was split open on the top from left to right. The right side of the face was sunken, and the left side bulged out. Humphrey saw a hole over one of the eyes big enough to insert two fingers.

Lount did not do an extensive cross-examination. He did, however, try to use Humphrey to account for the blood on the boxes sold to William Richie. "You say the blood was slowly dropping from the body when you removed it?"

"Yes."

"Did you rest the body on any of the boxes when you reached the ground floor?"

"No, I don't think we did."

Next, George Grundy and G.J. McConkey, both agents for New York Life Insurance Company, entered the box and recounted the history of the Hyams brothers and their adventures in insurance. Grundy produced the insurance policy and testified that Willie, at 22 years of age, got a premium rate of $384 per quarter. Harry, who was thirty-five at the time, could have gotten the same amount of insurance for $405 per quarter.

At the time of Willie's death, Dallas was carrying a total of $50,000 on his life in three policies. Harry took out the first policy, for $5,000 a few months before Willie's death. He purchased the second, for $25,000, on December 3, 1892. He got the third, for $20,000 on January 7, 1895. He allowed all these policies to lapse on February 7, 1895.[6]

On cross-examination Grundy testified that, although the policy was negotiated in the offices of the Hyams

---

[6] "The Hook Could Not Come Off the Weight," *Toronto World*, May 17, 1895; "A Conspiracy to Kill, the Crown Charges," *Toronto World*, May 16, 1895.

brothers, neither of them were present when Willie applied for the insurance. Grundy testified glowingly about what a sound investment Willie had made when he took out the endowment policy. When it came time for redirect examination, Osler pounced on Grundy's claim. "What would be the surrender value of a $30,000 policy at the end of five years?"

"About $4,000," Grundy replied.

"And you call that a good investment?"

"Yes, sir."

"After paying in over $8,000, the policy would be worth about half, at no interest. That was not the way you put it to him, was it?"[7] And with that parting shot, Osler concluded his examination.

Justice Street did not miss the import of this line of questioning. In his *Bench Book* he wrote: "Surrender value of Policy at end of 5 yrs [years] wd. [would] be about half what has been paid in the way of prems [premiums]."[8]

Osler then called Samuel Hughson of the Covenant Mutual Insurance Company and Dr. Thomas H. Little to testify about similar shenanigans with the $2,000 policy on Willie's life from Covenant Mutual. Harry paid the first premium on the policy. After Willie was insured, and shortly before his death, Harry applied for a $10,000 policy from Covenant Mutual. Dr. Little was called upon to perform the pre-insurance physical, but Harry avoided taking the

---

[7] "The Hook Could Not Come Off the Weight," *Toronto World,* May 17, 1895.
[8] Street, *Bench Book*, 14:3.

physical until after Willie died, and the policy was never issued because of the lack of a physical.[9]

Osler then turned his attention to proving that the weight could not have slipped off the hook. His first witness, David L. Graham, had been part owner of the printing business that occupied the warehouse before the Hyams brothers sublet it. The elevator had been installed in 1885, and it was used constantly. It performed "very well." The weight got caught on two occasions: once when a nail had been driven thought the boxing and into the weight shaft, and once when one of the boxing boards came loose. They never used a light weight to operate the elevator.[10]

Graham's partner, John Imrie, confirmed that the elevator was in good working order in November of 1892, when they sublet the warehouse to the Hyamses. The brothers paid $50 per month rent and kept the warehouse until the summer of 1893.[11]

James Rankin, who was foreman of the press department for Imrie and Graham, testified that he ran the hoist nearly every day from 1886, when he began working for Imrie and Graham, until 1892, when the press moved and the warehouse was sublet to the Hyams brothers. The elevator worked perfectly, and the only mishap with it occurred when a cat worked its way through the boxing of the weight shaft and was crushed by the weight. There was boxing all around the weight shaft from the top floor down

---

[9] "The Hook Could Not Come Off the Weight," *Toronto World*, May 17, 1895.

[10] Street, *Bench Book*, 14:4, 5.

[11] Street, *Bench Book*, 14:6

into the basement. The elevator shaft itself had doors on all floors except the basement floor.[12]

Charles Lee, an elevator repairman with 14 years of experience, testified next. He said that he performed repairs on the elevator cage in December of 1892. The brothers wanted a half-size counterweight, and Lee procured one for them. On the issue of the hook accidentally becoming detached from the weight, he said, "I don't think this weight could drop off the rope in the place it was in because there wasn't room enough." On cross-examination Johnston got Lee to admit that (1) the elevator cage was unsafe at the time he was called in to repair it, and (2) "I didn't pay much attention to the weight shaft."[13]

The next two witnesses cast grave doubt on the accident theory. John Fensom of Fensom Elevator Works contracted with the Hyams brothers to replace the hook on the 200-pound counterweight. He bought the hook from Joseph Wilson, who ran a hardware store. At first Fensom's worker, John Thompson, could not make the hook go into the hole in the counterweight. Thompson solved the problem by enlarging the hole with a chisel to make the hook fit snugly in the weight. Fensom testified, "I don't think the weight can come off the hook. I think it would be impossible for the weight to come off whether it were to catch either ascending or descending."[14]

The last witness of the day was Samuel Kidd, a carpenter. In late November or early December Kidd installed two doors on the elevator shaft, one on the first

---

[12] Street, *Bench Book*, 14:6, 7.
[13] Street, *Bench Book*, 14:7, 8.
[14] Street, *Bench Book*, 14:9.

floor and one on the second. On the second floor he opened the weight shaft and built a platform for the weight to rest on when the brothers changed it out for the lighter weight. Also, acting at the direction of the brothers, he took a portion of the boxing off the weight shaft to allow the weight to swing free when it was being changed. On cross-examination Johnston got him to say that the idea of building the platform may have come from him rather than the brothers.[15]

By the end of the day, if Osler had convinced no one else of the impossibility of the weight accidentally slipping off the hook, he had convinced the press. The *Toronto World* wrote:

> It is remarkable as showing the strength of the Crown's case . . . , that the witnesses who spoke of the possibility, or rather impossibility, of the weight becoming loosened from the hook while in the shaft were allowed to slip down from the witness box without a single challenge of their statements by the defense.

> It was also shown that the shaft in which the weight ran was continued down to the basement floor, when the prisoners took possession of the warehouse, and the Crown will ask the jury to believe that the facing of this shaft was cut off by the Hyams' in order to lend the color of accident to the murder they were planning. The evidence relating to the hoist and its general condition was the strongest feature of the Crown's case as presented yesterday, and, coming as it does from men who operated the hoist for years, goes far to offset the contention of the defense that it was a rickety, ramshackle, dangerous affair, unsafe for even ordinary

---

[15] Street, *Bench Book*, 14:10, 11

use. Of this evidence, possibly the most important part was that which proved that prior to the occupancy of the warehouse by the prisoners the weight shaft was absolutely free from obstruction of any kind and was only large enough to give the weight an inch and a half swing either way.[16]

Osler opened the eighth day of his case with more testimony about the elevator. Albert E. Fryer and Charles Hackney testified that they were procured by Expressman Fox to repair the elevator after Willie's death. They performed the repairs on January 23. They found several boards loose in the elevator shaft between the weight box and the wall. They also tore away the stand which had been erected to assist in getting off the weight. Witness Hackney said that Fox told him to look closely in the weight box for any projection which might be there. He sawed off about ¾ of an inch of the floor. The defense seized upon Hackney's testimony concerning the ¾ inch projection and made the most of it on cross-examination, but Justice Street must have felt that the small projection was insignificant. He took no notes on that portion of the testimony.[17]

Donald Craig, an elevator maker, gave expert testimony concerning experiments he made with the elevator to see if he could get the weight to fall off. He found that with the cage empty and the 200-pound weight attached, the elevator and weight balanced one another. The only way to get the cage to move up or down was to pull on the pull rope. Craig placed obstructions in the weight shaft to see how the weight would react to hitting an obstruction. When

---

[16] "The Hook Could Not Come Off the Weight," *Toronto World*, May 17, 1895.

[17] Street, *Bench Book*, 14:11; "Dallas Hyams Will Tell His Story," *Toronto World*, May 18, 1895.

the weight struck the projection, there would be so little slack in the rope that it was barely perceptible. Manipulating the pull rope would not increase the slack. He did not see how an obstruction could make the weight come off the rope.

Lount began his cross-examination by getting Craig to say that "accidents sometimes happen in elevators that one cannot account for."[18] Lount took the hook and placed it in the eye of the weight with the tip of the hook at the center of the eye. He then asked Craig which way the hook might slip if the weight hit an obstruction. Craig said the chances were even that the hook would either slip to fully engage the eye or slip off the weight. They made two experiments with the hook so placed. Once it fully engaged in the eye and once it slipped off the weight. In an article titled "Point for the Defence in the Hyams Case," The *New-York Herald* trumpeted this result, saying "It was from Builder Donald Craig, who knows all about hand elevators, that the defense drew the important admission that if only the point, or "nose," of the hook had been in the eye of the weight an obstruction or projection in the weight shaft might have released the mass of iron and allowed it to fall upon Wells. Craig made an experiment with the weight in front of the Jury box."[19]

Having emphasized this "point" scored on cross-examination, the *Herald* neglected to report what happened when Osler stepped up for redirect. The *Toronto World* covered the omission: "On behalf of the Crown the hook was again placed in position and a measurement

---

[18] Street, *Bench Book*, 14:12.
[19] "Point for Defence in the Hyams Case," *New-York Herald*, May 18, 1895.

made, which was compared with the dimensions of the weight box. The comparison showed that with the hook in the position suggested the weight could not be operated in the box."[20] Osler's demonstration that the hook could not have been in the position contended for by the defense caused the *New York Times* to directly contradict the *Herald*. In an article titled "Damaging to the Hyams Twins," the *Times* wrote, "At the Hyams trial to-day, Donald Craig and John Russell, elevator builders, testified that they considered it impossible for the elevator weight which killed Wells to have slipped off its hook by accident."[21]

The last witness called by the prosecution on the issue of the elevator was John Galt, a mechanical civil engineer with 22 years' experience. Galt testified that he inspected the elevator on May 16 and found it to be working in a jerky and irregular way. He tried everything he could to obstruct the weight and cause it to come off the hook and could not find any way that the hook and weight could accidentally become detached.[22]

The case was now drawing rapidly to a close. The only major element left to be addressed was expert testimony concerning the injury to Willie's head and how it might have been inflicted. Before launching off into the expert testimony on this issue, Osler did a little housekeeping. He called Detective Alf Cuddy to testify about the seizure and chain of custody on several items of evidence. In addition to this boring line of testimony, he did get Cuddy to relate a strange statement Harry had made immediately after Willie's death. Cuddy had interviewed Harry and asked if

---

[20] "Dallas Hyams Will Tell His Story," *Toronto World*, May 18, 1895.
[21] "Damaging to the Hyams Twins," *New York Times*, May 18, 1895.
[22] Street, *Bench Book*, 14:14.

Willie were insured. Harry said that Willie had some insurance, but he did not know how much.[23]

Dr. John Caven, who the autopsy on Willie in association with Coroner A.J. Johnson, took the stand as the first prosecution expert. His testimony tracked the testimony he gave at the preliminary hearing. Dr. Caven stunned the audience when he reached into his valise and pulled forth Willie's wired-together skull. Dallas and Harry became ghastly pale, and they averted their eyes from it. When Osler asked the jurors to pass the skull among themselves, they refused to touch it. Osler walked the length of the jury box holding the skull close to the jurors for their examination. None looked at it closely. After this demonstration Dr. Caven produced an undamaged skull for use in explaining the injuries.[24]

He concluded that to produce the injuries to the skull, it must have been resting on some solid base and force applied to the right side of the head. There were injuries to the base of the skull and to the vertebrae of the neck which must have been produced by a compressing force which brought the skull hard against the spinal cord. Dr. Caven concluded that there had to be more than one application of force to the skull to produce the injuries he saw. To produce the frontal injury to the skull, the force had to come from the front.[25]

---

[23] "Dallas Hyams Will Tell His Story," *Toronto World*, May 18, 1895.

[24] "Dallas Hyams Will Tell His Story," *Toronto World*, May 18, 1895.

[25] Street, *Bench Book*, 14:16-17; "Medical Evidence in the Hyams Trial," 455.

Johnston performed the cross-examination.[26] He began by trying to show that Dr. Caven, as an academic, had not actually practiced medicine for any great length of time.[27] Dr. Caven handled himself quite well, showing that he had several years of actual practice, that he had been on a hospital staff, and that he had devoted years to the study of disease and the examination of broken bones.[28] This line of questioning so impressed Justice Street that he did not take a single note on it. Johnston next tried to show that there were differences of opinion among the Crown's medical experts. Dr. Caven admitted that there were disagreements but testified that they were minor. Johnston then tried to demonstrate that Dr. Caven's testimony at trial differed materially from his testimony at the preliminary hearing. Dr. Caven stood his ground, arguing forcefully that his two statements were perfectly consistent,[29] but Justice Street's notes indicate that he believed Johnston was the winner of this contest.[30] Dr. Caven remained firm in his bottom-line opinion despite Johnston's heroics, but the *Ottowa Evening Journal* concluded that, "Owing to the careful examination of Mr. Johns[t]on, [Caven's] evidence was somewhat weakened."[31] The *New York Times*, on the other hand, reported that despite conducting "a most rigid cross-examination," the defense "failed to shake his main testimony in the slightest particular."[32]

---

[26] It appears that he and Lount had divided the burden of cross-examination by having Lount cross the lay witnesses and Johnston cross the experts.

[27] "Dallas Hyams Will Tell His Story," *Toronto World*, May 18, 1895.

[28] "Medical Testimony in the Hyams Trial," 455.

[29] "Medical Testimony in the Hyams Trial," 456.

[30] Street, *Bench Book,* 14:18.

[31] "How Wells Was Killed," *Ottawa Evening Journal*, May 18, 1895.

[32] "Damaging to the Hyams Twins," *New York Times*, May 18, 1895.

Coroner Albert Jukes Johnson, who had been in England at the time of Wells' death, took the stand next. Although at the time he was just one of several Coroners serving in Toronto, he would later be appointed Chief Coroner for the entire city.[33] He testified that the frontal injuries to the skull came from a slightly upward blow struck on the right side of the face. Another blow had been struck with great force on the right side of the head while the head was lying with the left side on a solid surface. Johnson believed that a third blow had been struck to the head, but he was not absolutely certain of this. On cross-examination Johnston did his best to discredit Johnson and to suggest that there were serious disagreements among the Crown experts. Dr. Johnson maintained that no differences of opinion existed as to the main point of the number of blows.[34] According to the *Toronto World*, "Mr. Johnston made a complete failure in his effort to shake Dr. Johnson in his testimony or lead him into contradictions."[35]

Dr. James Henry Richardson, Professor of Anatomy at Toronto University, was the last witness of the day. He swore that the injuries to the skull as revealed at the post-mortem examination could not, under any conceivable circumstance, be caused by one blow. Dr. Richardson's testimony so disconcerted the defense team that they held a hurried consultation.[36] After the defense team broke their

---

[33] Hassard, *Famous Canadian Trials*, 236.

[34] "Medical Evidence in the Hyams Trial," 456, 457; Street, *Bench Book*, 14:19-21.

[35] "Dallas Hyams Will Tell His Story," *Toronto World*, May 18, 1895.

[36] "Medical Evidence in the Hyams Trial," 457; Street, *Bench Book*, 14:21, 22.

huddle, Johnston "allowed Dr. Richardson to step down from the box without putting a single question."[37]

Osler attempted to begin the last day of the prosecution case with a little character assassination. The first witness was Detective Charles Heidelberg of the New York City Police Department. Heidelberg had arrested the Hyams brothers in November of 1881 on a charge of fraudulent theft, but the charges had been dismissed upon the conviction and sentencing of three of their accomplices.[38] After their close call with the law in New York, the brothers moved their theatre of operations to Jersey City, where they were convicted of insurance fraud and sentenced to three years in prison. After posting appellate bail in the amount of US$3,000, they jumped bail and moved to Canada. Detective Robert Pearson of the Jersey City Police Department was called to the witness stand to describe his investigation of the case, [39] but Justice Street quite properly ruled the testimony of both these detectives inadmissible.

Osler's next witness was Dr. Frederick Grassett, who testified that the injuries to the skull were produced by a "strong lateral force applied to the right side of the head, the head resting on the hard floor. I also think there is evidence of another blow from the front and side because the malar bones and angular process are broken and were driven in." Johnston again declined to cross-examine.[40]

Now would have been a suitable time to rest the prosecution case. Four experts had testified that there were multiple blows to the head; Johnston had failed to shake

---

[37] "Dallas Hyams Will Tell His Story," *Toronto World*, May 18, 1895.
[38] "How Wells Was Killed," *Ottawa Evening Journal*, May 18, 1895.
[39] "Hyams Twins Insurance Swindlers," *New York Times*, May 19, 1895.
[40] Street, *Bench Book*, 14:23.

the first two; and he had declined to question the last two. Lawyers frequently, however, succumb to the temptation of overproving their case; and this is what Osler did. He called several additional doctors, not as experienced and not as capable of withstanding cross-examination as the first four, and Johnston butchered them on cross-examination. The *New-York Herald* described the debacle in these words: "The Crown rested its case against the Hyams brothers at four o'clock this afternoon, after its medical experts had been most thoroughly overhauled by Mr. Johnston and had practically admitted that Wells' death might have been accidental."[41] After calling 68 Crown witnesses over a period of nine days, Osler rested his case; and the prosecution ended, not with a bang but with a whimper.

When the Crown rested its case at 4:00 pm, Johnston immediately demanded to know why Osler had not called Coroner William H.B. Aikins as a witness. Was the Crown trying to hide something from the jury by not calling the official Coroner who had investigated the death and found nothing suspicious about it? This, of course, was a bit of theatrics on Johnston's part. Almost all the court-watchers knew full well why Osler had not called Aikins. As the *New-York Herald* put it, "It has long been well known that Mr. Osler would omit Dr. Aikins' testimony and allow the defense to call him, in order that he might cross-examine him fiercely in the interest of the Crown."[42]

Dr. William H.B. Aikins was a prominent, well-respected member of the medical community and a pioneer in the use

---

[41] "Heidelberg Not Called to Testify," New York Herald, May 19, 1895.
[42] "Heidelberg Not Called to Testify," New York Herald, May 19, 1895.

of radiation therapy in the treatment of cancer,[43] but he had been a coroner for only two years when he handled this case.[44] As we have seen from the testimony of Expressman Fox and Undertaker Humphrey, he conducted only a superficial investigation.

Aikins testified as the first witness for the defense. Johnston went straight to the circumstances of the day Willie died. Aikins testified that he received a telephone call from Dr. King around 10:00 a.m. and went down to the warehouse on the streetcar. At the warehouse he found Harry Hyams, spoke with him briefly, and then, "I went down into the basement and saw a body there. The body was lying north and south, the head a foot or a foot and a half from the box containing the cage. There was no weight box in the basement. The trunk of the body was lying partly on its left side and partly on its back, the right side of the face being off. The easterly side piece of the weight shaft was in the basement, but there was no front on the box of the shaft. The weight was lying on its long narrow side close against the cage shaft. The head looked as if it had been drawn further from the cage. There were two pools of blood, there being more blood where the head lay than in the front."[45] Aikins did not see a wooden block at the bottom of the weight shaft.[46] This testimony is not clear, but it seems to indicate that the front of the weight shaft was open and that there was one pool of blood in front of the weight shaft and another under the head. Aikins saw a

---

[43] "Aikins, William Henry Beaufort, *Dictionary of Canadian Biography—Volume XV*,
http://www.biographi.ca/en/bio/aikins_william_henry_beaufort_15E.html.
[44] Street, *Bench Book*, 14:27.
[45] "The Hyams Case," Montreal Gazette, May 20, 1895.
[46] Street, *Bench Book*, 14:29.

blood trail between the two pools, but he did not testify to seeing a blood trail from the weight shaft to the first pool.

Upon examination of the head, Aikins found it to be "very much shattered, badly fractured." The scalp was broken at the top and possibly also at the back, and the sides of the head were crushed together and "considerably flattened." Aikins saw no spectacles or gloves on the body. Aikins then went upstairs to examine the top of the shafts and found the weight rope and hook there. He could not remember whether he examined any other floor. Under the circumstances he believed that he could not conduct an inquest. In cases of death by accident, mischance or natural causes, a coroner is not supposed to hold an inquest.[47]

The *New York Times* reported, "Coroner Aikins . . . spent an uncomfortable half hour in the witness box. He had been called by the defense, but under the fire of the Crown prosecutor's cross-examination made some very damaging admissions."[48] Osler inflicted his most damaging blow at the outset by getting Aikins to testify, "What I saw there was not incompatible with murder." Justice Street took the answer down word for word.[49] Unfortunately for the Crown, Osler seems not to have taken full advantage of this admission.

Francis Wellman, in his masterwork, *The Art of Cross-Examination,* popularized the maxim of cross-examination: "When you strike 'ile' [oil], stop boring, many a man has bored clean through and let the 'ile' run out of the bottom."[50] The point of the maxim is that the cross-

---

[47] "The Hyams Case," *Montreal Gazette*, May 20, 1895.
[48] "Hyams Twins Insurance Swindlers," *New York Times*, May 19, 1895.
[49] Street, *Bench Book*, 14:29.
[50] Wellman, *The Art of Cross-Examination*, 4th ed., 80.

examiner runs the risk of losing the point by trying to emphasize it. The witness will often catch on to the problem and mitigate the damage if the point is pursued. It takes great skill to keep the witness hooked, but it sometimes can be done. Osler did not maintain sufficient control of Aikins to keep him hooked:

Q: Did what you saw there negative murder?

A: The general appearance excluded murder.

Q: No, that is not what I asked. Was murder necessarily excluded?

A: I saw no conditions there compatible with murder.[51]

Q: You did not know of the motive? You did not know of the large insurance policy. There was nothing there to negative or exclude murder?

A: What do you mean?

Q: I mean exactly what I say. Was murder necessarily excluded?

A: Well, in answer to that I can say that I could form an idea of circumstances occurring there which might mean murder, but I don't think the conditions existing indicated murder.

Q: And what you were told assisted you in arriving at your conclusion?

A: Yes.[52]

---

[51] "Heidelberg Not Called to Testify," *New-York Herald*, May 19, 1895.

[52] "The Hyams Case," *Montreal Gazette*, May 20, 1895.

Osler lost the point by asking open-ended questions, but toward the end of the line of questioning he partially retrieved it. There was a better way to emphasize the point without losing it: The witness said, "What I saw there was not incompatible with murder." The phrase "not incompatible" is a double negative, the last resort of an expert who wants to camouflage an uncomfortable admission. Osler's task in this situation was to rip off the camouflage and allow the jury to see the admission in all its ugliness:

> Q: You said, "What I saw there was not incompatible with murder," didn't you? [Placing the stress on the "in-"].

> Q: "Not incompatible" means "compatible," doesn't it?

By repeating the witness's own words and tightly controlling the questioning, Osler could have driven the admission home without giving Aikins a chance to gracefully paper over it.

Three other damaging admissions involved basing his decision on hearsay from the Hyams brothers, being ignorant of how the tragedy occurred, and knowing nothing about the insurance on Wells' life. Osler hammered home on the point that Aikins had no idea how the death occurred. He asked repeatedly if Aikins had gotten any kind of a clear explanation of how the accident happened. Aikins finally fired back, "How could I, when there was no one there when it happened?"[53]

Osler then made the point that, although Aikins saw no reason for an inquest at the time of the death, he wanted

---

[53] "Heidelberg Not Called to Testify," *New-York Herald*, May 19, 1895.

to hold one after Willie's body had been exhumed and autopsied.

Q: You wanted to hold an inquest on the body two years after the death, did you not? Now, was that because of any new light on the subject?

A: I heard of the exhumation, and the law allows the Crown Attorney to order an inquest, so I saw Mr. Dewart on the matter.[54]

To summarize Aikins' testimony: He got there, saw the body, got a garbled explanation of what happened from Harry Hyams, had no idea how the death occurred, was unaware of the insurance angle, and even though the evidence did not rule out homicide he decided not to hold an inquest. To this summary we can add the testimony of Fox and Humphrey that Aikins' examination was both superficial and brief.

Osler ended his cross-examination on a high note with one more telling blow:

"Did you say to Dr. Bingham on one occasion that he should not make up his mind about this case, as there was money in it for the defense?"

Aikins' face flushed, and he replied, "I have no recollection of it."

"Will you swear that you did not say it?" Osler thundered.

Aikins hesitated to answer, but he finally spoke. "If I did it was only in a joking way," he said at last.

---

[54] "Medical Evidence in the Hyams Trial," 460.

"Ah!" Mr. Osler said, softly. He looked knowingly at the jurors and said, "Just a little joke, eh? You may stand down, Doctor."[55] Johnston tried to extract the venom of this last sting with one question on redirect. The precise wording of the question is lost to history, but Justice Street took down the answer verbatim:

A: I have spoken to many medical men.[56]

Court then recessed, and the day ended on Osler's triumphant cross-examination rather than the implosion of the prosecution case with the Crown's weak medical testimony. Perhaps the defense should have started off with a less vulnerable first witness.

---

[55] "Heidelberg Not Called to Testify," New York Herald, May 19, 1895.
[56] Street, Bench Book, 14:30.

CHAPTER TEN: THE DEFENSE CASE
DAYS ONE THROUGH THREE[1]

Johnston, who was becoming increasingly prominent in the presentation of the defense case, called Dr. Luke Teskey as the first witness of the day. Dr. Teskey was Professor of Anatomy at Trinity Medical College and a member of the staff at Toronto General Hospital. Teskey saw the body in the morgue after it was exhumed, but it was so decomposed that he could not tell whether there were any injuries below the head. He was present at the post-mortem examination made by Drs. Caven and Johnson. He also examined the weight. Based upon his observations and examinations, he felt able to give an opinion on how the injuries were inflicted upon the skull.[2]

Q: What do you say as to the injuries having been caused by that weight?

A: I believe that the injuries could have been caused by the weight falling upon the skull in a certain way. That is the easiest way I could account for the condition of the skull and the most probable way.

Questioned as to the damage to the bottom of the skull, he said the fracture of the small bones in the skull might result from a general crushing. He said that it was likely two blows had struck the skull. Using a book to simulate the weight, he demonstrated how the weight could have struck the head, how the head would have gone to the floor, and

---

[1] Monday, May 20, 1895 – Wednesday, May 22, 1895.

[2] The direct and cross-examinations of Dr. Teskey are taken from Street, *Bench Book*, 14:31, 32; "Medical Evidence in the Hyams Trial," 460-462; and "The Defence's Day in the Twins' Trial," *Toronto World*, May 21, 1895.

how the weight struck it a second time. The jury listened to this explanation with rapt attention. Teskey also said that if the weight hit Willie's head while he was standing, it might not have caused any fracture to the skull.

On cross-examination Osler emphasized the doctor's belief that two blows had been struck. Teskey said it was impossible to locate where the first blow landed or separate out any injuries the first blow could have inflicted.

Q: So you have the man knocked down by one blow and injured by the second blow. Now, might the blow have been struck with an axe or a sandbag?

A: Not with an axe, but it might with a sandbag.

Q: You are positive it could not be with an axe?

A: Well, it might; but I do not think so. An axe would leave a mark.

Q: So we have a man knocked down by one blow, probably rendered insensible, and then struck by some other blow and killed?

A: Yes.

By these questions, Osler had gotten the witness to agree that the Crown theory was as likely as Johnston's defense theory. He then worked to undermine Johnston's theory. Producing a diagram of the basement which showed the cellar to be 9'7" high, he asked: "Now, with the momentum of a fall of more than four feet would give such a weight, which would you expect to reach the ground first, the body or the weight?"

A: There is no evidence that the weight came down direct.

Q: Oh, then the weight hung in the air to allow the body to fall first?

A: Well, if you mean to the floor, the weight would reach the floor first.

Q: So, then the body ought to have fallen on the weight, and not the weight on the body?

A: Yes, but there is nothing to show that the weight reached the earth.

Q: No, it stuck in the air like Mahomet's coffin, suspended between earth and heaven, while the body reached the ground, then fell and battered his head in.

A: It might have remained suspended on the buffer; and while there, time would be lost.

"Oh, yes," Osler rejoined, "It remained there waiting. So that we have a case where a weight of two hundred pounds falls on a man's face and leaves no trace behind, then the man falls to the ground, reaching it ahead of the weight and the weight falls upon the head again."

"Your idea, Doctor," said Osler, "is that there is evidence of only one blow and that the blow was struck when there was resistance on the left side and the reasonable conclusion is that when that blow on the right side was struck the left side was resting on the ground?"

"Yes," replied Dr. Teskey, "that is a reasonable conclusion."

"And a man is not likely to lay his head down on the block?"

"Not in the ordinary course of things," Teskey said.

"It is likely to have been laid there for him," Osler replied.[3]

Dr. Irving H. Cameron took the stand next. On direct examination he testified that all the fractures to the skull may have been produced by one crushing blow. He saw no evidence of two lines of force. On cross-examination he backtracked. He said a single blow in the air, like the blow suggested by Johnston, would not produce all the fractures he saw, but a blow while the head rested on the ground would. He saw no indications of a second blow, but such a blow may very well have been struck.[4]

Dr. Bertram Spencer, who attended the autopsy, testified next. Aside from the fact that it took two hours to pick all the bones of the skull from the putrid remains of the head, he added nothing material to what had already been said by the previous experts. He could see evidence of only one blow, although the damage from another blow might have been obliterated by the crushing of the skull.[5]

The defense had reached the point of diminishing returns with the parade of experts, but just as the Crown had done, they soldiered on with additional experts. Justice Street took fewer and fewer notes on their testimony, and Osler was able to wring damaging admissions from them.

The parade of experts having ended, Robert Bruce Preston took the stand next to tell of seeing Willie Wells at the warehouse at noon on the Sunday before the death. He and his father were taking a walk, and the walk took them

---

[3] "The Defence's Day in the Twins' Trial," *Toronto World,* May 21, 1895.

[4] Street, *Bench Book,* 14:32.

[5] Street, *Bench Book,* 14:33; "Medical Evidence in the Hyams Trial," 463.

by the warehouse. Willie came to the door and invited Preston in. He showed Preston the improvements that had been made on the warehouse, including the door that had been added to the elevator shaft on the ground floor. They went into the cellar, where they found the elevator resting at the bottom of the shaft. Willie grabbed the pull rope and hoisted the cage up the shaft. As the weight came down, it got stuck near the ceiling of the cellar. Willie borrowed Preston's cane and poked at the weight until it came loose. Willie next showed Preston how to change the weight from the heavier one to the lighter one. Willie replaced the heavier weight and began to lower the cage. Preston saw that the hook was only partially engaged in the weight's hole and called this to Willie's attention. Willie let the weight back down. Preston told Willie to always make sure the hook was fully engaged in the weight. Preston walked away and didn't see whether Willie got the hook fully engaged in the hole. They went back upstairs and found Preston's father standing by the stove in the office. The Preston men then left the warehouse to finish their walk.[6]

After hearing of Willie's death, Preston the younger went back to the warehouse on January 18 and performed some experiments with the elevator. Two other men, James A. White and a Mr. Crone, went with him. They put the hook partially into the weight hole and tried to hoist it up into the shaft. It caught on the ceiling of the cellar because it didn't hang plumb. They let it down and pushed it to the side and were able to get it to go up the shaft.[7]

On cross-examination Preston said that as he and his father walked by the warehouse, he noticed that it had a

---

[6] Street, *Bench Book*, 14:35, 36.
[7] Street, *Bench Book*, 14:36, 37.

newly painted sign and crossed the street to take a closer look at it. As he was examining the sign, Willie came to the door and invited him in. Preston said he did not expect anyone to be at the warehouse when he approached it.

"What was the sign on the door," Osler asked.

"Toronto Warehousing Co.," said the witness.

"And when you were looking over the door Willie came to the door, eh?"

"Yes."

Osler then turned to Willie's demonstration with the elevator:

Q: Now, did you help manipulate the ropes or change the weight?"

A: No.

Q: He took the hook off the heavy weight without anyone's assistance?

A: Yes.

Q: And he didn't put the hook on with your help but changed and rechanged without your aid?

A: Yes.

Q: Now, show me how he put the hook so that it wasn't properly, fastened.

Preston indicated with the weight and hook the positioned in which he claimed the hook was. He fumbled with the hook, trying to get the point to engage, and finally admitted that the only way that the hook could be attached to the hole would be if all the slack was taken out of the rope.[8]

This last demonstration meant the only way the hook could be engaged with the weight in the manner that Johnston suggested would be if the person engaging the hook intentionally set the hook improperly and took the slack out of the rope to keep it improperly engaged until the weight of the cage was brought to bear on the rope.

Osler then asked Preston how he got the keys to go back on January 18 to perform his experiments. Preston said he didn't have the keys, when he and his companions got to the unoccupied warehouse the door was unlocked. In describing his experiments with the elevator, he admitted that he could never get the weight to become disengaged from the hook.

Preston claimed to have seen Willie almost daily before the warehouse opened. When he went to James A. White's tailor shop, he would stop by the Hyams brothers lending office at 11 King Street and borrow the telephone. He said he had been to the office at 11 King Street almost every day since Willie's death until the arrest of the brothers.

"Did you go there to loaf?" Osler asked.

"No, that's not the only reason I went there. I went to other places."

"Any financial transaction between you since with either of them?"

"No."

---

[8] "The Defence's Day in the Twins' Trial," Toronto World, May 21, 1895.

Osler then shifted directions "How frequently have you been to Mr. Horn's since the arrest?"

"Quite frequently, but I didn't always see Mr. Horn."

"Who did you go to see, then?" Osler wanted to know.

After a long pause, Preston replied, "A clerk named Nearny."

"What money have you got in this matter?" asked Osler.

"Nothing."

"What?" asked Osler, incredulous.

"Yes, no; yes, I did,"

"Well, which was it," asked Osler, "yes or no?"

"I got $10 for loss of time during the Police Court investigation."

"Nothing more?" Osler asked.

"No."

Preston's father, called to corroborate Preston, testified that he and his son went to the warehouse because his son wanted to visit with a young man who worked there.[9] This, of course, was in direct contradiction to what Preston had said. The jury put little stock in the testimony of either father or son.[10]

The last witness of the day was James A. White, the tailor who went to the warehouse with Robert Preston on January 18. On lifting the weight from the floor with the

---

[9] "Nearing Its Close Is the Twins' Trial," *Toronto World*, May 22, 1895.
[10] "Unanimous as to Guilt," *Toronto World*, May 25, 1895.

hook partially engaged it caught on the roof of the cellar. Preston shoved it into the shaft with his hands, and it went on up the shaft. Osler, seeking to show that there were no obstructions in the shaft itself, asked how far up the shaft they lifted the weight. Wright did not know.

Dallas Hyams' wife Annie entered the courtroom early in the morning and was allowed to have a private interview with her husband before court reconvened. The papers described her as pretty, brown-eyed, and clad in black. The *New-York* Herald reported that when the couple came back into the courtroom after the interview, she carried herself with "admirable composure," but Dallas had tears in his eyes.[11] The authorities allowed her to sit in the grand jury box, which was across the courtroom from the jury box. As she sat there facing the jurors, she repeatedly gave her husband encouraging smiles, and this cheered both her husband and her brother-in-law.[12] From the prosecution's viewpoint, this could not have had a favorable effect on the jury. Osler should have asked that she be moved to sit out of the jury's line of sight.

The first two witnesses, George Moyer, a builder, and his foreman, David Colley, sponsored a scale model of the elevator. In breadth and depth, it was supposed to be one half the size of the original, but the height was not to scale. On cross-examination Osler pointed out that the weight shaft was not to scale. It was depicted in the model as a trapezoid, wider on one side than the other, where the original shaft was perfectly rectangular. Colley said the

---

[11] "Good Defence of the Hyams Twins," *New-York Herald*, May 22, 1895.

[12] "Nearing Its Close Is the Twins' Trial," *Toronto World*, May 22, 1895.

model must have been tampered with, but he had no idea who did it or why it was done.[13]

Then came Donald McCarthy, whose testimony, if it were believed, could weigh heavily against the Crown. McCarthy had worked in the same building as the warehouse at the time of Willie's death. He oversaw the supplies for the Naismith Company, a restaurant which occupied the north side of the warehouse building. Naismith worked mornings in the basement of the company, where he gathered the supplies and hoisted them up to the ground floor for use in the kitchen. There was a stone wall about 14 to 18 inches thick between the two premises, but the basement wall had a hole in it between the two. The hole was large enough for a man to go through, but some planks had been nailed across the hole. McCarthy could not see through the planks into the warehouse cellar, but if he got close to the planking, he could look over the top plank into it. After Willie's death the hole was transformed into a door between the two cellars. When McCarthy worked in the restaurant cellar, he could hear people talking and moving about in the warehouse cellar.[14]

McCarthy would get to work on Monday mornings at approximately 6:30 so that he could go into the cellar and send up supplies to the restaurant. He would work until 8:45 or 9:00, sometimes until 9:30. He would eat his breakfast in the restaurant after working in the supply

---

[13] "Nearing Its Close Is the Twins' Trial," *Toronto World*, May 22, 1895.
[14] McCarthy's testimony is taken from Street, *Bench Book*, 14:41-45; "Nearing Its Close Is the Twins' Trial," *Toronto World*, May 22, 1895; and "Good Defence of the Hyams Twins," *New-York Herald*, May 22, 1895.

cellar. They stopped serving breakfast at 9:00, but they would feed him breakfast as late as 9:30.

On the morning of January 16 McCarthy heard sounds coming from the warehouse basement. He said, "I was in the habit of hearing sounds every morning. This morning I heard a man whistling, then I heard other noises, nothing unusual, but it might have been coal. After the whistling and the noise made by the coal I heard an unusual crash—first a heavy thud, and then a crash. I took it that something unusual had happened."

"Were the sounds far apart?" Johnston asked.

"No, one followed the other. I thought something had happened to the elevator."

"Was there any whistling after that?"

"No. There was silence for about fifteen minutes. Then I heard footsteps in the Hyams' cellar, and a shout or cry, as of one calling to another. The steps sounded as if someone were coming from the street. The cry sounded like 'Will' or 'Wells.'"

McCarthy heard of Willie's death later that day, and he reported what he heard to his manager, John Thomas Bragg and a friend named James Rosvear. Both these men corroborated his story, saying that they spoke to McCarthy shortly after Willie's death.[15]

After leaving Naismith McCarthy went bankrupt trying to make a go of the grocery business. He then left Canada to work in various U.S. cities in New York, Pennsylvania,

---

[15] "Good Defence of the Hyams Twins," *New-York Herald*, May 22, 1895.

Ohio, and Michigan. He had recently returned to Canada from Detroit.

Osler spent two hours cross-examining McCarthy. McCarthy told Osler he and his family had been living in Toronto since March 8, 1895, and during that time he had earned a grand total of $10 doing odd jobs.

"Did that keep your family?" Osler asked.

"No, it did not."

McCarthy denied that anyone had come to see him in Detroit on behalf of the defense. He said that after his return to Toronto the first man he spoke to about the case was his father-in-law.

"You stopped earning money in Detroit, came to Toronto and next day spoke to your father-in-law about the defense?" Osler asked.

"Yes."

Osler asked about his employment in Detroit and learned that McCarthy could earn US$3.00 a day in that job.

Osler: "And yet you left that position and remained here 2 1/2 months and earned but $10 in that time, not sufficient to keep your family; is that correct?"

"Yes." [16] What Osler was implying by this line of questioning was obvious—McCarthy was being compensated for his testimony out of the Hyams' war chest. Often on cross-examination it is far more powerful to raise a suspicion of wrongdoing than to outright suggest it by asking a direct question which is certain to be denied.

---

[16] "Nearing Its Close Is the Twins' Trial," *Toronto World*, May 22, 1895.

One line of questioning that Osler did not pursue could have gone something like this:

Q: When you heard the crash, you called out to the other room asking what had happened?

Q: When you heard the man call out "Will" or "Willie," you called across to ask if Willie was hurt?

To corroborate the testimony of McCarthy, the defense next read the deposition of John Thomas Bragg into evidence and called James Rosvear to the stand. Both men corroborated McCarthy's description of the layout of the cellars, the hole in the wall, and the ability to hear conversations coming from the warehouse cellar. Neither, however testified that McCarthy had told them about what he purportedly heard in the basement on the morning of the tragedy.[17]

Duncan McDermott, a carpenter, testified next. He said he made some changes to the warehouse cellar after the Hyams brothers vacated it. He found no box for the weight and nothing to prevent it from swinging side to side. When he made other changes to the cellar in January of 1893, the weight shaft had been partially boxed.

Osler asked two questions on cross-examination: "Then, if there were sides to the weight box in January and not afterwards the sides must have been removed for some purpose?"

"Yes,"

---

[17] Street, *Bench Book*, 14:45; "Nearing Its Close Is the Twins' Trial," *Toronto World*, May 22, 1895.

"And you have a very hazy remembrance of seeing a block there?"

"Yes, very hazy." [18]

Joseph McMillan, who operated the elevator before the twins took over the warehouse, testified that the elevator was a "miserable affair," and he wouldn't trust his life on it. During the ten months that he worked for Imrie and Graham, the weight got caught in the chute half a dozen times, and McMillan recalled the weight slipping off the rope one time and falling into the basement.[19] He said that when he took a board off the weight shaft in the basement and inspected the chute, he found a piece of flooring projecting into the chute about the level of the ground floor. He nailed the boxing back onto the chute without trying to do anything to fix the projection.

Osler was careful to point out on cross-examination that the hook that was on the weight when it slipped and fell was not the hook that was on the weight at the time of Willie's death. McMillan further admitted that he never told either Imrie or Graham about the weight catching, the weight falling off, or the board projecting into the weight chute. "I wasn't in the habit of running to the boss about everything," was his excuse.

"What you did speak to them about," said Mr. Osler, "was that the cage caught and that the rope required splicing, and these defects were remedied."

---

[18] "Nearing Its Close Is the Twins' Trial," *Toronto World*, May 22, 1895.
[19] "Good Defence of the Hyams Twins," *New-York Herald*, May 22, 1895.

"Yes," said McMillan, "and these defects were remedied." [20]

The defense next called a series of witnesses to testify that the weight might fall off the hook if the conditions were right. The witnesses were examined, cross-examined, and asked to perform tests and experiments. The testimony was contradictory, and the experiments proved unhelpful in establishing that the weight was likely to slip off the hook. Justice Street was so unimpressed by these witnesses that he took only a line or two of notes for each of them.[21] Perhaps the most entertaining of these witnesses was H.A. Leighton, an expert on elevators, who provoked peals of laughter in the courtroom when he testified that if the weight came off the hook, it would fall, and that's all he knew about it.[22] The *New-York Herald* said of the experiments that were performed: "Mr. Johnston, for the prisoner, and Mr. Osler, for the Crown, made experiments with the hook and weight for the benefit of the jury. ... [T]he jury seemed more amused than convinced by the efforts of both learned gentlemen."[23]

Mary A. Burgess, a hotel owner who had known the Hyams family for years, testified to receiving an undated, hand-delivered letter from Miss Latimer sometime in January of 1893. On cross-examination she told Osler she had no idea why the letter was hand-delivered. The Hyams brothers knew her mailing address.[24]

---

[20] "Nearing Its Close Is the Twins' Trial," *Toronto World*, May 22, 1895.
[21] Street, *Bench Book*, 14:47.
[22] "Nearing Its Close Is the Twins' Trial," *Toronto World*, May 22, 1895.
[23] "Good Defence of the Hyams Twins," *New-York Herald*, May 22, 1895.
[24] "Nearing Its Close Is the Twins' Trial," *Toronto World*, May 22, 1895.

Matthew Rammage, an engraver and calligrapher from Philadelphia, testified next. His testimony had been taken by commission because he lived outside Canada, but he decided to appear in person and give live testimony. Rammage had lived in Toronto until May of 1893. He knew the twins, and, unlike most of the witnesses, could tell them apart. On the day of Willie's death, he left his home about 8 o'clock and reached the office where he worked about 8:30. When he found it locked, he decided to take a walk. He met Harry Hyams a few minutes later in the north side of Victoria Street, near Adelaide Street. A young man joined Hyams at that point. The young man, who was aware of Rammage's skill as a calligrapher, said that he wished to take some writing lessons from him. The three walked along Adelaide Street to Toronto then across King to Leader Lane and then along Colborne Street to the warehouse. Harry gave the young man some instructions and the young man unlocked the door to the warehouse and went in. This was about 8:40. Hyams returned with Rammage to Leader Lane, where Hyams entered the barber shop at approximately 8:45. Other than raising some question about the witness's character and motivation for testifying, Osler did little to undermine the gist of his story.[25] And with this witness, the second day of the defense case ended.

On this, the third and last day of the defense case, Annie Hyams again came early to court, walked over to the dock where her husband Dallas sat, shook hands with her husband and brother-in-law, and whispered words of encouragement to the two pale-faced men. As the jury filed in, she grabbed her husband around the neck and pulled him close to her. Lifting her veil, she kissed him, and his chalky paleness disappeared as he flushed to the brows.

---

[25] "Nearing Its Close Is the Twins' Trial," *Toronto World*, May 22, 1895.

The blush quickly gave way back to pallor, and Mrs. Hyams resumed her seat in the grand jury box facing the jurors across the courtroom. The day before, she had worn her veil over her face, but on this day she kept it raised, giving the all-male jury a much better view of her beautiful face.[26]

The defense opened the day with two witnesses intended to prove that the twins had entered the warehouse business in good faith. James Langston and Charles J. Palin both testified to the brothers engaging in activity consistent with the legitimate opening of a warehouse, and Palin's books were introduced into evidence to show the business that the brothers had transacted with him. Palin testified, however, that the building was totally unsuited to the operation of a warehouse. One of the major deficiencies of the building was the inadequacy of the elevator. Palin testified that it was not really an elevator, which was mechanically powered and had safety brakes, but was a muscle-powered dumbwaiter with no safety brakes. Palin pronounced the dumbwaiter unsuited to the moving of heavy goods from floor to floor. On cross-examination Palin admitted that although his books showed numerous transactions with the Hyams brothers, only three of them were dated before Willlie's death.[27]

The defense then offered an alibi for Dallas Hyams. John Neil, a photographer, saw Dallas at his 11 King Street office between 8:30 and 9:00. Joseph Jessamin, a tailor, saw Dallas at the office "around 9:00." John Collins, a stencil maker, thought he saw Dallas climbing the stairs to his King

---

[26] "The Fate of the Twins May Be Known Tonight," *Toronto World,* May 22, 1895.
[27] "The Fate of the Twins May Be Known Tonight," *Toronto World,* May 22, 1895.

Street office sometime between 9:00 and 10:00. The best witness for the alibi was Rod Westcott, a barber in a Jordan Street barbershop, who testified that. beginning at 9:00 or 9:10, he gave Dallas a shampoo and a haircut and singed his hair, and then gave him a shave. The whole operation took 52 minutes. Of this evidence the *Toronto World* said these witnesses "established a complete alibi for Dallas Hyams up to 10 o'clock a.m., but as the Crown holds that the alleged crime was committed later this evidence may be useless."[28]

The last significant witness called by the defense was William T. Murphy, a clerk at the Canadian Express Company. Murphy testified that during the five years preceding Willie's death, Harry and Dallas and their mother had received at least $200 per month, sometimes from New York, and sometimes from New Orleans. Attorney Lount concluded the direct by announcing "We have shown that in five years $20,000 has been received altogether." Osler's cross-examination made Lount eat his words. He first established that all but one of the payments were to Mrs. Clara C. Hyams, the defendants' mother, and they merely acted as her agents to pick up the checks. The one payment made directly to the Hyams brothers amounted to $150. "Then," said Osler as he turned to the jury, "taking the date of the killing as January 1983, prior to the killing all the money consigned to the prisoners personally was $150." He repeated himself for emphasis, "The $20,000 prior to the killing thus comes down to $150." The courtroom erupted in laughter, and the jury joined in.[29]

---

[28] "The Fate of the Twins May Be Known Tonight," *Toronto World,* May 22, 1895.
[29] "The Fate of the Twins May Be Known Tonight," *Toronto World,* May 22, 1895.

The defense could not rest at this point. They had to call some witnesses to erase the embarrassment of Murphy's testimony and end the case on a victory. They called two more witnesses to testify that there was indeed a hole in the wall between the two basements in the Colborne Street building, and then Johnston proposed to read portions of the preliminary hearing testimony of Mr. and Mrs. Aylesworth which he contended were inconsistent with the testimony they gave in court. Osler objected. Justice Street properly ruled that the statements could not be read into evidence. The defense had not confronted the Aylesworths with the purported statements and given them a chance to admit, deny, or explain the alleged inconsistencies.[30] The defense thus had to rest their case on a defeat.

Even though the defense had begun their case with Osler's triumph over Dr. Aikins and ended their case with the discrediting of their claim that the brothers had received a $20,000 allowance from their relatives, they had presented a persuasive case in the middle. They had organized their presentation much better than the Crown had, and if the lay witnesses could be believed they had put on fairly good alibis for Dallas and Harry.

Osler got off to a good start with his rebuttal, calling Francis Brodie of the Montreal branch of the Bank of Toronto to testify that evidence offered by the defense of Harry's solvency was fraudulent. The defense had put in a passbook showing a $7,950 deposit. Brodie testified the entry was not in Harry's handwriting and the deposit was never made. Next, over strenuous objection from the defense, Osler called David Miller, the manager of the

---

[30] "The Fate of the Twins May Be Known Tonight," *Toronto World,* May 22, 1895.

Toronto branch of the Merchant's Bank. Using bank records, Miller traced $1,600 from Martha's insurance payment into the bank account of Dallas Hyams.

Then the rebuttal went off the rails. Osler called Barrister Edward Fenton to impeach the testimony of Matthew Rammage, but Justice Street ruled his testimony inadmissible. Osler recalled John Fensom Jr. and asked him: "It was sworn here that Wells took the weight off the hook unaided on Sunday. Is that possible?" asked Mr. Osler. The defense objected strenuously, and Justice Street sustained the objection.[31]

Finally, Osler attempted to counter defense evidence that the younger Preston could see over the lettering on the entrance to the warehouse, called John Galt, a civil engineer, and asked: "There was a painter here this morning who swore that he did the lettering on the door. Now, Mr. Galt, what is the height of that lettering?" Justice Street sustained the defense objection to this testimony on the grounds that the painting was done two and one half years prior, and it had changed in the interim. Then Osler attempted what was the most important impeachment. He tried to have Galt testify that McMillan's testimony about removing the board from the weight shaft and finding an obstruction was impossible. Galt stood ready to testify that the board McMillan claimed to have removed ran below the floor and above the ceiling of the cellar. The defense objected before Galt could get the words out of his mouth, and after a lengthy argument, Justice Street ruled, "I think it will be safer not to receive the evidence." [32] It was

---

[31] "The Fate of the Twins May Be Known To-Night," Toronto World, May 23, 1895.

[32] "The Fate of the Twins May Be Known To-Night," Toronto World, May 23, 1895.

certainly safer for the Hyams brothers. This was crucial evidence for the prosecution which should have been admitted, but Street's long string of rulings against the Crown had conditioned him to disallowing testimony.

Thus, the Crown's rebuttal started with a bang and ended with a whimper. Osler had intended to start strong with the two bankers and end strong with Galt, but the disallowing of the minor impeachments in the middle sabotaged Galt's major impeachment at the end. It would have been far better if Osler had called only Galt and the two bankers.

"That is the reply," Osler said, and with that announcement he ended the evidentiary portion of the greatest trial that Canada had ever witnessed. It was now time for the lawyers to make their speeches. Twenty first century lawyers would call the speeches "final arguments," but the lawyers of the Victorian Era called the speeches "summation." Each side would get one chance to speak, and the Crown would go last. Justice Street called a brief recess before the speeches began. (See Appendix C for the arguments of the lawyers.)

CHAPTER ELEVEN: THE JUDGE SUMS UP.
THE JURY SPEAKS[1]

The bells chimed noon as Justice Street began his summing up to the jury. He spoke for approximately two hours.[2] The pundits raved about Street's encyclopedic knowledge of the evidence pertinent to all the issues, and almost everyone regarded it a fair and impartial analysis of the evidence "although it was considerably in favor of the prisoners, in that His Lordship left to the jury as an important consideration the improbability that the prisoners, although alleged to have schemed carefully, had made no preparation, when it came to the crucial point of giving a reasonable explanation of the accident."[3] When Street concluded, Wellman marched up to the bench, shook hands with the judge, and congratulated him on the "fairness" of his address. Although Street tried mightily to be impartial, his "summing up" was like a third argument for the defense. The prosecution can seldom survive such a blow. The *Toronto World* had this to say about Justice Street's summing up:

> His Lordship's charge wonderfully changed the aspects of the prisoners. Before the judge commenced his remarks and Mr. Osler's damning impeachment was fresh in the minds of the jurors, dark visions had opened up before the twins; but now things looked brighter, and Harry conversed smilingly with his custodian, while the features of Dallas lost the look of anxiety which has

---

[1] Friday, May 24, 1895.

[2] The following account comes from "Unanimous as to Guilt," *Toronto World*, May 25, 1895. Details from other sources are duly noted.

[3] "Unanimous as to Guilt," *Toronto World*, May 25, 1895.

characterized both prisoners for 14 days. Mrs. Dallas Hyams also looked much relieved and smiled hopefully.

"The evidence here," Justice Street began, "is circumstantial, as distinguished from direct evidence. In many serious crimes, there can be, from the nature of them, no direct evidence. Then you must take the evidence of circumstances."

"In this case it is denied, and strenuously denied by the prisoners, that a crime was committed. You must, therefore, first decide whether this evidence points to the commission of a crime and if a crime was committed did these prisoners commit it?" Justice Street then told the jury that if they had any substantial doubt about whether the death was accidental, then they need look no further. If, on the other hand, they decided that accident was highly improbable, then they should look to the evidence of motive, means, and opportunity."

Street then turned to the evidence of Donald McCarthy, the cellarman at Naismith's who testified that he heard whistling and a crash in the adjoining cellar. He discussed the Crown's attack on his memory and concluded his remarks on McCarthy by saying that although they might have reason to question his vivid memory, "You may, if you like, conclude that he heard part of what he said he did. You may conclude that it is probable he may have heard the whistling, and he may have heard the fall."

Street next addressed the differing testimonies of the experts for the prosecution and defense. He told the jury that their disagreements were immaterial. Everyone, he said, agreed that two blows had been struck to Willie's head. The question was how the blows were delivered. "Of course," Street said, "the theory of the Crown is that the first blow was struck by one of the prisoners and while the unfortunate boy was lying on the ground the weight was used to crush his head. The theory of the defense, on the other hand, was that the weight caught and upon Wells looking up the shaft fell, knocking him to the ground and afterwards followed and tilted over upon his head, giving the second blow, and crushing the skull." Street neglected to mention the problem with this theory. Nobody testified that there was blood on the side of the weight. The only blood seen was on the bottom. Osler also overlooked this point, which could have been used on cross-examination of the defense experts.

Street then discussed the confusion over the gloves and the glasses. Dr. King, the first on the scene, was positive Willie had on no glasses and almost positive he wore no gloves. Expressman Fox, next on the scene was adamant that Willie had on glasses and gloves. This suggested that the Hyams brothers may have "posed" the body after Dr. King left to make it look more like an accident. Adding to the confusion, Fox swore he never touched the body until after Coroner Aikins and Undertaker Humphrey arrived. Neither Humphrey nor Aikins saw gloves or glasses on the body. Street concluded his remarks on this issue by saying that, instead of attributing evil actions to the twins, "You may come to the conclusion that either Fox was mistaken or that the Coroner and Humphrey were mistaken."

Speaking to the $1,000 owed by the Hyams brothers to Willie and Willie's many efforts to get repaid, Street reminded the jury that Dr. Macpherson and Richard Lane had testified about the $1,000 loan the brothers had negotiated. Street said that this evidence proved the twins could pay the debt without having to kill Willie. Street then turned to the $30,000 insurance policy which Willie could in

219

no way afford. He reminded the jury that, "The answer of the defense is that it was an excellent investment. It is for you to say whether you think that is the reason why the insurance was placed or whether it was a part of a scheme to make $30,000 at the expense of the life of Wells."

Street then addressed the Crown's contention that the Hyams had employed Willie, Aylesworth, and Latimer at the warehouse in furtherance of their murder scheme: "It is said that the employment of these three was a blind. There was, however, some evidence undoubtedly before the jury that the prisoners were commencing in the mercantile business. As to the envelopes addressed by Miss Latimer. If she did nothing else while at the warehouse those produced [by the Crown] would hardly be all those she addressed. It is not unreasonable to find that some of the envelopes had been sent out.

Addressing the twins' constant tinkering with the elevator, Street said, "Perhaps the prisoners having nothing to do, occupied themselves with keeping the elevator in order." In like manner he discounted the evidence of changing the weight and the hook, and he answered the Crown argument that there was no conceivable use for the platform which they had added by saying "It is to be recollected that they told Fox that they built it to change the weight."

Getting to the end of his summation, Street told the jury:

Let me lay before you a consideration. It is the Crown's theory that for months and weeks before this occurrence the prisoners had been laying plans with the greatest possible care and preparation so as to dispose of this young man without leaving suspicion on

220

themselves. How did it happen that when it comes to the crucial point of the whole case no preparation was made for a reasonable explanation to be given of the accident? The evidence is that the weight would not come off the hook in any ordinary way, that if the hook was put in the eye it could not come out unless the weight tilted over to one side. Supposing the coroner had that morning asked an explanation, according to the evidence the prisoners would have been entirely without explanation. If it were not for that discovery which has been made that the weight would hang on the nose of the hook, the prisoners would have been without any apparent reason for the occurrence.

You must consider whether the prisoners, who planned this crime so carefully, would have left themselves open to this position that they were alleged to have killed a man, and accounted for it by an accident which could not possibly have taken place, because there is no evidence that they knew of this peculiarity about the weight at all. If they had discovered that there was some way in which the accident might happen would they have kept silent about it when they were giving a reason for the death of this boy, would they not have made use of it to allay suspicion and point out that the weight might have come off the hook?

In closing, Street said that the twins' machinations and misrepresentations with the $30,000 policy might have been made because the brothers were "insurance cranks." His last words to the jury tended to discredit the Crown's evidence of the Hyams brothers profiting from Willie's death to the tune of several thousand dollars: "Admitting that the prisoners had absorbed the insurance money the jury should recollect that the prisoners were not being tried for dishonesty. They were being tried on the serious charge of murder."

Thus ended the longest trial in Canadian history, almost doubling the previous record of eight days set in the trial of John Hendershott and David Welter for the insurance murder of William Henry Hendershott, another case prosecuted by B.B. Osler which resulted in a conviction and two hangings.

The *Toronto World* did not err when it called the Hyams trial "the greatest trial in the history of Canada."[4] The *World* summarized the statistics of the trial as:

Length of Trial: 14 days

Empanelment of Jury: 90 minutes

Osler's Opening Statement: 1 hour

Crown Witnesses Examined: 60

Crown Testimony: 9 days

Defense Witnesses Examined: 41

Defense Testimony: 3 ½ days

Rebuttal Evidence: 1 hour

Pages of Testimony: 2,400

Words of Testimony: 720,000

Number of Exhibits: 85

Johnston's Speech for the Defense: 3 hours, 35 minutes

---

[4] "Unanimous as to Guilt," *Toronto World*, May 25, 1895.

Lount's Speech for the Defense: 5 hours, 15 minutes

Osler's Speech for the Prosecution: 3 hours, 15 minutes

Street's Summing Up: 2 hours

Justice Street excused the jury to deliberate on its verdict and declared the case in recess until 5:00. Because the jury had made little progress when court reconvened, Justice Street again recessed until 9:00. On their first ballot, the jurors voted 7 to 5 for conviction. On their second ballot, the vote stood 9 to 3 for acquittal. After seven hours of deliberation, the vote stood 10 to 2 for acquittal.

At 9:00 Justice Street reconvened the court. When Harry and Dallas were brought back into the courtroom, they had a look half of fear and half of hope. Dallas appeared near collapse. When Justice Street began to address the jury, the twins trembled violently, and their faces grew colorless. The judge addressed the jury: "As you have been locked up for seven hours, gentlemen, I have sent for you to ask if there is any further instruction you desire, or if there is any prospect of your coming to a decision before morning."

Foreman John Gregg replied, "There is no prospect of agreement, my Lord."

"I should very much like to avoid an abortive trial;" Street said, "but if there is no prospect of any agreement, it is no use my keeping you longer."

"I could not speak on behalf of the other jurors," said Foreman Gregg.

Street then addressed the panel as a whole, "Have any of you other gentlemen any idea of any prospect of agreement?"

Juror Malcolm Cameron replied: "I myself think there is no prospect of an agreement, My Lord."

"In that case," Justice Street said, "I have nothing to do but discharge you. You are discharged from further attendance." He set the case over for retrial in the Fall Assizes, which were scheduled to begin in November.

When officers escorted the brothers back to the holding cell just off the courtroom, Dallas immediately began to take his clothes off. This prompted speculation in the press that the trial had unhinged him,[5] but both defense counsel and jail officials discounted the speculation.[6] The deputy governor of the jail assured reporters that Dallas was "acting rationally and taking his meals regularly."[7]

Reporters buttonholed the jurors for comments as they left the courthouse. Juror John Jenkins said: "There was not a man on the jury who did not believe them guilty but there seemed to be a missing link somewhere in the Crown's evidence. Had the penalty been anything but hanging we would have given a verdict of conviction in short time, but we did not like to send the men to the gallows on the evidence put in. Of course, we knew of outside things, but it was not given to us in evidence, and we couldn't act upon it. The majority of the evidence put in by the defense we did not believe at all. We did not attach any importance to the evidence of the Prestons or of McMillann, but as it was uncontradicted, we had to consider it."

Juror Abraham Torrance said, "We were unanimous as to their guilt, but we did not think the Crown had produced

---

[5] "Failed to Agree," *Springfield (NY) Journal*, May 30, 1895.
[6] "From the Queen City," *Montreal Gazette*, May 29,1895.
[7] "There Was Money in It," *Ottawa Journal*, May 29, 1895.

sufficient evident to justify us in convicting them. Of course, we knew of the attempt to insure the wife's life, but the judge said we must confine ourselves to the evidence."

All the jurors who spoke to the press agreed that if evidence of the attempt to insure Martha Wells' life had been admitted, they would have convicted.

Foreman John Gregg said that when the jury retired, someone suggested that they immediately take a ballot. Gregg objected, "It's no good taking a ballot until we have discussed the matter." After a short debate, they voted 7 to 5 for conviction. More discussion followed, and the final tally was 10 to 2 for conviction. The holdouts for conviction were George Munro and James Crichton. Gregg said he was unconvinced by the testimony of the Aylesworths and Mrs. Hyams. "After hearing that evidence, I could never have found the prisoners guilty."

Gregg was one of the jurors approached by the mysterious "Mr. Pender," who was believed to be the infamous New York City jury-fixer, Col. Foster. "Mr. Pender" had called on Gregg on the Sunday before the trial began. "Pender" came to Gregg's home and sounded him out regarding his views on capital punishment and the guilt of the Hyams brothers. Gregg said that he told "Pender" he had no opinions on the matter and would be guided by the evidence. Gregg denied that "Pender" made any improper proposals.[8]

As soon as the trial had ended, lawyers for both sides began diligent work on shoring up their cases for the next trial. The Crown made an exhaustive investigation of all the evidence introduced by the defense, and the defense began

---

[8] "There Was Money in It," *Ottowa Journal*, May 29, 1895.

a hunt for corroborating witnesses for the ones they had called at trial. They announced to the press that they had uncovered a number of new witnesses who would "endorse some of the most important points in the defense."[9] T.W. Horne, who acted as solicitor for the defense trial team and was credited with putting the defense case together, set sail for Germany on June 5 to do a background investigation on the brothers time at Heidelberg University.[10]

On a somewhat macabre note, the *Manitoba Morning Free Press* reported that Willie Wells' body was still being held at the undertakers and would probably not be reinterred until after the second trial.[11]

The *Toronto World* ran an editorial complaining of the treatment of the Crown witnesses in the Hyams case. Although they were treated no different than Crown witnesses in other cases, they had suffered a much greater hardship. Prosecution witnesses went unpaid unless they were indigents or were experts, a situation which was also common in the United States at that time. In the normal case this might not be too great a hardship, but the Hyams witnesses had attended court for days and weeks on end at the preliminary hearing, before the grand jury, and at trial. They confronted the prospect of again attending court for another two weeks at the retrial. This stood in stark contrast to the situation of the defense witnesses, who had received reimbursement for their lost time.[12]

It should be obvious that the defense was far outspending the prosecution. They had engaged Pinkerton

---

[9] "From the Queen City," *Montreal Gazette*, May 29, 1895.
[10] "The Hyams Case," *Manitoba Morning Free Press,* June 5, 1895.
[11] "The Hyams Case," *Manitoba Morning Free Press,* June 5, 1895.
[12] "Payment of Witnesses," *Toronto World*, June 15, 1895.

detectives to dig up dirt on Aylesworth. They, or someone acting on their behalf, had commissioned the services of a New York jury-fixer. They had imported, at great cost, New York's finest criminal lawyer to assist the Canadian lawyers, and they stood ready to spend even more for the defense at the second trial.

One burning question on the minds of the press concerned whether the Crown would be able to introduce the evidence which the first jury said would have tipped the scales to conviction. Deputy Attorney General Cartwright answered the question with a definite maybe. A different judge would try the case in the Fall Assizes, and he would not be bound by the decision of Justice Street. Cartwright summed up the probabilities by saying it was possible the new judge would allow the evidence, but the issue was still "a matter of doubt."[13]

The police announced that they had uncovered some "startling new evidence" which made them confident of a conviction on the retrial.[14] This new evidence was most likely the testimony of Journalist Hector Charlesworth about the offer of a $5,000 bribe to kill the story which prompted the prosecution. Charlesworth and his news editor, Walter Wilkinson, had discussed whether the prosecution should be made aware of the offer, but they decided to keep it secret. Wilkinson had suggested that Charlesworth should reveal the bribe, but Charlesworth was adamant that he shouldn't. He later explained that "It would undoubtedly have injured the lawyer who had put me on the track of the original 'scoop,' and I argued that if *World* reporters got the reputation of disclosing private

---

[13] "Prospects for the Hyams Trial," *Ottawa Journal*, June 27, 1895.
[14] "Second Trial of the Twins, *Toronto World*, June 27, 1895.

conversations with their legal friends it would be an end of our getting scoops at all."[15]

Between the first and second trials, Wilkinson left the *World*, and a new editor was appointed. This editor had a different view of journalistic confidentiality, and he told Crown Counsel Walter Curry of the bribe offer. Shortly after the second trial began, a constable detained Charlesworth and took him to the courthouse. The constable escorted Charlesworth into a private room, where Crown Counsel Curry confronted him. Charlesworth's new chief was also present to contradict him if he denied that the attempt had been made. Charlesworth underwent a rigorous interrogation. As Charlesworth later recalled, "Curry, since he had known me from childhood, thought himself at liberty to bully me; and would not listen to my objections that I would be injuring a man who had treated me with confidence throughout the case, and had done me kindness in other matters." Curry broke down Charlesworth's resistance, and Charlesworth gave a full written statement about the incident.[16]

After giving his statement, Charlesworth was released, and he left the courthouse "in high dudgeon." He didn't know it at the time, but Curry had detailed plainclothes detectives to tail him. Charlesworth sent word to the lawyer, Samuel Smoke, that he urgently needed to meet him at a secret rendezvous. They met that night under the watchful eyes of the police detective tailing Charlesworth, and Charlesworth told Smoke how he had been coerced into giving a sworn statement to the prosecution.

---

[15] Charlesworth, *Candid Chronicles*, 227.
[16] Charlesworth, *Candid Chronicles*, 228.

"Well, Hector," Smoke said, "I'm sorry, but if you tell that story in the witness box, I shall be obliged to take the stand and swear that you are a liar. I have too much at stake to do otherwise." Luckily for Smoke, the undercover detective was too far away to hear the substance of the conversation.

Not long afterward a law student came to Charlesworth and escorted him to the law office of Britton Bath Osler. Charlesworth would later recall, "It was my first meeting with him, and I never met a man more kind." Osler showed Charlesworth the written statement taken by Curry and asked him if he intended to tell the truth when he took the stand. "Of course," Charlesworth replied, but he renewed his protests about having to do so. Osler said he knew Charlesworth's feelings and appreciated them profoundly. "But," Osler said, "there are times when duty to the community must override private feelings."[17]

Ironically, while Charlesworth was trying to evade giving evidence in the Hyams case, the *Toronto World* was patting itself on the back for the great service it had done law enforcement by exposing the crime:

The Hyams tragedy was brought to light through the investigations of this paper. While coroners, detectives and other public officials were asleep the *World* investigated the case on its own account, with the result that the greatest criminal trial Canada has ever witnessed was set in motion through our efforts. ... Again, the press is shown to be the best detective of the age. And in the scouting out of news the *World* is away ahead of all its contemporaries.[18]

---

[17] Charlesworth, *Candid Chronicles*, 228.
[18] "The Latest Horror," *Toronto World*, July 16, 1895.

In July, the papers began to report that Solomon Hyams, the reclusive millionaire who was helping to foot the bill for the twins' defense, had disappeared from his hermitage at the Gilsey House Hotel. Grief stricken by his nephews' predicament and debilitated by gout and arthritis, Solomon took the advice of his physician and took a train to Hot Springs, Virginia, on July 5. Speculation in the press that he would never return to New York City[19] proved true. After a mere two weeks in Hot Springs, he died. His brother, Chapman Hyams returned the body to New York City, where it was buried in Woodlawn Cemetery. The *World* attributed his death to the prosecution of his nephews. "Disgraced by his own kin," the paper wrote, "He is unable to bear up under the infamy."[20] Solomon's death prompted speculation in the press that the twins' defense had run out of money. Francis Wellman put the speculation to rest by making an announcement that "the defense had just as much money as it ever had."[21]

Solomon Hyams was not the only one who had been prostrated by the first trial. Martha Hyams had been in a very weak condition ever since her appearance as a witness against her husband in the first trial. She arrived in Toronto from Pickering on October 26 and immediately checked into the Bellevue Private Hospital. Her attending physician, a Dr. Temple, told the press that she suffered from "nervous prostration."[22] The defense team were certain she would not testify in the second trial, saying they had an affidavit

---

[19] "Hermit Hyams," *Ottawa Daily Citizen*, July 12, 1895; "Disliked the Notoriety," *Toronto World*, July 12, 1895.

[20] "Death of 'Hermit' Hyams," *Toronto World,* July 23, 1895.

[21] "Trial of the Hyams Twins," *Ottawa Daily Citizen*,

[22] "To Stop the Hyams Trial," October 28, 195; "Hyams Twins Again," *Ottawa Evening Citizen*, October 28, 1895.

from her which "tells the reason why she claims she was persuaded to testify and in which, it is alleged, she agrees not again to be a witness."[23]

The final pretrial blow to the prosecution came with the announcement of the presiding judge—Justice Thomas Ferguson. Historian Edwin C. Guillet wrote in his account of the trial: "The result was pretty much a foregone conclusion when the Judge was announced, for it was known that he had an exaggerated—not to say perverted—notion of what constituted fairness to the accused."[24] There's an old joke among trial lawyers about a judge who took the bench at the beginning of a criminal trial and asked, "Is the prosecution ready?" When the prosecution announced ready, he turned to the defense and asked, "Are we ready?"

---

[23] "A Chance for the Twins," *Ottawa Daily Citizen*, October 9, 1895.
[24] Guillet, *Insurance Murderers*, 53.

CHAPTER TWELVE: THE SECOND TRIAL
THE PROSECUTION CASE[1]

In the lead-up to the second trial, a theatrical man, a friend of Hector Charlesworth, happened to be in Toronto. He asked Charlesworth if there might be a big trial in the offing, and Charlesworth replied that the Hyams case was about to be retried. The theatrical man said he thought so. He told Charlesworth that he had seen Col. Foster in town. He knew Foster from the time that Foster ran the Boston Ideal Opera Company, and he told Charlesworth that Foster had become the most notorious jury-fixer in the Tammany Hall political machine. The theatrical man told Charlesworth that back in New York he had heard Foster boasting about a "job" he was going to pull off in Canada. Apparently, Foster had changed his tactics from the first trial and recruited a group of men to work under his direction, because as soon as the jury panel had been pulled a group of strangers visited the prospective jurors' homes posing and book salesmen, photo-enlargers, and sewing machine salesmen. Their conversations with the jurors always seemed to get around to the Hyams case, and the strangers started presenting the jurors with arguments for the defense. Nobody reported being offered money, as had some of the prospective jurors from the first trial, but it is likely that such offers were made.[2]

Finally, the day for the trial came. On Tuesday, November 4, 1895, Justice Ferguson called court to order. Six other murder cases were set for the Assizes, but the Hyams case took precedence over all others. The Crown had

---

[1] Monday, November 4 – Thursday, November 21, 1895.
[2] Charlesworth, *Candid Chronicles*, 229, 230.

subpoenaed ten new witnesses and the defense twenty-five. Pundits predicted the trial would last three weeks. Martha Hyams had grown weaker and more prostrated with each passing day as the trial approached, and her physician, Dr. Temple, had declared her unfit to testify. Retrials after hung juries were rare. It had happened in a murder case only once in journalistic memory, and the defendant was discharged after the jury hung a second time.[3]

The *Toronto World* proclaimed the lawyers assembled to try the case "from among the most brilliant legal minds on the American continent." Attorney General Cartwright; B.B. Osler, Q.C.; and Crown Attorneys Dewart and Curry appeared for the prosecution. W. Lount, Q.C., and W.G. Murdoch represented Harry. E.F.B. Johnston, Q.C., and T.W. Horne appeared for Dallas. Francis Wellman and his partner W.W. Gooch sat at counsel table to advise; no effort having been made to get Justice Ferguson to allow them to appear in the case. The first order of business was impaneling and instructing a new grand jury. By two o'clock, grand jury proceedings concluded, and the brothers entered the courtroom. Dallas was decked out in a cut-away coat and vest, a spotless white shirt with a blue tie, carefully pressed trousers, and highly polished shoes. Harry wore a similar outfit. They both looked hale and happy, confident of the outcome. Jury selection commenced promptly at 2:10 p.m., and they had a jury by 5:50, at which time Justice Ferguson recessed court. Harry had excused seventeen prospective

---

[3] "Hyams Trial Tomorrow," *Toronto World*, November 4, 1895; "Seven Charges of Murder," *Toronto World*, November 5, 1895.

jurors, and Dallas had excused nineteen. The Crown excused seventeen.[4]

The next morning two burly constables with drawn truncheons escorted the twins into the courtroom. Harry and Dallas came to court wearing the same suits of clothes, but they were slightly paler than the day before. Osler had brought the tangible evidence from the first trial into the courtroom and piled the pieces around the prosecution table: the 200-pound weight, the smaller weight, boxes full of addressed envelopes, and sacks and baskets of various other things Osler hoped to get into evidence. He put Willie's skull, in a sealed handbag, onto counsel table. The first order of business that morning was Osler's opening statement. If anything, he gave a more powerful speech than the one he gave at the first trial. Next came the calling of witnesses, and here Osler showed that he knew his case much better than he did the first time around. Last time he called Aylesworth as one of his first witnesses, and the defense had a field day sniping at him and making him look untrustworthy. Osler would bury Aylesworth deeper in the procession of witnesses and start off with a surveyor who had drawn a floorplan of the warehouse and a photographer who had taken pictures of the warehouse's interior. Next, he called Dr. E.E. King, the Hyams family physician whom Harry had summoned to the warehouse, Undertaker Benjamin D. Humphrey, and Expressman Joseph Fox. But they weren't there. Constables were dispatched to take the three into custody and bring them to court. The rest of the morning was a waste. Justice Ferguson recessed court until 2:00 p.m. That afternoon Dr. E.E. King gave lengthy testimony for the Crown. His

---

[4] "The Hyams Twins on Trial," *Toronto World,* November 6, 1895; "Hyams Twins on Trial," *New-York Herald*, November 6, 1895.

testimony was the same as at the first trial, but he did add one detail. He did not believe that the falling weight hit the buffer block at the bottom of the shaft. He saw some blood spatter on the block, but there was no indentation in it as would have been if the weight had violently hit the block.[5] Both in his opening statement and in his direct examination of King, Osler attacked the judgment of Coroner Aikins in refusing to hold an inquest in the case and announced he would not call Aikins as a witness because Aikins was prejudiced in favor of the defendants.[6]

Few observers had come for the first day of testimony, and this trend continued the second day. Empty seats far outnumbered spectators. Undertaker Humphrey testified as the first witness. The *World* said that despite "his inclination to contradict himself whenever closely pressed by counsel," he made an excellent witness for the Crown. Dr. King's testimony the day before had materially helped the defense because his description of the wounds to Willie's head were consistent with the defense theory of accident. Humphrey's testimony about the damage to the head completely negated King's testimony on this point. Humphrey had a much better opportunity to observe the wound, as he prepared the body for burial, and his testimony strongly supported the prosecution theory. He said the right side of the head, not the front of the head was the point of greatest impact, disputing the defense theory that Willie was looking up the shaft when he was struck. Humphrey also testified that the body was not in the same position as testified by Dr. King, suggesting that the brothers posed the body after King left. The *World*

---

[5] "Osler's Arraignment," *Toronto World,* November 7, 1895.
[6] "Two Surprises in the Hyams Trial," *New-York Herald*, November 7, 1895.

explained: "The theory, of the crown is that when the prisoners learn[ed] that the coroner was coming, and fearing he would suspect foul play, [they] changed the position of the body and placed the glasses on the face and the gloves on the hands to give color to their story that an accident and an accident alone had robbed poor Willie Wells of, his life." Humphrey also testified that one of the brothers (he didn't know which) told the coroner that the weight came off the hook and fell down the shaft. They didn't know just how the weight hit Willie, but they heard the weight fall, and they supposed Willie was looking up the shaft at the time. Osler had to work to get one more admission out of Humphrey. He tried to refresh Humphrey's recollection with the transcript of his testimony at the preliminary hearing, but Lount said that he "decidedly objected" to that tactic. After a brief argument, Ferguson ruled for the Crown. This was one of the few rulings that he made in the Crown's favor. Using the prior testimony as a corkscrew, Osler finally got Humphrey to say that one of the brothers told the coroner that the weight fell from the third floor. Johnston nitpicked Humphrey's testimony on cross-examination, and the two got into a "wordy entanglement," but Justice Ferguson calmed the witness by telling him that on cross-examination, lawyers were justified in asking questions that often seemed "impudent or absurd."[7]

Expressman Fox took the stand as the next witness. It was necessary to call him as a Crown witness, but his smiles toward the defendants in the box, "his ready replies and hearty assent to all that Mr. Lount, counsel for the defense, asked or suggested, plainly indicated his sympathy with the twins. Contrary to the assertion of Dr. King, Fox said he saw a slight dint in the buffer block, but it appeared to have

---

[7] "Jos. Fox on the Stand," *Toronto World*, November 8, 1895.

been made some time prior to Willie's death. Fox testified that while he and Harry were alone in the basement, Harry told him, "Dallas and Willie Wells were fixing the elevator, and the weight broke loose and killed Willie." Osler had to extract this statement from Fox by use of the transcript of his prior testimony at the preliminary hearing. On cross-examination Lount got Fox to say that he thought the brothers "appeared to be doing a quite profitable business" at the warehouse. The lengthy cross-examination made a favorable impression for the defense. One dramatic moment came when Fox testified that only a big, strong man could lift the 200 -pound counterweight. Lount immediately had Dallas come down from his seat and stand by Fox. Having the 5'2", 110-pound Dallas stand in the shadow of Fox's 6', 200-pound muscular physique strongly suggested that the Hyams brothers were weaklings incapable of lifting such a huge weight. Osler repaired the damage on redirect by forcing Fox to admit that he had often seen the brothers take the heavy weight off the hook and replace it with the lighter one. Although "Mr. Fox appeared to be somewhat in the nature of an unwilling witness for the Crown," said the *Toronto World*, "On the whole it would appear that the Crown had found rather a good witness in Mr. Fox,"[8] and most of the papers concurred with the *World's* assessment.[9]

Although the overall tenor of his testimony was unfavorable to the defense, Fox also gave some favorable testimony. He testified that the windows on the ground floor of the warehouse were large enough for passersby to

---

[8] "Changing the Weights," *Toronto World*, November 9, 1895); "Jos. Fox on the Stand," *Toronto World*, November 8, 1895.

[9] "Fox's Damaging Testimony, *Victoria Daily Times*, November 8, 1895; "Another Long Trial," *Portland Oregonian*, November 8, 1895.

see everything going on inside on the ground floor as well as in the basement. He also softened his testimony about the message the Hyamses sent to Undertaker Humphrey. At the previous trial he testified that they told Humphrey to keep his mouth shut. His new version of the message was: "Tell Humphrey, if anyone comes to him about the death of Wells, to tell them to go to h—. They are trying to blackmail us."[10] This caused the *Ottawa Daily Citizen* to report that, "His [Fox's] evidence was, on the whole, favorable to the prisoners."[11]

On the fifth day of the trial the prosecution dropped a bombshell. Osler called a Mrs. Caroline Wells, who was no relation to Willie. Mrs. Wells testified that she was a friend of Willie's, and that he was a patient in her dental practice. When she heard that Willie had been killed, Mrs. Wells went to the Aylesworth's home to view the body. She saw an ugly, indented, triangular wound over Willie's left eye which the undertaker had filled with plaster of Paris. She covered the plaster with pink powder to keep it from looking so ghastly. Although Lount subjected her to a vigorous cross-examination, trying to get her to say that the wound was over the right eye, Mrs. Wells remained unshaken. Lount reminded her that Dr. King, Undertaker Humphrey, Expressman Fox, and the coroner disagreed with her.

"I can't help it," she replied, "I am not mistaken."

Lount concluded his cross with an aphorism: "When a woman says she will, she will, and that's an end on it; But when she says she won't, she won't, and you may depend on it." This testimony was important because all previous

---

[10] "Hyams Brothers Trial," *New-York Herald*, November 8, 1895.
[11] "Dominion of Canada," *Ottawa Daily Citizen*, November 8, 1895.

testimony had the only wound on Willie's face being a protrusion of the right eye caused by the compression of the skull. If there was such a wound over his left eye, it meant that he had been struck in the face, rendered unconscious, and then had the weight dropped on his head. Osler followed Mrs. Wells with more witnesses to testify positively that they had seen the injury over the left eye. Mrs. Lydia Leveritt, a professional nurse called to the Aylesworth's to attend Martha, testified that she saw the injury and helped the lady dentist cover it over with pink powder. Joseph Rowley and his son Ernest saw the wound over the left eye at the undertaker's. The son was particularly positive. He saw the wounds over both eyes, and the one on the right far overshadowed the one on the left. His mother, Mrs. Joseph Rowley, saw the injury at the Aylesworth's. She thought the wound was ghastly and covered it with flowers. She was positive the injury was on the left side because she stood to the left of the coffin and did not see the right eye. Johnston cross-examined her, and his examination stood in stark contrast to the courteous examination conducted on Mrs. Wells by Lount. Try as he might, Johnston was getting nowhere by conventional means. Deciding that the situation called for drastic action, Johnston attempted a stunt which shocked the spectators and sickened the witness. Johnston grabbed a skull off the prosecution table and held it at arm's length in front of himself as he advanced across the courtroom toward Mrs. Rowley. Osler and Curry both admonished him to stop, but he continued toward the witness. As Johnston thrust the skull toward her face, a look of horror came over Mrs. Rowley's face and she nearly fainted. She avoided falling by immediately grasping the railing in front of her. Osler again urged Johnston to stop, and he returned the skull to the prosecution table. He had shaken the testifier, but not her testimony. The *World* called his action deplorable. The final witness to testify to the injury over the left eye was Uriah Jones, who saw the body at the cemetery when it was interred.

The defense had contended that Harry went looking for Dr. King at 9:00 on the morning of Willie's death, but the Crown presented evidence that the streetcar Harry took to Dr. King's had not been running at 9:00. Osler offered the records of the streetcar company to prove that the car started its runs that day at 10:45 a.m., but Justice Ferguson reserved ruling on the objection of the defense, and the lawyers had to wait until the following Monday for his ruling. That ended the first week of the prosecution's case.[12]

On Monday morning Justice Ferguson hobbled the prosecution by ruling that the records of the streetcar company could not go into evidence. Justice Street had allowed the books into evidence, and they had shown that Harry could not have left the warehouse in search of Dr. King until 10:42 a.m. This testimony would have seriously weakened the brothers' contention that Willie died while they were in the barbershop getting their hair cut. Osler tried to recover from this blow by calling David Carney, the car starter for the streetcar company, who testified that the streetcar's regular hours of operation began at 10:42, and that the car started operating on schedule the morning of the death. Ferguson ruled this testimony inadmissible because Carney had refreshed his recollection by looking at the books which had been ruled out of evidence.[13]

---

[12] "A Sensational Day," *Toronto World*, November 11, 1895.
[13] "A Day of Sparring," *Toronto World*, November 12, 1895.

The testimony and evidence Ferguson ruled out on this issue appears to be admissible on any of three well-established principles of Canadian evidence law. First, the books were admissible as regularly kept business records.[14] Second, the man who made the entries could testify that they were past recollection recorded.[15] Third, under the doctrine of present recollection refreshed, it was proper for David Carney to refresh his recollection by reference to the books.[16]

Eldridge Stanton, another new witness, ran a photography shop at 11 King Street, the same building where the Hyams brothers had their money lending business. Shortly after learning of Willie's death, Stanton asked one of the twins (he didn't know which) what had happened. The twin told him that Wells had been tinkering with the weight and it fell on him and killed him. The twin said that his brother heard the crash and went downstairs to see what had happened. He was so overcome by the sight that he fainted and had to go home in a cab. The defense let Stanton step down from the witness stand without asking him a single question.

Osler then called a series of witnesses to testify that the elevator was operating properly. His last witness of the day was Civil Engineer John Galt, who testified that he saw no way for the hook to have become detached from the weight as claimed by the defense. He further testified that any obstruction in the shaft which might block the weight would make the grip of the hook more secure. On cross-examination Lount tried to set the hook into the weight so

---

[14] Grain Workers' Union Local 333 v. Viterra Inc., 2021 FC 920 (CanLII).
[15] R. v. Richardson, 2003 CanLII 3896 (ON CA).
[16] R. v. Kassam, 2007 ONCJ 239 (CanLII).

that the weight was balanced on the point. After much effort he finally got the weight balanced. Just what effect might such a positioning of the hook have on the probability that the weight would fall off? Galt admitted that in such a situation the weight might slip off, but it would be far more likely to slip into its proper place.

"How would you account for the hook getting into such a position?" asked Galt.

"Well, some person may have placed it in that careless manner. No one, of course you understand, would think of doing such a thing willfully, but accidents will happen," Lount replied.

"Possibly," Galt said.

Justice Ferguson adjourned court with Galt still on the stand.[17]

The next morning, outside the presence of the jury, Justice Ferguson heard arguments on whether to allow the brothers' attempt to insure Martha for almost $300,000. Both sides had already submitted legal briefs on the issue, and Osler argued the admissibility on different grounds. They had engaged no fewer than nine different insurance agencies to insure Martha for an aggregate of $290,000. There was no way the chronically penurious brothers could pay the premiums on all this insurance. They must not have planned to pay the premiums for any length of time. If they did not plan to pay the premiums, then they must have planned to kill Martha. The situation was almost identical to Willie's insurance. They couldn't pay the huge premiums on Willie. They didn't pay the huge premiums on Willie. They

[17] "A Day of Sparring," Toronto World, November 12, 1895.

murdered him and collected the insurance. After due consideration, Justice Ferguson announced his ruling. He thanked the lawyers on both sides for providing him with legal authorities and said that he had never taken such a deep interest in any legal question. He said he had gone into the arguments with his mind firmly made up not to be governed by the action of any former justice. With this preamble, he ruled the evidence inadmissible.[18] Justice Ferguson's ruling served to nail the lid tightly shut on the Crown's hopes for a conviction. He had other nails to add to this one. It will be recalled that the first jury said they would have convicted if the insurance fraud with Martha had been introduced in evidence.

The Hyams case was just one of a long line of cases ruling similar fact evidence inadmissible, and the law has now developed in Canada to the point that appellate courts will defer to the trial judge's ruling if the evidence is held out, but will not hesitate to reverse if the trial judge lets it in.[19]

Was there anything that the Crown could have done that they left undone to render the evidence admissible? There are two "thinking outside the box" strategies which might have salvaged the evidence. We have previously discussed the tactic of holding off on the indictment for the murder of Willie and indicting the brothers for insurance fraud and conspiracy to murder Martha. With a conviction for conspiring to kill Martha on the books, that transaction looks a lot more relevant to the murder of Willie. The Crown could also have included counts of insurance fraud and

---

[18] "A Variegated Day," *Toronto World,* November 13, 1895.

[19] R. v. B. (C.R.), 1990 CanLII 142 (SCC), [1990] 1 SCR 717; R. v. Bush, 2017 ONSC 422 (CanLII); R v Whitehead, 2022 SKCA 19 (CanLII).

conspiracy to murder in the murder indictment. The brothers' activity insuring Willie was almost identical to their activity insuring Martha. The Crown cannot be faulted for using neither of these tactics. They are known to work,[20] but it takes imagination to conceive of them.

Osler recalled Engineer Galt and concluded his testimony. He then brought to the stand the rest of the carpenters, technicians, and experts who had testified in the previous trial, and he hadn't quite finished with his last witness when Justice Ferguson recessed court for the day.[21] The twins were all smiles at the end of the disastrous day for the Crown. They would soon have reason to lose those smiles.

The next day began well enough for the defense, with Justice Ferguson disallowing testimony from the Crown's elevator experts, but then the Crown did something remarkable. They had Carpenter John Aldridge disassemble the weight shaft, and they brought it into the courtroom for examination piece by piece. As more and more sections of the shaft made their way into the courtroom the twins became more and more tense and unhappy. Finally, Justice Ferguson asked, "Did the owner give the Crown permission to tear down the building?"

One portion of the shaft made the twins uneasy. It was the piece of the shaft which contained the protruding wood that the defense claimed had caused the weight to stick in the shaft and become dislodged from the hook. A thorough examination and experimentation with that portion of the shaft lead the *World* to proclaim: "There is not projection enough to arrest a feather in its downward flight, let alone

---

[20] They have worked in several of my cases.
[21] "A Variegated Day," *Toronto World,* November 13, 1895.

a ponderous iron casting weighing more than 200 pounds."[22]

Many witnesses' inability to conform their current testimony to their previous testimony proved a recurring theme. Almost invariably the new testimony proved helpful to the defense, but the Crown had a ready remedy. Using the transcripts of the witnesses' testimony from the preliminary hearing and the first trial, Osler coaxed them back. He would read the conflicting portion of the transcript to the witnesses and asked them to either affirm or deny the correctness of their previous statements. The defense repeatedly objected to Osler's method of refreshing the witnesses' recollection, and Ferguson repeatedly overruled the objections.

Justice Ferguson was a jovial, good-natured gentleman, but the repeated objections from the defense wore on his patience. Finally, by midafternoon he had enough of the defense's obstructionism. "How many rulings do you want on that point?" he exclaimed, "Is this trial going to be all rulings and nothing else? If this thing is going to come up so often, I think it would be better to have another officer appointed to make the rulings while I try the case." The audience laughed at this remark, but the constables quickly restored order.

The Crown's attitude toward adverse rulings by the judge stood in stark contrast to the attitude of the defense. Where the defense repeatedly objected to evidence previously ruled admissible and repeatedly argued for its suppression, Osler accepted the judge's ruling with equanimity and moved on. When Justice Street ruled the testimony of Osler's first elevator expert inadmissible, he

---

[22] "The Hyamese Twins," *Toronto World*, November 14, 1895.

announced that based on that ruling he would excuse several other elevator experts from attending. Once you've lost a point, the only thing you can accomplish by continuing to argue the object is to alienate the judge. One way to preserve the point for appeal is to simply say, "Same objection, your honor, same grounds," to which the judge can reply, "Same ruling," and the case moves on expeditiously.

Robert Wright, a close friend of Willie's, again described his examination of the weight shaft shortly after Willie's death. Harry Hyams was with Wright for the examination and showed him where Willie's body was found. Harry said that Willie's head was just outside the shaft with the weight resting on it. Wright thoroughly examined the shaft from top to bottom and found it in good order. On the day of Willie's funeral, Wright again had an opportunity to speak to Harry. Wright asked, "How did the accident happen?"

"I was sitting in the office at the time," replied Harry, "and I heard a noise, and ran over towards the hoist, and in going downstairs to the basement, I met Dallas, who told me that Willie had been killed. I then went down and took the weight off Willie's head, and Dallas went upstairs to the office."

Having met with a setback over the experts, the Crown had recovered well and scored some telling points, but it was now time to call Brother-in-Law Aylesworth to the stand. Osler got off to a rocky start when Aylesworth didn't answer to the calling of his name. He had left the courthouse for some reason, and Justice Street had to recess court until the following morning.[23]

---

[23] "The Hyamese Twins," *Toronto World*, November 14, 1895.

The next morning when the twins were escorted into court their faces appeared paler than usual, and they had worried expressions on their faces. Harry's hand shook as he handed his lawyer a sheaf of notes he had taken in his cell. Aylesworth took the stand and spent four hours and fifty minutes retelling the story he had told on direct examination in the previous trial. He retraced the circumstances of his employment with the brothers; retold the story of how Willie came to be insured; described the sham business being conducted at the warehouse; recounted the events of the day Willie died; and described how the Hyamses milked Martha of almost every penny of the insurance money. Osler attempted to end his direct examination on a high note by having Aylesworth testify that Martha was now penniless, but Justice Ferguson refused to allow the question.

After the defense team held a brief whispered consultation Mr. Lount began his cross-examination. Aylesworth fared much better on cross than he did at the last trial. He had a ready answer for every embarrassing question Lount could ask. According to the *Toronto* World, "Mr. Lount and the witness became engaged in a lively tilt of cross-firing, in which the witness came out of it a little ahead." Court recessed at 4:10 with Aylesworth still on the stand.[24]

The following day Aylesworth endured five more hours of cross-examination by Lount and emerged with his testimony intact. Aylesworth had learned much from the thrashing he received in the first trial, and he adjusted accordingly. In the previous trial the *Toronto World* had

---

[24] "Aylesworth in the Witness Box," *Toronto World*, November 15, 1895.

described him as giving his testimony with an air "between ennui and impertinence;"[25] in this trial the *Word* described him as a "shrewd witness." One thing that Lount accomplished on cross was to have Aylesworth contradict the prosecution evidence about the wound over Willie's left eye. Aylesworth, who had inspected the body at the funeral home, did not remember it, and he was sure that if there had been such a wound, he would remember it. Osler immediately followed Aylesworth with the Reverend C.W. Watch, who conducted Willie's funeral. Rev. Watch distinctly remembered the wound over Willie's left eye. Randolph Wright, a pallbearer at Willie's funeral, testified that Harry had said he injured his hands lifting the 200-pound weight from Willie's head. Wright remarked that Harry was a "pretty small man to tackle so big a proposition." Harry replied that he had hurt his back lifting the weight. After a few more relatively minor witnesses, Annie Aylesworth took the stand. Her testimony had not concluded when Justice Ferguson called a recess for the day.

---

[25] "The Hyams Twins on Trial," *Toronto World*, May 10, 1895.

JUSTICE FERGUSON[26]

The next day the *New-York Herald* ran a picture of Justice Ferguson.[27] This came about because of Francis Wellman's campaign to ingratiate himself with the judge. Early in the trial, Wellman saw Ferguson reading the *Herald* during court recesses. Wellman telegraphed the *Herald* and offered to pay the expenses of a reporter if the paper would send one to Toronto. The reporter came, and Wellman later wrote in his memoirs:

> As the defense was paying all his expenses, I was able, to a certain extent, to mold his impressions of the evidence; and I took special pains to see that he made frequent references to the extreme impartiality shown by the presiding judge in the conduct of the trial. I even succeeded in buying a photograph of the judge, taken in his robes, and had it reproduced in the *Herald's* account of the trial. It was with no little satisfaction, then, that I thought I could detect just the suggestion of a smile on

---

[26] *New-York Herald*, November 16, 1895.
[27] "Minister in Hyams Trial," *New-York Herald*, November 16, 1895

the judge's face as he read the *Herald's* reference to the "British fair play" shown toward the American boys on trial for murder in Canada. If the judge, at the start of the trial, actually did share in the general prejudice against the prisoners, I was sure it had all been removed when I heard his summing up to the jury. He gave us the benefit of every doubt, and there was not a single incident in our favor during the long trial that he failed to call to the attention of the jury.[28]

One major hurdle for the prosecution to overcome in proving motive on the part of the twins was that they could not be assured of receiving the insurance benefits only if Martha were Harry's wife. On the final day of the second week of the trial, Osler worked hard to minimize the problem. Since Harry was engaged to Martha, there could be no suspicion whatsoever that he might have been involved in killing Willie. Therefore, the twins contrived to convince everyone that Harry was not at the warehouse when the death occurred. In the days following Willie's death, the brothers told everyone that only Dallas was in the warehouse at the time of Willie's death, and that Dallas and Willie were trying to repair the elevator when the weight fell. The second point Osler made came from the mouth of Annie Aylesworth, Martha's sister. She testified that Harry's wooing of Martha kicked into high gear after Willie's death, and that his appeals to Martha were so earnest that Mrs. Aylesworth herself was moved by Harry's efforts. She frequently burst into tears during her testimony, but Justice Ferguson was one person she failed to impress. He repeatedly warned her to get to the point as she told her story in a roundabout way.

---

[28] Wellman, *Gentlemen of the Jury*, 119, 120.

Mabel Latimer, on the other hand, had Justice Ferguson beaming down at her while she gave her testimony calmly and precisely. She said the brothers never told her what their business was or why they kept her busy addressing envelopes that were never mailed. Then she told of the day of Willie's death. She had been sent early that morning to deliver a message that could easily have been mailed and did not get to the warehouse until 11:00. When she got there, she found the door locked. Harry came to the door and told her a terrible accident had occurred. He said that Dallas had been fixing the weight and that it had slipped and killed Willie. Harry told her to go home as the place was unfit for her to enter and to come back in the afternoon.

Osler called Samuel Smoke, Martha Hyams' solicitor, to testify to his dealings with the Hyamses on her behalf. Although he had been allowed by her to testify at the previous trial, he appeared in court with a letter from her directing him, "Please do not testify." Justice Ferguson put off ruling on whether Smoke should be allowed to testify until Monday morning when the court would reconvene.

The next important witnesses were moneylenders Sam Grandage and Dr. Macpherson, who were put on the stand to testify that during the time the twins undertook to carry the heavy burden in insurance premiums on Willie's life, they were so hard up for money that they habitually borrowed money at 2 per cent, compounded monthly. Macpherson was still on the stand when court recessed for the weekend.[29]

The following Monday found the Crown sailing in rough seas, as Osler was handicapped by witnesses who refused to cooperate and a defense team that objected at the drop

---

[29] "A Tearful Witness," *Toronto World*, November 18, 1895.

of a hat. Justice Ferguson repeatedly sustained the defense objections, causing the *Toronto World* to quip, "If the twins are hanged for the murder of Willie Wells it will not be because of the admission of any evidence that might be termed doubtful." Ferguson spared the Crown total defeat by reserving ruling on the two biggest issues until Tuesday—whether Smoke should be compelled to testify and whether Martha's testimony from the previous trial should be read into evidence.

It was an open secret that great pressure had been brought to bear by the Hyamses on Martha to convince her not to testify at the second trial. As she had succumbed to Harry's pressure to turn the insurance money over to him and as she had succumbed to his pressure to marry, she succumbed to this pressure and decided not to testify. And her decision extended to revoking her waiver of attorney-client privilege and directing Samuel Smoke not to testify.

Osler's argument for the admission of Smoke's testimony rested on two grounds: First, once Martha waived attorney-client privilege and the testimony was heard, she could not later "unwaive" it in a second proceeding. Second, Osler assured the court that attorney-client privilege did not apply because he had no intention of questioning Smoke on communications between Smoke and Martha but would confine his questioning to what Harry Hyams had told Smoke. On Osler's first contention, lawyers for both sides had diligently searched the English and Canadian authorities for a case on point, but they found nothing. Osler had extended his search to cases from U.S. courts and found one which had ruled on almost the exact point in question. *McKinney v. Grand Street Railway Company*, 104 N.Y. 352, 10 N.E. 544 (N.Y. 1887), confronting an issue of doctor-patient privilege, had ruled that once the privilege had been waived it could not be "unwaived." On Osler's second point, Ferguson said he thought Osler's "discrimination was rather fine." What Ferguson meant was that Osler was making "a distinction without a difference" when he distinguished between what Martha told Smoke and what Hyams told Smoke. On the main point of whether a waiver of privilege could be withdrawn, Justice Ferguson said, "I have a very strong impression that the Crown should make out its case against these men without a straining after evidence that rests on doubtful grounds." Ferguson nevertheless reserved ruling on whether Smoke should be compelled to testify.

Osler then called Martha's attending physician, Dr. Temple, who testified that she was too ill to attend court and give testimony. He then announced his intent to read Martha's previous testimony into evidence. The defense team smiled at this announcement, and Justice Ferguson asked, "Have you any more points hidden away, Mr. Osler?"

"Yes," replied Osler, "I still have one or two more tangles for Your Lordship. I can't help these points arising, it is my duty to present them, and the defense seem to think it is their duty to object."

Osler continued to have rough sailing when he called moneylender Richard Lane. Lane could remember little about his transactions with the twins, even when confronted with photographs of his entries in the book where he recorded his dealings with the Hyamses. Despite Lane's evasions and Ferguson's adverse rulings Osler eventually proved that the twins were tottering on the brink of bankruptcy when Willie died and flush with cash after the insurance was paid. On cross-examination by Mr. Johnston, Lane said he advised the brothers to go into the warehouse business because they couldn't lose much money and might even make some. Johnston asked, "What kind of businessmen were they?"

"Of the worst kind," Lane replied, "as they never made a success of anything they went into."

Osler then called the insurance agent, George Grundy, to testify about the issuance of the policy. In persuading Willie to take out the insurance, Harry had said that he wanted to take out insurance on his own life, but the cost of the premiums would be too high. Osler tried to impeach this statement by having Grundy testify to the difference in premiums between insuring Willie, who was twenty-two, and Harry, who was thirty-five. The defense objected on grounds that there had been no proof of Harry knowing what the premiums were. Ferguson ruled that the Crown must prove that Harry knew the difference in rates before he would allow Grundy to testify to the difference in rates.

Osler did win a minor victory when Ferguson allowed him to offer evidence of the insurance on Dallas' life. In persuading Willie to agree to take out the insurance, the twins had told him that Dallas was carrying a $50,000 policy on his own life. The truth was that he had only a $5,000 policy for which the annual premium was $268.20, a far cry from the $384 per quarter premium on Willie's policy. Grundy proved eager to help the defense on cross-examination, and when it was concluded Osler threw him a bombshell question on redirect. "Do you owe the Hyamses any money?" he asked. This ignited a firestorm of objections from the defense. Osler replied that he proposed to show that Grundy had gotten money from the Hyamses after the insurance was paid. "I propose to show," he said, "that this witness has been utilized by the defense. I propose to show that he is a hostile witness, as is my right." At this time one of the spectators in the courtroom fainted, and Ferguson recessed court without making a ruling. He never made a ruling on the objection, and the testimony went unheard, but the jury had heard Osler's argument.

The day ended with another wrangle as Osler called the court reporter from the previous trial to read Martha's prior testimony into evidence. This predictably caused the defense to object, and Ferguson reserved ruling until the following morning.[30] He ruled both inadmissible.

The contemporary news articles do not report on why Justice Ferguson ruled the prior testimony of Martha Wells Hyams inadmissible. The common law of Canada held that prior testimony could be read into evidence by the prosecution if the witness had died, become insane, was being withheld by the defense, or was too ill to come to court.[31] The issues had to be the same and the defense had to have had an opportunity to fully cross-examine the witness, but if those criteria were met the testimony was admissible.[32] The eminent legal scholar John Henry Wigmore made two observations on the interpretation of this common law. First, he wrote that, "The situation is one that calls for common sense and liberality in the application of the rule, and not a narrow and pedantic illiberality."[33] Second, he wrote that statutes seeking to allow for the admission of prior testimony frequently make it harder to admit because of poor wording of the statute, especially when "the statute merely secures admissibility in certain

---

[30] "A Day of Argument," *Toronto World*, November 19, 1895.

[31] Tremeear, *Criminal Code and Law of Criminal Evidence in Canada*, 785.

[32] Wigmore, *Anglo-American Evidence*, § 1387.

[33] Wigmore, *Anglo-American Evidence*, 65.

instances, and is not intended to forbid admission in other instances.[34] Under the common law Martha's prior testimony was admissible. At the time of the trial, however, the common law of Canada was augmented by statute. The statute provided that preliminary hearing testimony of an unavailable witness could be read in at trial, and it set out a procedure for the reception of the evidence. The procedure required that the deposition be signed by the witness and the judge before whom the testimony had been taken.

From the state of the law at the time of the trail, we can infer why the judge ruled the testimony out. The letter of the law did not specifically say that testimony at a prior trial was admissible, and it required that the testimony be signed by both the witness and the presiding judge.[35] After the trial, the statue was amended to make prior trial testimony admissible and to drop the requirement of for the witness to sign the testimony.[36] The spirit of the common law allowed prior testimony into evidence, but the letter of the statutory law did not include prior trial testimony. Justice Ferguson perpetrated an injustice by strictly adhering to the letter of the law, and to correct this injustice, the law was changed to specifically state that prior trial testimony was admissible. Wigmore would say that Ferguson did not exercise "common sense and liberality in the application of the rule," and instead applied a "narrow and pedantic illiberality" in construing the statute. There's an old proverb that "the letter of the law killeth, the spirit

---

[34] Wigmore, *Anglo-American Evidence*, 67-71.
[35] Crankshaw, *Criminal Code of Canada and Canada Evidence Act*, 638.
[36] Tremeear, *Criminal Code and Law of Criminal Evidence in Canada*, 784.

giveth life."[37] Ferguson's ruling on this issue went a long way toward killing the Crown's case.

The defense team was confident this ruling meant that the Crown could not prove that the twins bilked Martha of all the insurance proceeds, but Osler was nothing if not relentless. He called D.T. Ames, New York's most eminent examiner of questioned documents to testify that Harry forged the endorsements of four checks totaling $8,000. Harry had gotten Martha to write checks to imaginary people and then endorsed the checks himself and got the proceeds. This put the defense into panic mode because it looked like Ferguson was finally going to overrule one of their objections. Instead of trying to stop Osler's thrust, they opted to parry it, thereby receiving a lesser wound than would otherwise have been inflicted. To forestall the evidence that Harry was a forger, they offered to admit that the brothers made off with Martha's money. Osler objected to the stipulation and fought to get in the evidence because a bald stipulation does not carry the same persuasive force as proof by testimony. Ferguson ruled that the admission was accepted, and he further ruled that this admission made Smoke's testimony unnecessary. The Crown thus could show that Martha received $29,900 insurance proceeds for Willie's death, that the twins made off with $22,800 of that money, that Mrs. Aylesworth got $4,750, and that Martha was left with less than $2,000.

Here was another missed opportunity for the Crown to shore up its case. Had they included four counts of forgery in the indictment for murder, the defense would have had much more difficulty keeping the evidence out. Rules pertaining to joinder and severance of charges were more

---

[37] Based on 1 Cor. 3.6 (KJV).

stringent in the 19th century than they are today, and the defense quite possibly could have gotten the counts severed for separate trials. If so, the Crown could have convicted Harry on the forgeries before trying the twins for murder. As the saying goes, a hit with a .22 is better than a miss with a .45.

It should be easier to employ this stratagem today than it was in the Victorian Era. Modern Canadian law provides that "any number of counts for any number of offenses may be joined in the same indictment,"[38] but if a defendant is charged with murder, no count may be added to the murder charge unless the non-murder count charges an offense that arose out of the same transaction as the murder.[39] The forgeries were arguably part of the same transaction as the murder because they were perpetrated to reap the fruits of the murder. Were the murder to have happened in the U.S.A. today, the brothers could be charged with Racketeering, rendering all the forgeries, the insurance fraud with Martha, and conspiracy to kill Martha all chargeable in the same indictment.[40]

To prove that Willie and Aylesworth were given useless tasks in copying out old lists, Osler called Herbert Waddington, a clerk at the Might Directory Company to testify to the percentage of change from year to year in the directory. Ferguson ruled the testimony inadmissible.

Then Hector Charlesworth, much against his will, took the stand to testify about the bribe attempt. He had nothing to fear. The defense argued that the bribe was offered in relation to the insurance scam involving Martha, not the

---

[38] Canadian Criminal Code, R.S.C., 1985, c. 46, § 591(1).
[39] Canadian Criminal Code, R.S.C., 1985, c. 46, § 589(a).
[40] See generally Fla.Stat. Ch. 895, and specifically Fla.Stat. § 895.03(3).

insurance scam involving Willie. Ferguson bought the argument and suppressed Charlesworth's testimony.[41] "I was ordered to step down, greatly to my relief," Charlesworth wrote in his memoirs, "Had the evidence been taken, the defense would have proclaimed me a particularly ruthless perjurer, and I would have had small chance of being trusted with confidences by any member of the legal profession."[42]

The prosecution case was winding down, and Osler embarked upon the final phase of his presentation—the medical testimony. Dr. John Caven took the stand and repeated the testimony he had given at the previous trial. Osler brought out one additional significant fact:

"Does one blow account for all you see there?" Osler asked.

"I don't think so," Caven replied, "From the condition of the right side of the face and the breaking off of the right internal angular process, I would say that two lines of force had been applied."

"Can you indicate the line from which the force would come to break off the angular process?"

"It must have been from before, backwards."

"A witness has described the breaking up of the right eye of the spectacles and the bending in of the frame, and another has told of the finding of a piece of glass in the right eyebrow. Do these statements assist you in coming to a conclusion as to this second line of force?"

---

[41] "H.P. Hyams a Forger," *Toronto World*, November 20, 1895.
[42] Charlesworth, *Candid Chronicles*, 229.

"As to the driving in of the eye," Caven replied, "that is a physical impossibility; it might have been ruptured to cause it to look like a driving in. If the glass were firmly imbedded, I would say that it had been driven in by force applied from before."

As the prosecution got into the medical evidence, the objections from the defense became fewer and farther between. Johnston objected once to a hypothetical question asked by Osler, but the judge quickly ruled the question proper. The Crown called fewer experts than in the first trial, and the presentation was lucid and easy to follow. The *Toronto World* summarized the testimony of the six medical witnesses:

> In concise form it is simply this, that two distinct lines of force were necessary to produce the conditions found in the skull; one delivered from the front, fracturing the cheek bones and the internal angular process, which the Crown claim was struck while Wells was standing erect; and the second the heavy crushing blow, upon which both sides agree.

The controversy over the disputed line of force centered around injuries to the internal angular process of the right mandible. The Crown contended that a separate, lateral force caused the injury, while the defense attempted on cross-examination to explain the injury by "the transmission of force on the principle of vibration." Mr. Johnston tried mightily on cross-examination to get Dr. Caven to agree that vibration from the crushing blow could have produced the injuries to the jaw. Dr. Caven replied that it was "within the possibilities" that part of the injuries to the jaw could have been caused by the crushing blow, but not all of them. Dr. Caven's summarized his position on the vibration theory by saying, "The defense theory is capable of reasonable argument, but personally I cannot agree with it." Lengthy cross-examinations by both Johnston and Lount failed to move Caven from his opinion that two lines of force caused the injuries.

Dr. Arthur Jukes Johnson testified that the crushing blow to the skull came while the head was lying on the floor, and that the injuries to the jaw were "accounted for by other lines of force."

"There has been evidence of a wound over the left eye. How would that be produced?" Osler asked.

"There is no evidence here in this skull that would account for that wound. It could not be produced by the bursting of the skull." Johnson was unshaken on cross-examination.

Four more medical men testified that the skull gave evidence of two lines of force. The crushing blow came from the side while the head lay on a flat surface, and the blow to the jaw came laterally from the front of the face.

Osler announced to the defense that he would conclude the prosecution case early the next morning, and they should be ready to proceed with their evidence at that time.[43]

---

[43] "Two Lines of Force," *Toronto World*, November 21, 1895.

CHAPTER THIRTEEN: THE SECOND TRIAL
THE DEFENSE CASE[1]

On the morning of November 21 Osler presented a few more doctors to corroborate the testimony from the day before and introduced a perjured affidavit by Harry. In connection with the insurance claim on Willie, an affidavit from a disinterested party had to be submitted. Harry supplied the affidavit claiming he had no interest whatsoever in the policy on Willie's life. This last piece of evidence was hardly necessary. The jury certainly had already concluded that Harry was a liar.

Then it was the defense turn. Johnston's first witness was Dr. Luke Teskey, who testified that downward was the only direction from which the force came against Willie's head. He posited a theory that Willie was standing looking up the shaft when the weight first hit him, that he fell to the floor, that the weight bounced off the buffer block and hit Willie's head a second time. He agreed with the prosecution experts that Wille's head was resting on the floor when it was crushed. It all sounded so convincing until Osler began his cross-examination. Osler carefully shepherded Teskey through the details of his explanation until he had boxed the doctor into a trap. Using a book as a stand in for the 200-pound weight, Osler had Teskey demonstrate how the weight contacted the head for the first blow and then for the second. Teskey testified that when the first blow was struck, Willie's head fell to the floor ahead of the weight and was then crushed when the weight bounced on it.

Having carefully lead Teskey out onto the limb of improbability, Osler then sawed it off: "How do you

---

[1] November 21-30, 1895.

reconcile your theory of the two positions of the head and your testimony that the head would fall directly to the floor when struck with the obvious fact that in order to get into position for the second blow, the deceased would have had to turn a somersault after he received the first blow?"

Teskey backpedaled: "Surely I have made an error somewhere." Even Justice Ferguson was incredulous about the testimony, saying that he could not understand how the change in position of Willie's head could be brought about.

Pointing to the 200-pound weight lying in front of the jury box, Osler asked, "It looks like a ball that would rebound, doesn't it, Doctor?" Both judge and jury erupted in laughter at the question. Osler then concluded his cross-examination by calling Teskey's attention to the testimony about glass imbedded in the bone over the right eye. That was evidence that the head had been struck by a blow coming from the front, wasn't it? Teskey agreed.[2]

The defense followed Teskey with a parade of medical experts, but only one of them proved a strong witness. Dr. Irving H. Cameron, professor of clinical surgery at Toronto University, peppered his testimony with arcane scientific terminology. The *Toronto World* wrote that his testimony "proved interesting and instructive to those whose mental power was sufficient to follow through its mazes." Cameron held that it was quite possible for Willie to be holding the pull rope in his right hand looking up the shaft when the weight came loose and hit his head. Willie could then have fallen to the floor ahead of the weight, and his head could have been crushed when the weight hit the buffer block and

---

[2] "Crown Case Closed," *Toronto World*, November 22, 1895.

fell over on his head. This made for a more plausible scenario than Dr. Teskey's bouncing weight.

Osler worked diligently on cross-examination to weaken Cameron's testimony, using two small mannequins from an art supply store to illustrate the postures of Willie's body. The courtroom again was filled with laughter, but this time the laughter came at Osler's expense as Cameron deftly parried his every thrust.

The defense closed out the day with the testimony of Dr. W.A. Powell, who thought that a single blow would account for all the injuries to the skull. As to the injury to the internal angular process of the jaw, the injury relied upon by the Crown to establish the blow from the front, Powell said that bone was weak and could be broken off by the pressure of a thumb. He was still on the stand when court recessed for the evening.[3]

One interesting development occurred outside the courtroom. The *Toronto World* had started calling Harry and Dallas "the Hyamese Twins," an obvious allusion to Chang and Eng Bunker, the conjoined twins who billed themselves as "Siamese Twins" when they toured the U.S. and the British Isles.[4] The *World* continued to call them "Hyamese" even after the trial was over.[5]

More medical testimony followed the next day, and then the defense turned to proving the unsafe condition of the elevator. The witnesses testified in chorus about the elevator's antique pattern, loose construction, and unsafe

---

[3] "One Crushing Blow," *Toronto World*, November 23, 1895.

[4] "Hyamese Twins," *Toronto World*, November 14, 1895.

[5] "The Hyamese Acquitted," *Toronto World,* December 2, 1895; "Hyamese Again Remanded," *Toronto World*, December 24, 1895.

character, but the only accident they could describe was the crushing of the ill-fated cat. The first defense witness, Shipp, developed such a case of stage-fright when he took the stand that he could not tell a coherent story on direct examination. The second, Mr. Brimsmead, testified about changing out the weight. He hurt the defense case by admitting that he had to take a hammer to the hook to make it come loose from the weight.

JOSEPH McMillan, who worked for the previous tenants of the warehouse, testified that he frequently used the elevator and found it rickety and unsafe. He testified about an obstruction in the elevator shaft that frequently caught on the weight. It was a board that protruded about two and a half inches into the shaft. He told of how he took the weight shaft apart and chiseled the protruding board flat. He remembered one time that the weight came off the hook, but he replaced it with ease. He did not fare well on cross-examination. Osler brought the portion of the elevator shaft which McMillan had supposedly chiseled and asked him to point out the chisel marks. He could find none. Osler continued to work on him, and "before he got down from the witness box his story was as full of holes as a fanning-mill sieve, and he was the laughingstock of the whole court."[6]

When the defense turned to the barbershop alibis the direct examinations went much as they had in the first trial, but the cross-examinations were more brutal. Osler, armed with the transcripts of the witnesses' prior testimony, used them to good effect. Using the transcripts, he was able "to tie up with a plenitude of contradictions every man who entered the witness box." The witnesses could recall with

---

[6] "Drawing to a Close," *Toronto World,* November 25, 1895.

remarkable precision the events of January 16, 1893, but they had small ability to recall events of much more recent vintage.

The witnesses unanimously swore that the brothers were not in the warehouse at 9:00, the time set by the defense for Willie's death; but they could not agree on where the brothers were at that hour. Three witnesses swore they saw Dallas in his 11 King Street office at 9:00, but then other witnesses put him in the Jordan Street Barber Shop from 8:30 until 9:20. Matthew Rammage saw Harry Hyams at the corner of Adelaide and Victoria Streets around 8:30. As they stood there talking, Willie Wells came by, and the three of them walked down to the warehouse. Willie entered the warehouse while Rammage and Hyams walked on. Rammage forgot all about the meeting until two years later, shortly after the arrest of the twins. Solicitor Horn came to Philadelphia, where Rammage was then living, and suggested to him that he had met Willie and Harry on the morning of January 16. Rammage recalled the meeting with remarkable detail, but he could not distinguish between what facts he independently remembered, and what facts Horn said the defense wanted to prove. Would Rammage swear that Horn did not tell him that the meeting occurred at 8:30? No, he would not.

Osler concluded his cross-examination by asking, "Will you swear that all the evidence you have given here today was not suggested by Mr. Horn at that first interview?"

"Not wholly suggested," Rammage replied.

While Harry and Rammage were escorting Willie to the warehouse, it appeared Harry that simultaneously sat in the barber's chair at the Leader Lane Barber Shop. Barber A.J. Gardipey testified that he shaved Harry from 8:35 to

8:55 that morning; and at 9:15, immediately after Harry left, another customer came in and reported Willie's death. He had no occasion to recall that morning until February of 1894, shortly after the twins' arrest, when Solicitor Horn came to him and reminded him of the incident.

John Neil, a photographer, testified that he met Dallas or Harry at the 11 King Street office that morning between 8:30 and 9:00. On cross-examination he admitted that he did not remember the meeting until Lawyer Horn reminded him of it. Joseph Jessiman saw either Dallas or Harry at the King Street office at exactly the same time as Neil, but Neil was nowhere around.

John Collins was sure it was Dallas whom he saw at the King Street office at 9:00, but his testimony as to the details of the sighting were very different from the details which he described in the first trial. He said he could place the time so precisely because he was attending to some recently arrived press parcels, but on his prior testimony he could not recall whether the parcels came in the forenoon or afternoon. He admitted that Mr. Horn had gone over his testimony with him about two weeks ago.

At the time Dallas was being seen by so many men at his King Street office, he was simultaneously in the barber chair at the Jordan Street Barbershop of Rod Westcott. According to Westcott, Dallas came in around 8:20 or 8:30 and was in the barber chair receiving a haircut, a shave, and a shampoo for the next 50 minutes. On cross-examination Westcott was adamant that Dallas had been in his barbershop from 8:30 until 9:20 that morning, and he was prepared to contradict anyone who said anything different.

"If three men would swear that they saw him somewhere else during that hour, you would say they were mistaken, would you?" asked Osler.

"Yes, I would," Westcott replied. Coincidentally, the first person to ever speak to him about the January 16 shave, haircut, and shampoo was Solicitor Horn.

Donald McCarthy, who worked in the basement adjacent to the warehouse, then took the stand to testify about hearing the crash in the warehouse basement shortly before 9:00 on the morning of January 16. He heard whistling through a hole in the wall and then a crash, as if the elevator had fallen, and then he heard footsteps and someone calling Willie's name.

"How much money did you get for the last trial?" was one of Osler's first questions. McCarthy said he got $60, which was less than he expected. He also admitted that before the first trial Lawyer Horn paid off a debt which McCarthy owed to a Queen Street businessman.[7]

The defense attempted to corroborate McCarthy's testimony with James Rosvear, who sometimes worked in the basement assisting McCarthy. He vividly recalled the hole in the wall dividing the two basements, describing it as about two and a half feet square. On cross-examination, however, Rosvear said the hole did not penetrate into the Hyams' basement; it simply went into a small dead chamber between the two basements that was not used for any purpose.

Coroner Aikins took the stand to testify concerning his decision not to hold a coroner's inquest, but he did reveal

---

[7] "The Barber's Alibi," *Toronto World*, November 26, 1895.

one unhelpful detail that was not brought out at the previous trial. While he was in the basement Harry showed him a short-nosed hook and told him that it was the one in use at the time of the death. Cross-examination revealed that the short-nosed hook very definitely was not the hook attached to the weight that morning. The defense tried to attribute this discrepancy to faulty memory on Aikins' part, but the Crown insisted that Harry showed him the short - nosed hook in order to lead him to believe the hook could easily come off the weight.

"Did you know that there was a large insurance on the boy's life and that a heavy premium was due in a few days?" Osler asked.

"No, I did not," Aikins replied.

"Would it have made any difference to you if you had known?" This question prompted a vigorous objection from the defense. After a lengthy argument, Justice Ferguson sustained the objection, and the question went unanswered.

Osler ended his cross-examination with a series of questions concerning a conversation Aikins had with one of the Crown experts.

Q: Do you remember the interview with Dr. Bingham?

A: Yes, I do.

Q: Did you tell Dr. Bingham that there was money in it for the defense?

A: I may have said it in a jocular manner, but in earnest, no.

Q: What did you say to him?

A: I said jestingly that he should not be in a hurry to make up his mind as there was money in it for the defense.

Q: And you knew then that Dr. Bingham was in consultation with the Crown officers at the time?

A: Yes, I knew he had seen the skull, and had not made up his mind.

Next the defense put on the testimony of the Prestons about Willie being at the warehouse the Sunday evening before his death. The younger Preston testified that Willie took him into the basement and showed him how the elevator operated. The weight got stuck, and Willie asked to borrow Preston's cane to dislodge it. Willie then lowered the weight into the basement and showed Preston how the weights could be changed. When he put the hook back into the 200-pound weight, Willlie only partially engaged the hook into the eye of the weight. Preston pointed out the dangerous condition of the hook, but Willie did nothing to correct it. Preston also testified that on the Wednesday following Willie's death, he went to the warehouse to make experiments with the elevator weight to see if the weight would fall off if the hook were not properly engaged. Osler tried to inflict "death by a thousand cuts" upon Preston's credibility by pointing out the many discrepancies between his present story and his previous testimony, but the *Toronto World* concluded that "Mr. Osler's cross-examination did not materially affect the testimony of the witness."

Finally, the last day of testimony came, and spectators packed the courtroom to hear the best trial lawyers in Canada argue their cases in what the *Toronto World* called "the most remarkable murder trial ever held in Canadian courts." Mrs. Dallas Hyams sat in the grand jury box next to Francis L. Wellman's wife, the famous opera singer Emma Juch. Mrs. Justice Ferguson and her daughters joined them in the grand jury box.

The defense ended with a whimper rather than a bang when they called a clerk in the offices of the Canadian Express Company to testify that large sums of money had been shipped from the U.S. to the brothers between May 9, 1889, and October 14, 1894. On cross-examination the witness testified that before January 16, 1893, the twins had received only $150, the rest of the money being sent to their mother in installments of $200 per month. The $200 payments ceased between December 13, 1892, and June 9, 1893, while the mother was in Florida.

In rebuttal Osler called Samuel W. Hughson of the Covenant Mutual Insurance Company to testify that he was present when Preston did the experiments with the weight, that the experiments occurred on the Thursday following Willie's funeral rather than the Wednesday following his death. Harry Hyams was present for the experiments, and they were not conducted in the manner described by Preston. Ferguson decided that Hughson was obviously talking about a second set of experiments and would not allow his testimony before the jury unless Osler could prove that the warehouse was locked on the Wednesday following Willie's death. And with the suppression of Hughson's evidence, the Crown rested its rebuttal.

At 3:00 Johnston rose to give his final argument. It was an eloquent plea, full of sound and fury, and its theme was the relentless unfairness of the prosecution. The Crown had retained Canada's greatest criminal lawyer, and he was assisted by a staff of eminent co-counsel. He had left no stone unturned in dredging up evidence against the brothers, he had tried hard to taint the defense witnesses with moral infamy. He had been assisted by one of the shrewdest criminal investigators in Toronto, Detective Cuddy. Cuddy had seized the brothers' most sacred property and Osler had paraded it before the jury. Not even the love letters between Harry and Martha were safe. "We have had our lives laid open and bare to the investigation of the clever, ingenious, shrewd men, skilled in criminal prosecution; men whose business it is to prosecute criminals; a detective whose duty it is to work up cases of this kind." And the twins' last bulwark of defense was the twelve good men and true who were going to hold the Crown to its high burden of proof.

Eventually, Johnston got around to talking about the evidence in the case. He began by pointing out contradictions among the prosecution witnesses. The contradictions alone were enough to warrant the jury in acquitting. He then spoke of "one of the most remarkable pieces of evidence ever placed before a jury, the wound over the left eye, which their own evidence showed did not exist." He then cataloged each piece of evidence tending to indicate guilt and gave an innocent explanation for everything. The plausibility of those innocent explanations might be open to question, but he made them, nonetheless. The constant tinkering the twins had done with the elevator showed how solicitous they were for the safety of their employees. The many contradictory stories the brothers told about how the death occurred was proof of their innocence, not their guilt.

"Suppose one of you should commit a crime," Johnston said, "would you not, when people came to question you of it, have a ready story which you would tell to everybody? Is it likely that a guilty man would tell one man one story and another man another? These conflicting statements on the part of the prisoners, the Crown will ask you to believe are evidences of guilt. But I ask you, as reasonable men, are they not rather the strongest possible proof of the innocence of the accused?" At 5:30 Johnston said he could not finish his address in a reasonable time, and Justice Ferguson recessed court for the day.[8]

Ironically, on the same day that Johnston complained about how the vast resources devoted by the Crown to the case had overwhelmed the hapless brothers, the *Toronto World* ran a story on the cost of the case. Adding up the expenses of the second trial, the *World* found that the Crown had spent "the magnificent sum of $9056.50" toward convicting the brothers. The defense, in contrast, had spent $26,000, most of which went to attorneys' fees. One telling statistic was the amount of money spent by both sides on witness fees. The Crown had paid out $350 in witness fees, while the defense had spent $6,500 on Pinkerton detectives and witnesses. This last amount was more than the $6,000 spent by the Crown on counsel fees and detectives.

The entire next day was consumed by the speeches of the defense counsel. After speaking for a total of six hours, Johnston ceded the floor to Lount. When the day ended, Lount had barely begun his speech. Johnston continued to hammer away at each circumstance in the Crown's circumstantial evidence case, finding a plausible explanation for each. The brothers were trying hard to make a go of the warehouse; they had good reason to have

---

[8] "Fate of the Twins Soon to be Told," *Toronto World*, November 28, 1895.

their clerks copying outdated information sheets by hand; they certainly did borrow money at high interest rates, what's criminal about that? Johnston's argument was the standard "divide and conquer" used by the defense in a circumstantial evidence case. They argue that the individual items of evidence, standing alone, fail to prove guilt. But one individual circumstance, standing alone, seldom proves guilt—it is the cumulative effect of all the circumstances taken together that proves guilt.

In conclusion Johnston made an eloquent and impassioned plea for the lives of the twins: "No higher stake can be battled for than the life of a fellow-being…. I ask you for what I have been striving here and fighting against terrible odds—the lives of two human beings. Will you give me those lives, or will you give them to the hangman; will you, upon the evidence which I have endeavored to review and place before you, say that your minds are fully satisfied or that my request is an unreasonable request? … Let your duty be performed on what has been presented before you; let your judgment be the judgment of God-like justice tempered with mercy; weigh well the facts that have been presented to you and then come to the best conclusion you can. I have endeavored to do my duty; no man can do more."

Then it was Lount's turn to talk. His reputation for eloquence outstripped all the other lawyers in the case, and his speech did nothing to call that reputation into question. He plowed the same furrows which Johnston had plowed, but he asked for even more than Johnston did. Johnston had called upon the jury to acquit because of reasonable doubt. Lount urged them to proclaim the brothers completely innocent by their verdict.[9] His speech consumed less time than Johnston's had, and before the day was over, he had ceded the floor to the prosecution. Osler was still speaking when Justice Ferguson recessed court for the day.

At 9:15 the next morning the twins arrived at the courthouse in the custody of their jailers. As they stepped from the coach which had brought them from the jail a crowd of onlookers greeted them. As the crowd surged forward to get a better look at the twins, Harry took notice of Hector Charlesworth in the crowd. Charlesworth bade Harry a "good morning," and Harry returned the greeting.[10] Then his custodians closed ranks around him and his brother and pushed them through the crowd into the courthouse. The defense team arrived at 9:45, and they were roundly criticized by some of the bystanders as they pushed through the crowd.

Because there were far more would-be spectators than the courtroom could accommodate, a phalanx of officers guarded the door and denied admittance to all but a select few. The courtroom filled by 10:00, and the guards turned everyone else away. Charlesworth was amused that two attractive young girls were able to sneak in past the guards. They had already been turned away, but when they saw Justice Ferguson arrive, they pretended to be with him. They accompanied him as he pushed his way through the jostling crowd and slipped past the guards into the courthouse.

All day long people surged around the entrance to the courthouse trying to get in, and the constables repeatedly

---

[9] "Great Forensic Battle," *Toronto World*, November 29, 1895.
[10] The identity of the reporter to whom Harry spoke is inferred from the fact that he was a reporter for the *Toronto World*.

had to use rough means to keep them out. One barrister who tried to gain admittance so that he could keep an appointment in the Civil Assize Court found himself turned away. He insisted upon gaining admission; and when words failed, he tried to push his way through the wall of constables standing in the door. A scuffle ensued in which he found himself outnumbered and ill-used by the constables. Charlesworth noted that he "made a good fight against big odds," but he was finally ejected and deposited on the ground. His clothing was torn, and he had several bruises, but the greatest injury was to his dignity as a group of young ladies laughed at his predicament. He gathered himself up, went back to his chambers, and dashed off an angry letter to Sheriff Mowat demanding that amends be made to him and that the offending constables be punished. Several other citizens joined him in complaining about the ill-use they received at the hands of the constables.

At 10:00 sharp Osler resumed his argument. He first described the financial predicament of the brothers leading up to the death and their settling of longstanding debts afterward. Then he turned to the day of Willie's death: "Now, what happened on the morning of the 16th? That, of course, gentlemen, is the all-important question. Did the prisoners keep the appointment they had made the night before with Wells? He was wanted early; he was wanted to meet the prisoner H. P. Hyams on some business. What business? Is it shown there was anything to be done In the warehouse? … Is there anything suggested which would occasion their meeting on that morning in the warehouse? The occasion would be within the prisoners' knowledge; It is a matter they could suggest to their counsel; it is a matter that could be hunted out, but there is absolute silence with reference to it." This argument came close to commenting on the defendants' exercise of their right to remain silent.

"Now what is the first development we have? The first development is from Dr. King's testimony; and the importance of that development is that we find that dead boy in the possession of these prisoners—killed by violence. Ad if you find two men in a room and the body there of a third, fresh killed by violence, what presumption arises?"

Osler then reminded the jury that the defense experts did not clear the brothers of the charge of murder. In fact, they agreed with the Crown's experts. All agree that two blows were delivered to Willie's head. All agree that the second, crushing blow came when Willie was unconscious on the floor. The defense expert, Dr. Cameron testified that, upon the assumption that the brothers were innocent, the defense theory of how death occurred was a possibility— not a probability. In light of it being a possibility rather than a probability, "You must look at the light of what went before and what followed after, and then see if you can take that possibility in."

Osler then addressed the conflicting stories told by the brothers. According to Dallas' first story, he was not at the barbershop, but was at the warehouse when Willie died: "I was there. I heard it fall. I went down. The weight was on him. I fainted." Osler then asked whether that first version did not "stamp [the barbershop alibis] with more than doubt?" Dallas had other versions. In one he was on a floor above Willie adjusting the weight when it fell and killed Willie. In another version, Dallas was writing in the office and heard the crash of the falling weight. Harry told Dr. King that Willie had been struck by the weight and they had gotten the weight off his head. In all his descriptions of the accident to Dr. King, he never mentioned that he was at the barbershop when it happened. Harry told Undertaker Humphrey that he (Harry) heard the weight fall. It must have made quite a racket for Harry to hear it while blocks away at the barbershop. In none of his earliest statements did Harry claim to have been at the barbershop. They both admitted to being at the warehouse when the death occurred. They both admitted hearing the crash. With these admissions, what possible weight could be given to the alibis?

Osler then assailed the credibility of the defense witnesses. He spoke of the improbability of the witnesses' excellent memories. He spoke of the conflicts in their testimony. He reminded the jury of how they fared poorly on cross-examination. Then he concluded his remarks with an eloquent peroration. His last words to the jury were: "You have got to follow [the evidence in] all its complications; you have got to take their financial condition; all the acts of preparation; you have got to take the medical and mechanical evidence; you have got to take the supposed evidence of alibi; you have got to take the results, the fruits of the crime, coming to them; take all these things into your consideration, gentlemen, and simply do right." While Osler spoke, the twins became more and more glum, their faces drained of color, but their countenances brightened considerably during Justice Ferguson's address.

At 12:20 Justice Ferguson began his address to the jury: "The counsel on both sides of the case have come to the conclusion of their labors. The time has come for me and you to commence the performance of our duties." He then commenced a two-hour speech which sounded very much like an argument for the defense. In his address he enumerated and rebutted each of the Crown's arguments. "Admitting that the prisoners got more than $22,000, is that any reason these men should be condemned? These men were in sore need of the money, it is true, but may Wells not have been killed by an accident, or in an ordinary case, some person else might have killed him?" Ferguson then repeated the defense timeline for the fatal day, and reconstructed the events of the death by saying that Wells wanted to start a fire in the heater and went down to the basement to get coal. The elevator cage was on the top floor and the weight in the basement. As he lowered the cage and lifted the weight, the weight got caught at the first floor. Wells looked up the shaft to try to diagnose the problem, and the weight fell on him. He observed that Wilie was so careless in working the hoist it was no surprise that he got himself killed.

According to Ferguson, the barbers were worthy of belief for many reasons, and the Crown medical experts were not. If there had been a blow to Willie's face as Dr. Caven had said, there was absolutely no evidence of it; and Dr. Johnson had simply adopted Caven's opinion; and the statements of the other Crown experts did not negate the theory that one crushing blow would cause all the injuries. The defense experts, on the other hand, were men high in their profession, and they deserved praise for the clear and satisfactory manner in which they gave their testimony. Justice Ferguson reviewed the defense theory of how the death occurred and commented favorably on it.

On Osler's argument that a presumption of wrongdoing arose from the defendants being found in the warehouse with the body, Ferguson said: "It is not right to say the body was found there and the prisoners were seen there, and have to account for it; the question is has the Crown proved enough? ... Are you satisfied that [the defense theory of how the weight fell] is proved? If you are, that alone would show the innocence of the prisoners. If you are not satisfied that that is proved, are you satisfied that that is not so beyond a reasonable doubt?"

Ferguson concluded by saying, "If you are satisfied that the prisoners are guilty beyond a reasonable doubt, find them guilty like men without regard to the consequences. If you are in doubt, if you are left in hesitation, if there is a reasonable doubt in any of the ways I have mentioned, then find the prisoners not guilty. ... Perhaps I ought to have gone through the evidence on a wider range, but for my own part I do not see I could do any good by doing so. But I will leave you with what I have said, with one thing more—a proposition that may seem inherent in criminal justice—that it is better that very many persons who are guilty escape, than that one innocent person should suffer. Now, gentlemen, I leave the case in your hands."

The *Toronto World,* in its subheading of the article on the day's events, described Ferguson's address in the following words: "The Summary of the Case, as Submitted to the Jury by His Lordship One of the Most Remarkable, In Many Respects, Ever Heard in a Canadian Court."

No sooner had the jury retired than Osler stood and asked Ferguson for a reserved case on twelve grounds. He urged that the judge had committed error in:

(1). The exclusion of the evidence of the conspiracy to insure and murder Martha Hyams.

(2). The exclusion of the evidence of the time at which the streetcar ran.

(3). The ruling that the Crown must accept the defense offer to admit that the twins received the insurance money, which rendered much Crown evidence inadmissible.

(4). The exclusion of the testimony of Hector Charlesworth about Dallas' attempt to bribe him.

(5). The refusal to allow the Crown to present evidence concerning the difference in premiums on Harry Hyams and Willie Wells.

(6). The refusal to allow the Crown to ask Dr. Aikins whether he would have ordered an inquest if he had known about the insurance on Willie's life.

(7). The exclusion of Samuel Hughson's rebuttal testimony contradicting Preston's description of the experiments he conducted with the elevator weight.

(8). The exclusion of testimony by the Pickering telegraph operator about the delivery of a telegram to Uriah Jones, Willie's uncle.

(9). The exclusion of expert testimony concerning the elevator.

(10). The exclusion of expert testimony concerning mercantile agencies.

(11). The refusal to allow the Crown to ask Aylesworth the purpose of a trip he made to Montreal.

(12). All the other rulings excluding evidence tendered by the Crown.

Osler also said that he believed he had grounds for a reserved case based on some of the statements made by Ferguson to the jury, but he did not urge this point.

Ferguson listened attentively to all the assignments of error made by the Crown, but he did not rule on them. To have these issues reviewed, the judge had to allow the reservations, and if the reservations were allowed, then the prisoners would stay in jail or under bond until the review was completed.

The jury had been out seven minutes when they knocked upon the door of the jury room. There was a bustle of excitement as the spectators anticipated the announcement of a quick verdict. They were disappointed when it turned out that the jury simply wanted some sheets of paper to use as ballots. After 37 minutes of deliberation, the jury was ready to report its verdict.

The jury filed into the courtroom, and High Constable Jones was taking the roll of the jury when the jailers brought the twins into the courtroom. It was evident from the smiles on the twins' faces that they anticipated an acquittal. When everything and everyone was in place, Constable Jones asked: "Gentlemen of the jury, have you agreed upon your verdict.

Foreman William Frisby replied in a soft voice, "We have." There was an awkward silence as Frisby waited to be asked another question. Finally, he realized that he was supposed to announce the verdict without prompting. He then boomed out, "NOT GUILTY!" and sat back into his chair with a sigh of relief. Dallas' face grew ashen pale, but he finally smiled. Harry's head sank into the corner of the dock, but a broad grin could be seen on his face. Sheriff Mowat and the constables quickly suppressed a smattering of applause from the audience.

Johnston and Lount rose and asked that the prisoners be discharged from custody. Crown Attorney Dewart asked that they be held to answer charges of conspiracy to commit insurance fraud and to murder Martha Hyams. Justice Ferguson discharged the twins, thereby rendering Osler's reserved case moot, but the twins had only a few moments to enjoy their freedom before Detective Cuddy served them with warrants for conspiracy to commit insurance fraud and murder.

The jurors in the first trial were more than willing to speak about their assessment of the evidence, saying that they thought the twins probably guilty but that there was a reasonable doubt. The jurors for the second trial appeared to be reluctant to speak of their deliberations or their views on the evidence. Only one anonymous juror made a terse statement to Hector Charlesworth. He said that Justice Ferguson's charge strongly favored the defense and that only one ballot was taken, and it was unanimous for not guilty.

Martha Hyams had spent most of the trial confined in a private hospital, and she was unable to leave her sickbed during the trial's last week. When she was notified of the verdict, she said that she was satisfied the twins had murdered her brother, but she felt that she was at the end of her own life and did not want to have her last hours made unhappy knowing that she had assisted in sending her husband to the gallows.[11]

---

[11] "The Hyamese Acquitted," *Toronto World,* December 2, 1895.

Charlesworth had the opportunity to meet Col. Foster toward the end of the trial. There appeared to be scant reason for Foster to remain in Toronto at all, which led to the natural inference that he stayed in Toronto for the duration of the trial so that he could pay off the jurors he had subverted when they returned a not guilty verdict. Charlesworth instantly disliked to Foster. Charlesworth walked up to his theatrical friend as Foster berated a lady singer under the friend's tutelage.

"Your star isn't worth a curse," Foster said, "Just a silly amateur."

Although he hadn't been formally introduced, Charlesworth felt compelled to come to the young girl's defense. "I think she is a lovely and talented girl," he said.

"Who is this young cub?" Foster asked the theatrical man in a whisper that could be heard in a sawmill.

"The young lady's backer," the theatrical man replied in an exaggerated stage whisper.

"Of course, I want you to understand I was just kidding, boy," Foster said as he put his arm around Charlesworth, "You may be losing a little money now, but you will get it back and plenty more. She's a 'comer' alright."

Charlesworth told Foster that he agreed. Foster, who was an expert card shark and pool hustler, then began to try to con Charlesworth. If Charlesworth had enough money to back a theatrical performer, Foster could separate Charlesworth from some of that money at the pool table.

"Like to play a game of billiards, boy?" Foster asked.

"No," Charlesworth replied.

"Well, let's get up a little game of poker—I'm sort o' lonesome tonight," Foster countered.

"No," Charlesworth again said, "I must get over and see how the show's going." With that he took his leave of Foster and the theatrical man. The total of Charlesworth's wealth at that time was the two dollars that he had in his pocket.

Years later, when Charlesworth wrote his memoirs, he closed out his chapter on the Hyams trial with the comment, "Personally I think the insinuating Foster had as much to do with the acquittal of the Hyams brothers as anybody."[12]

We already saw that Edwin Guillet believed the appointment of Justice Ferguson to preside at the second trial sounded the death knell of the prosecution case. He concluded his monograph on the trial by saying: "Due regard to all the circumstances suggests that if anything in this world would justify lynching it was the way in which Harry and Dallas Hyams got away with murder in January 1893—and twice more in 1895."[13]

Wallace W. Stewart, writing in 1931, attributed the acquittal to the twin influences of Justice Ferguson's "perhaps … exaggerated idea of fair play toward prisoners on trial for their lives" and the machinations of "the insinuating Foster." Stewart observed that Ferguson not only excluded evidence which Street had allowed in, he excluded much new evidence as well, and then gave a summation which "could hardly have [given the jury] a stronger hint" that they should acquit. He made special mention of Ferguson's exclusion of the railway company's

---

[12] Charlesworth, *Candid Chronicles*, 230, 231.
[13] Guillett, *Insurance Murderers*, 57.

time records which "might have upset the alibi set up by the prisoners." [14] According to the defense, Harry got to the warehouse, found Willie dead, and immediately jumped on a tram headed to Dr. King's office to get Willie help. Dr. King got to the warehouse, sized up the situation, and called the coroner at 10:00.[15] The problem with this timeline is that the tram Harry took to Dr. King's did not start running until 10:25 that morning, giving Harry and Dallas plenty of time after their alleged haircuts to kill Willie.[16]

Albert Hassard presented the minority report in his *Famous Canadian Trials*. He noted that in Justice Ferguson wrote in his Bench Book, "The Crown commenced and prosecuted upon the assumption of guilt of the prisoners, instead of respecting the legal presumption of innocence till the contrary is shown, and neglected all duty towards the accused." Justice Ferguson further wrote that because the Crown displayed a "greediness for blood," they were eminently unfair to the defendants. Hassard concluded, "Would that there were more Justice Fergusons upon the judgment seats of all civilized lands, not that guilt might escape its necessary punishment, but that innocence might receive its just rewards!"[17]

Prosecutors are supposed to believe that the people they prosecute are guilty. It is unethical for a prosecutor to pursue charges against someone believed to be innocent. To seek the death penalty against men believed to have committed a horrific murder neither displays "a greediness

---

[14] Stewart, "The Hyams Twins Case," *Maclean's: Canada's National Magazine*. https://archive.macleans.ca/article/1931/6/15/the-hyams-twins-case.

[15] Street, *Bench Book*, 14:27.

[16] "Mrs. Harry Hyams Again a Witness," *Toronto World*, May 15, 1895

[17] Hassard, *Famous Canadian Trials*, 246.

for blood" nor is it eminently unfair. Justice Ferguson appears to have decided early on that the defendants were innocent and was offended that the prosecution team disagreed with him. Once the judge abandons the role of impartial arbiter and begins to advocate for the defense, it is near impossible for the prosecution to prevail.

This observation leads us to ask a series of questions. First, were Hyams brothers guilty? Second, should they have been prosecuted? Third, should they have been convicted? This may seem to be asking the same question in three different ways, but the three questions are separate and distinct. The first question asks whether the accused is guilty of the alleged crime as a matter of real-world truth. The prosecutor should never file criminal charges unless satisfied that the accused is guilty. The Canadian courts disagree with me on this point. *Miazga v. Kvello Estate*, 2009 SCC 51 (CanLII), [2009] 3 SCR 339, holds that a prosecutor may proceed with a prosecution even though doubtful of the defendant's guilt. The rationale for this decision is that the prosecutor should not usurp the function of judge and jury. Things are a little different in the United States. Doubt about the guilt of an accused is specifically recognized as a factor to consider in making the charging decision.[18] This is a reasonable rule. If you can't convince yourself that the defendant is guilty, how can you convince a judge and jury?

In answering this first question, we are not bound by rules of evidence and may certainly consider things that a jury would never hear. For example, suppose Dan Defendant is suspected of abducting and killing Valerie

---

[18] Standard 4-1.3(a), *National District Attorneys Association National Prosecution Standards*, 3rd ed.

Victim. Officers unlawfully arrest Dan and then coerce him into confessing to murder. In his confession he divulges the location where he buried the victim. The victim is found in an unmarked grave exactly where Dan said he put her. Dan is charged with murder, but his confession is suppressed because it was the product of an unlawful arrest and unlawful coercion. The evidence found in the grave is suppressed because it is the product of the coerced confession and therefore "fruit of the poisoned tree." The fact that Dan will never get convicted of killing Valerie is irrelevant to the fact that Dan is guilty as a matter of real-world truth.

What is the real-world truth about the Hyams brothers' guilt or innocence? We can consider all the evidence put before the jury, but we need not limit ourselves to that. We can consider all the evidence that Justice Ferguson ruled inadmissible. We can even consider evidence that the Crown never attempted to put before the jury. All things considered, the twins murdered Willie Wells. We will not perform a thorough review of the evidence, which we have fully discussed in the preceding chapters, but we will mention several salient points supporting our conclusion.

First, the brothers initially admitted to being at the warehouse when Willie was killed. They quickly modified their stories to claim they were elsewhere, but this is a common occurrence when a guilty party unwittingly makes an incriminating statement. There are differences between cunning and intelligence, and the cunning frequently lack foresight. Upon realizing that the initial story won't do, the perpetrator produces a better one. We have two sources of corroboration for the brothers' first statements, neither of which was heard by the jury.

Hector Charlesworth reports a candid conversation he had with the Hyams brothers' "own confidential solicitor" shortly after the brothers departed Canada. Charlesworth did not name him, but it was most likely T.W. Horn. "Of course Harry was guilty," the solicitor said, "but nobody will ever convince me that Dallas would hit anybody with an axe. If anyone accused Dallas of slipping poison in his tea, I would believe that, but he was too yellow to do anything violent."[19]

The next item of corroboration comes from the pen of Francis L. Wellman. According to Wellman's memoir, *Luck and Opportunity,* the death occurred this way: "He [Wells] had been sent down to the cellar by the brothers-in-law to hold the rope connected with the elevator-weight ... while the two defendants were in the loft examining the weight which seemed to be jammed in some way so that nothing would go up or down. It was claimed that the brothers in the loft had called to their brother-in-law in the cellar to look up and see if he could discover if the rope had become entangled, and while in this exposed position, the weight had fallen into the cellar, striking the head of the youth looking up the elevator shaft and instantly killing him."[20] Where could Wellman have gotten such a sequence of events if not from the mouths of his clients?

The brothers were up the elevator shaft finagling with the counterweight while Willie stood at the bottom of the shaft holding the rope when suddenly the weight "accidentally" fell, killing Willie and enriching the brothers to the tune of $22,000. This was a story which the jury could never hear if the defense were to have any hope of an

---

[19] Charlesworth, *Candid Chronicles*, 229.
[20] Wellman, *Luck and Opportunity*, 94.

acquittal. So, an alibi was concocted—an alibi which would have been destroyed if Justice Ferguson had allowed evidence of the trolley schedule on the day of the death.

Add these facts to the ones presented at trial and the ones suppressed by Justice Ferguson, and the conclusion is inescapable that the brothers were guilty of murder. As to the defense evidence, we have good cause to discount it: The defense spent more money on witnesses ($6,500) than the Crown spent on attorneys' fees ($6,000). The defense witnesses had remarkable memories for the events of a day which had occurred two years before. Cross-examination by Osler should have discredited most of them in the eyes of any impartial factfinder. The first jury, although they hung, were unanimous in pronouncing the defense witnesses unworthy of belief. The second jury, with Justice Ferguson's endorsement of the credibility of the defense witnesses the last thing they heard before retiring to deliberate, understandably found the brothers not guilty.

Which brings us to the second question. Should the brothers have been prosecuted? A prosecutor in a common law jurisdiction should never file criminal charges simply because the defendant is guilty.[21] What is the requisite evidence? (1) Does the prosecutor have probable cause to believe the defendant guilty? (2) Is the quantum of available evidence sufficient to give the prosecutor a reasonable prospect of conviction?[22] The standard is not "a

---

[21] "It is a well-accepted principle of law in Canada and throughout the Commonwealth that a prosecution should be undertaken only where the requisite evidence exists and a prosecution would best serve the public interest. It has never been the rule that a prosecution will occur solely on the basis that there is sufficient evidence to support a charge." *Public Prosecution Service of Canada Deskbook*, 3.2.

[22] *Public Prosecution Service of Canada Deskbook*, 3.1.

certainty of conviction," but "a reasonable prospect of conviction." Prosecutors are not prophets, and there is nothing so uncertain as a jury verdict.

Crown Counsel were confronted with a botched death investigation in a two-year old case. Given the facts that botched investigations have doomed many cases and that a criminal case, unlike wine, does not get better with age, Crown Counsel would have been justified in declining to prosecute the case. They were equally justified, however, in bringing charges. Given the serious nature of the crime, and given the fact that Crown Counsel were satisfied of the brothers' guilt, and given the fact that the only way to achieve justice was to file charges, they were justified in indicting the brothers.

Twenty/twenty hindsight, however, tells us that they charged the wrong crimes. They had an excellent case against the brothers for insurance fraud and conspiracy to murder Martha, and the evidence of their enrichment from Willie's death would have made excellent evidence of motive. Martha could have weathered the rigors of testifying much better in a noncapital case, and the Crown could have revisited the question whether to charge murder after the brothers were convicted and sent to prison.

The third question, whether the brothers should have been convicted, is a question of the available courtroom proof. No matter how guilty the accused may be, if the courtroom proof falls short of the reasonable doubt standard, the defendant should be acquitted. At the first trial before Justice Street, the prosecution was rough, disorganized, and disjointed. A jury would have been justified in acquitting based on the poor showing of the prosecution. In the second trial before Justice Ferguson, the prosecution had mapped out a more organized, more persuasive case with additional evidence of guilt. Had they gotten all their evidence before the jury, and had Justice Ferguson not given such a one-sided summation, the prosecution should have prevailed. Given the evidence which did get before the jury in the second trial, they would have been justified in convicting, but it is unsurprising that they acquitted.

CHAPTER FOURTEEN: THE AFTERMATH

On Monday, December 2, 1895, the twins appeared again before Judge Denison in Police Court and entered pleas of not guilty to the charges of insurance fraud and conspiracy to murder. E.F.B. Johnston, who represented the twins in Police Court, did not ask for bail and none was given. The twins were all smiles at the arraignment, happy that they had escaped the gallows. Crown Counsel announced that they intended to file additional charges of forgery and advised Judge Denison that there was a warrant for forgery against Harry from Montreal.[1]

They were back before Judge Denison on December 23 for their preliminary hearing, but Crown Counsel Curry said he could not proceed until the next Monday. Johnston objected and demanded that the preliminary hearing begin immediately, but Judge Denison put the case over until the following Monday and remanded the twins to custody.[2] On December 30 the brothers were back in court before Judge Denison. The Crown leveled new charges of forgery against them, and they pleaded not guilty to all charges. In light of the new charges, Johnston asked that the case be put over again. Denison remanded the twins to custody and set their next hearing date for January 6, 1896.[3]

Finally, the preliminary hearing began. After calling a few witnesses to the application for insurance on Martha, Crown Counsel Curry asked that the case be adjourned on grounds that he wanted to obtain the originals of the insurance applications, which were now in England. Judge Denison said he did not feel justified in postponing the case

---

[1] "In Their Old Quarters," *Toronto World*, December 3, 1895.
[2] "Hyamese Again Remanded," *Toronto World*, December 24, 1895.
[3] "Hyams Plead Again," *Duluth News-Tribune*, December 31, 1895.

for such a long time, and Curry countered that he had additional important evidence to offer, including the testimony of Martha Hyams, who was still confined to her sickbed. Judge Denison continued the case until the following day.[4]

On January 20, the case came back up for hearing, and Crown Counsel Curry announced that an essential witness, a Mr. St. Marie, had relocated to the United States in connection with his job and would be out of Canada for a year. St. Marie refused to appear in court any earlier unless he was indemnified for coming back to Canada. Judge Denison said he would not believe such a witness under oath, and Curry dropped his attempt to procure St. Marie as a witness.

Curry then proposed to drop the conspiracy to murder charges against Harry Hyams and use him as a witness against Dallas. Johnston said that if Curry tried to call Harry as a witness, he would advise Harry to refuse to answer questions. Johnston reasoned that being in jail for contempt was no worse than being in jail on criminal charges. Curry dropped the charges against Harry and put him in the witness stand over Johnston's objection. The direct examination proved brief.

"Where do you reside, Hyams?" Curry asked.

"I live in Toronto Jail."

"Are you married?"

"Martha Hyams is my wife."

"Where did you reside in the summer of 1894?"

---

[4] "News from Toronto," *Montreal Gazette*, January 7, 1896.

"I refuse to answer."

"I appeal to the court," Curry said.

"I'll adjourn for a week to consider the question," Judge Denison replied. Even though conspiracy to murder charges had been dropped against Harry, Denison remanded him to jail on the forgery charges.[5]

On January 28 Denison convened the conspiracy case against Dallas at the Aylesworths' residence, where Martha was confined to her sickbed. She appeared frail from the four months she had spent in bed. The examination lasted an hour and a half, and it did nothing to improve either her health or the Crown's case. She appeared in shock from the strain of having testified.

She said that in June of 1984, when she and her husband were living in Montreal, they applied for a $10,000 policy on her life, but the application did not go through. As far as she knew, Dallas had nothing to do with that application. In December of 1894 she and Harry decided that a $50,000 policy on her life would be a good investment. She went to Toronto to get the policy. While in Toronto, the insurance agent told her that Harry had applied for a $100,000 policy on her life. This news frightened her, but Harry reassured her that the agent was mistaken about the amount of the policy. Again, as far as she knew, Dallas had nothing to do with this second application. She said she had done her husband a great injustice in saying anything that might suggest he planned to kill her. Curry asked if she would give evidence against her husband. She said most emphatically that she refused to testify against him.[6] The conspiracy case

---

[5] "The Hyams Twins," *Windsor Star*, January 28, 1896.
[6] "The Hyams Case," *Montreal Gazette*, January 29, 1896.

against the Hyamses having collapsed, Denison dismissed the case. There were still those forgery charges to detain the brothers, though.

On Saturday morning, February 1, 1896, Wellman and Johnston met with Attorney-General Sir Oliver Mowatt to try to work the case out. They reached an agreement that the brothers would be admitted to bail in a small amount and that they would immediately leave the country, forfeiting their bail. If they ever returned to Canada, the authorities would immediately arrest them on charges of failure to appear for the forgery charges. On Monday, February 3, the brothers appeared in court for the final time. Magistrate Hugh Miller set bond at $750 cash for each of the men, and when the bond had been posted, Wellman took them in a hack directly to Union Station, where they boarded a special train for the United States.[7]

The train had gone barely a dozen miles when Wellman realized that the train had started moving at breakneck speed. "I noticed we were going around the bends and curves at a speed well up to seventy miles an hour. The car window-shades literally stood out at right angles." Wellman called to the conductor and asked that he order the engineer to slow down, or they would all be killed. The conductor replied that he had no way of communicating with the engineer, and that he was just as frightened as Wellman. "You see," he said, "this man has never in his life before handled a passenger train—he's a freight engineer."

The train stopped in Buffalo, where Wellman breathed a sigh of relief to board a regular passenger train for New York City. Wellman persuaded the conductor to have the train stop a few miles short of the terminal, and he loaded

---

[7] "Hyams Twins Gone," *Windsor Star,* February 3, 1896.

the two brothers into a carriage which transported them to Wellman's home. There was still that outstanding warrant from New Jersey for bail jumping, and Wellman did not want to take any chances on the twins getting arrested again.[8]

Wellman reboarded the train, and when he arrived in Grand Central Station the waiting reporters were disappointed to see that he did not have the twins with him. "I do not care to say," he told the reporters, "where I left the Hyams brothers, and I purposely refrained from asking them about their future plans. All that I do know is that these much-persecuted men have gone West with the intention of beginning life all over again. Having gone through so much, it is well to allow them to drop out of sight. Though they have been proved entirely innocent of the crimes imputed to them, they have no redress, because the prosecution was conducted by the officers of the British Crown." Some unnamed informant told the reporters that the Hyamses had parted company with Wellman in Buffalo and taken a train for Chicago, with their eventual destination being either Dakota or Kansas.[9]

Of course, the press had been fed a load of poppycock. The twins hid out at Wellman's home until he could book passage for them on a steamer headed for South America. The twins boarded the steamer and sailed off to Spain, where they spent several weeks deciding where to settle. The decided upon Buenos Aires in Argentina. Since Argentina had no extradition treaty with the United States, it was a perfect refuge for American fugitives from justice. The brothers set up a real estate agency and a brokerage,

---

[8] Wellman, *Luck and Opportunity*, 99.
[9] "Did the Twins Go West?" *Buffalo Evening News*, February 5, 1895.

where they undoubtedly continued the sharp practices which got them in so much trouble in the U.S. and Canada. Harry made no attempt to communicate with Martha, and she never heard from him again.[10] This was not the last she heard from the Hyams family, though. Chapman Hyams set up a trust on her behalf in the sum of US$20,000, with annual payments of the interest to be made to her.[11] The first payment came to her upon her release from the hospital. Her health was recovering quite well, and she left Toronto for a place with a better climate.[12]

Martha's endowment stands in stark contrast to Chapman Hyams' treatment of the Canadian lawyers who defended his brothers. He decided he had spent enough money in Canada and refused to pay the bills of the brothers' Canadian defense team. Francis Wellman stepped in to mediate the dispute, and finally persuaded Chapman Hyams to make payment to them. His fee of US$40,00, however, dwarfed the US$23,000 to be split among the four Canadian defenders. Chapman's treatment of the men who fought so hard to save Harry and Dallas gives good reason to believe that he was not motivated by altruism when he settled the trust on Martha. That US$20,000 trust probably bought her failure to cooperate with the subsequent prosecutions of the twins.

Britton Bath Osler's fame as a barrister of unparalleled ability continued to grow until he became known as the "Tartar of the Bar" because of his matchless ability to conduct cross-examinations of lying witnesses. He continued to try cases at breakneck speed until his health

---

[10] "The Hyams Twins," *Ottawa Daily Citizen,* May 15, 1896.

[11] "Martha Wells Hyams Well Provided For," *The Buffalo Commercial,* February 5, 1896.

[12] "The Hyams Twins," *Ottawa Daily Citizen,* May 15, 1896.

failed in 1901, and he died the following year at the age of sixty.[13]

William Lount went on to become a Justice of the High Court of Ontario and served as a judge until his death in 1903.[14]

Ebenezer Forsyth Blackie Johnston's efforts in the Hyams case gained him a sterling reputation as a criminal defense attorney. He came to be a regular adversary of Osler in the criminal courts, and he gained a reputation as a cross-examiner almost on a par with Osler. According to Hector Charlesworth, "[He] lacked the personal authority and distinction of Osler, and he was less suave and fair in cross-examination." Johnston died at the age of 67 in 1919 after an illustrious career at the bar.[15]

Francis L. Wellman went on to a long and prosperous career as a civil trial lawyer, avoiding criminal cases like the plague. He did, however, defend two more murder cases in New York City, both of which he won.[16] Wellman also gained fame as an author of books on trial advocacy. One of those books, *The Art of Cross-Examination*, is still in print today. Wellman's private practice clientele consisted

---

[13] Brode, "Osler, Britton Bath," *Dictionary of Canadian Biography*; "Mr. B.B. Osler," *Canada Law Journal, 35(9):289-291;* "A Personal Sketch of the Late B. B. Osler," *Canadian Law Journal,* 1:284-285; Hassard, "Great Canadian Orators: Britton Bath Osler," *The Canadian Magazine,* 54(4):353-360.

[14] Johnson, *Canadian Directory of Parliament*, 342.

[15] Bryson, "Johnston, Ebenezer Forsyth Blackie," *Dictionary of Canadian Biography.*

[16] "The Acquittal of Davis," *New-York Tribune*, March 2, 1901; "Garvey's Defence Is an Effort to Prove Alibi," *New-York Tribune,* December 21, 1911; "Taxicab Murder Trial Ends; Judge Frees Prisoner," *New York Evening World*, December 22, 1911.

mainly of lawyers who retained him to try cases for them. In this sense, his practice was close to that of the traditional English barrister, and he liked to call himself a barrister rather than a trial lawyer. Wellman died in 1942 at the age of eighty-seven, having outlived all other lawyers involved in the trial of the Hyams case. At the time of his death, he was credited as being the deadliest prosecutor in the United States, having gotten more guilty verdicts in first degree murder cases than any other American prosecutor.[17] It is unlikely, however, that he sent more men to the electric chair than Britton Bath Osler sent to the gallows.

Hector Charlesworth outlived Wellman, dying in 1945 at the end of a distinguished career as a journalist, author, poet, and chairman of the Canadian Radio Broadcasting Commission. Of all the principles in the case, Charlesworth was the man most responsible for setting in motion the chain of events which resulted in the prosecution of Harry and Dallas Hyams.[18]

---

[17] "Francis Wellman, Lawyer Author, 87," *New York Times*, June 8, 1942.
[18] "Hector Charlesworth, Author and Critic, Dies Suddenly," *Ottawa Journal,* December 31, 1945.

APPENDIX A: BRITTON BATH OSLER'S OPENING STATEMENT[1]

The Introduction:[2] You will have to prepare yourself for the solemn duty imposed upon you by casting aside all you have heard and read. Try and eliminate everything concerning the case and have your minds free to receive the evidence. There is a duty thrown upon you of protecting the community; there is also the duty of protecting and guarding the prisoners. The Crown has to make out its case beyond reasonable doubt. The prisoners cannot be condemned upon suspicion: they cannot be convicted because you think a foul crime has been committed and a scapegoat must be found.

In all crimes of deliberation of purpose, all homicides which are the result of quick passion, it is seldom there is in eye to see or an ear to hear, and in cases of that kind the Crown is necessarily driven to circumstantial evidence. If circumstantial evidence was not allowed, the worst class of crime— the crime of design—would go unpunished. You have nothing to do with the responsibility or with the result, that is for the law. The juror who does not believe in capital punishment and, therefore, finds a verdict of not guilty, is usurping the powers of the legislature. It is not for him to correct the laws which he thinks are erroneous. It is for him as a good citizen to live up to those laws.

The Statement of the Case: Life insurance is one of the most beneficial schemes of modern times. A plan by which the breadwinner of his family can provide for their

---

[1] May 8, 1895.

[2] The text of Osler's speech is taken from "The Hyams Twins on Trial," *Toronto World*, May 10, 1895, and "The Hyams on Trial," *Windsor Evening Record*, May 10, 1895.

necessaries after he is gone is a good one. The allegation of the Crown is, however, that what is most beneficial has been used by the prisoners to gratify their greed, and that they killed a man, by marriage akin to one of them, in order that they might reap the benefits of life insurance to the extent of some C$ 31,000 or C$ 32,000.

The Division: You have to consider, do the circumstances point to the prisoners? Is the appearance of innocence that has been given only an appearance that was designed?

The Confirmation: In the fall of 1889 there was a growing family of four—two women and two men. They were orphans. There was a little money in the family. They had an uncle in Pickering who looked more or less after them. There came to this city the two prisoners, the wife of one of them and the mother. These prisoners came from the United States. The prisoners came to know that the Wells family had some money. The elder brother of the Wells died, leaving William, the alleged murdered boy, and two sisters, Mrs. Aylesworth, and another supposed to be married to Harry Hyams.

In 1892 an agreement was arranged by which the Hyams secured C$ 2700 from Wells and his sisters for the purpose of investing, agreeing to pay therefor C$ 30 a month; to pay the whole back after notice had been given to them to do so, and to pay 13 1/3 per cent interest for the money in the meantime. Eventually the amount of the loan was made up to C$ 3000, C$ 1000 being subscribed by the dead man and C$ 1000 by each of the sisters. Connected with the loan was an agreement to provide for the employment of the deceased and also for his brother-in-law, Aylesworth. This shortly was the relationship as it started. H. P. Hyams subsequently married one of the Wells sisters.

The prisoners had an office at 11 King-street west. It will appear before you that there was not much business carried on. In November 1892, they took a warehouse in Colborne-street and called themselves the Toronto Storage Company. From November 1892, until a period three months after the death of Wells the prisoners ostensibly carried on business in the warehouse. I say ostensibly, because part of the Crown's case is that little or no business was carried on. In that warehouse were employed William Wells, Aylesworth and Miss Latimer. They were paid weekly wages. In the basement of the warehouse on Jan. 16, 1893, William Wells was killed, and the question is whether he was there murdered or whether his death was, as the prisoners allege, caused by an accident by reason of the weight in the elevator shaft falling upon him. You are to ascertain whether that death was by accident or design.

Why should they kill him? In August a life insurance policy was taken out in the New York Life Insurance Company for C$ 30,000, made payable to Martha Wells. There were also in addition a Covenant Mutual policy of C$ 2000 and another policy of C$ 1000 in the New York Life; all these amounts being payable to Martha Wells. The premium on the C$ 30,000 policy had been paid by the Hyams, and H.P. Hyams' bargain with regard to that insurance was that he was to pay the premium and was also to pay Wells in three years C$ 2500 for the use of his money. Harry Hyams also claimed the right to name the beneficiary. There was some talk of making the two sisters the beneficiaries, but Harry Hyams claimed that as he was paying the premiums, he had the right to name the beneficiaries. The first quarter's premium was paid by money handed by one of the prisoners to Wells, who in turn paid it to the agent. Another quarter's premium would have fallen due shortly after the date on which Wells was killed, and this premium would have had to be paid in order to keep the policy alive. Only one quarter's premium was therefore paid. The premiums were payable to Martha Wells.

Now, Harry Hyams and Martha Wells had continued along their courtship, without any talk of marriage, until shortly before New Year's, when marriage was proposed by Harry Hyams, and pressure was brought upon Martha Wells to induce her to consent to become his wife.

Wells' share of the C$ 3000 advanced by himself and sisters to the Hyams had not been paid when the tragedy occurred in the Colborne-street warehouse. Young Wells had gone down to Pickering a few days before and arranged for the purchase of a small farm, it finally being settled that Monday, Jan. 16, Wells and his sister were to go to Pickering to close the negotiations for the purchase of the farm. This was on the explicit understanding that on the 16th Hyams would pay young Wells the C$ 1000 they owed him. Therefore, you see the necessity existed for the payment of the C$ 1000 on the morning Wells was killed.

About the time Wells was killed insurance was placed on the life of the prisoners or one of them. Was that not part of the scheme to throw the insurance company off their guard; to make them think the prisoners had a sort of craze for insurance? It will appear that these policies on the life of the prisoners were allowed to lapse shortly afterwards.

There was little business done in the Colborne-street warehouse, as I have said. It will be for you to say whether the renting of that warehouse was not part of the scheme which culminated in the death of Wells. It will appear that in that warehouse a young woman was employed whose sole occupation was to address envelopes that were never mailed. Now, was that warehouse merely rented to give an appearance of a business with the realization of the insurance on young Wells' life as the ultimate result?

[Osler then turned to the elevator, he described how little-used it was, how the brothers nevertheless continually tinkered with it and made alterations to it. Alterations without which, it would have been impossible for the weight to have fallen on Wells.]

Do all these things lead up to the realization on the policy? Having regard to the limited use of the hoist, what was the object of these changes? The Crown says that, considering the business done in the warehouse, there was altogether too much attention paid to that elevator—that there was an object.

[Finally, he described the events of the day Wells died:]

In the order of events the prisoners, Wells, Aylesworth and Miss Latimer should be at the office that Monday morning. Saturday night Miss Latimer is given three letters to deliver on Monday morning before she comes down. The Crown suggests that was in order that she might be out of the way. That left Aylesworth, however. On Sunday, an order is left for Aylesworth to go over the Don and make some enquiries. Aylesworth is thus out of the way. An order is given for Wells to be down early at the office. Wells is going to Whitby with his sister on the midday train to make the payment on the farm. There is no reason given why he should be down. There were no goods to take in, nothing to be moved from flat to flat. Wells is found dead.

[Osler then recounted some of the inconsistent stories told by the brothers:]

One story in explanation is that Dallas was writing in the office, heard a great noise, ran down, and seeing Wells fell over his dead body in a faint. Another story is that both prisoners heard the noise, and they lifted the weight off the dead boy's head. The prisoners were the only ones there. The Crown says they were designedly the only ones there. There will be some evidence to show than both doors of the warehouse were locked.

The Refutation: It is claimed that the weight slipped from the rope. Were this so, the gravity would bring that weight down pretty straight, even if it had caught. The Crown claims that there was not enough play in the box to give the weight tilt enough to slip off the rope. It will be submitted that the weight could not come off the hook in the shaft as sufficient slack could not be obtained by the rope to slip out of the eye which had to be cut in order that the hook could be inserted. It is suggested that the deceased put his head partly in the shaft to look up to see what prevented the weight coming down. It is apparent that that is the only way there could have been impact between the weight and the head. The weight is found on the head six or eight inches from the platform of the weight shaft.

You have evidences of witnesses as to the condition of the skull as it appears now. The Crown will suggest to you that it was impossible for the weight striking the head, to have caused the wounds found thereon. The Crown will suggest to you that the chief force that came upon that head was a force from the side. The Crown will seek to convince you that there was more than one application of force upon that head to bring it into the condition that it was. It will be for you to say whether a weight falling upon a man under any circumstances could produce the lines of force from different directions found on this head.

Shortly, then, we say, that it is impossible with relation to the elevator shaft and the position of the body that the weight could have caused that death. We say that the head tells the same story. You will have evidence as to the bloody hands of Harry Hyams and the contradictory stories of the prisoners. You must give due weight to these. You will have the evidence of Dr. King, who was first summoned to the warehouse. and of Dr. Aikins, the coroner. Without desiring to reflect in the slightest upon the professional character of these gentlemen, you will recollect that they passed upon the matter at the time of the accident, and that their conduct at the time in so doing is more or less in review. You may or may not consider that that will or will not affect their evidence in the slightest degree.

The Conclusion: I have referred to the courtship of Harry Hymns and Martha Wells. Shortly after the accident, Harry Hyams, who seemed to have Martha Wells pretty well under control, commenced to obtain cheques from her until two amounts of C$ 1700 and C$ 2500 were obtained. About this time, a friend told her that the house and office furniture of the Hyams' were under chattel mortgage. Then she became alarmed and consulted a solicitor. Subsequently she went into retreat in a church school, with a view of breaking off all relations between them. Harry Hyams found her location, visited her, conversed with her and as a result induced Martha to marry him on the following Tuesday. As a result of this marriage, with the exception of C$ 4000 or C$ 5000, given by Martha Wells to her sister, Mrs. Aylesworth, the prisoners have absorbed every dollar of the insurance money. If the prisoner, Harry Hyams, thought in marrying Martha Wells he would have influence enough to secure the insurance, he thought correctly. If their object was to kill in order to get the money that object has been attained.

APPENDIX B: ORDER OF WITNESSES AT FIRST TRIAL
PER JUSTICE STREET'S BENCH BOOK

WITNESS	SYNOPSIS OF TESTIMONY
1: Baker, Francis L.	Architect who made drawings of warehouse floorplan.
2: Aylesworth, Ebeneezer W.H.,	Entire story of the relationship between the Wellses and Hyamses. Events of the fatal day. Statements by the brothers.
3: Bryce, Fraser	Photographer who took pictures of warehouse.
4: Dickie, John	Telegrapher. Identified messages from Willie to his uncle in Pickering.
5: Aylesworth, Annie	Entire story of the relationship between the Wellses and Hyamses. Events of the fatal day. Statements by the brothers.
6: Winters, John R.E.	His business produced some of the information sheets which Willie, Aylesworth, & Miss Latimer copied.
7: Hyams, Martha Wells	Entire story of the relationship between the Wellses and Hyamses. Events of the fatal day. Statements by the brothers.
8: Rice, Omer F.	Banker. Details relating to Martha's bank account.

WITNESS	SYNOPSIS OF TESTIMONY
9: Hogarth, George	Telegrapher. No telegram sent to Uriah Jones on 1/15/1893.
10: Curry, Isaac	Druggist & agent of telegraph company. No telegram sent to Uriah Jones on 1/15/1893.
11: Patton, Harold	Banker. Details of bank accounts of Willie and Martha Wells.
12: Jones, Uriah	Purchase of farm by Willie.
13: Fox, Joseph	Expressman. Circumstances surrounding Hyams' occupation of warehouse & death of Willie.
14: Chambers, James	Liveryman. Rented a coupe driven by James Lavelle to Harry Wells on the morning of January 16, 1893.
15: Lavelle, James	Drove Dallas home on morning of January 16, 1893.
16: Riordan, Jeremiah	Railway conductor who took Harry to get doctor.
17: Nix, William H.	Railway company employee who helped establish time Riordan picked up Harry.
18: Henley, William Herbert	Railway company employee who helped establish time Riordan picked up Harry.

WITNESS	SYNOPSIS OF TESTIMONY
19: Howden, John	Railway company employee who helped establish time Riordan picked up Harry.
20: Gardipey, A.J.	Barber who shaved Harry on the morning of 1/16/1893.
21: Latimer, Mabel Emily	Worker in warehouse. Type of work done there.
22: Henley, William Herbert	Recalled to produce record book.
23: Carney, David	Railway company employee who helped establish time Riordan picked up Harry.
24: Curry, Thomas Allen	Railway company employee who helped establish time Riordan picked up Harry.
25: Hyams, Martha Wells	Cross-examination by the defense.
26:Steen, William	Established approximate time of Dallas sending message to Humphrey to keep his mouth shut.
27: Pengilly, Eliza	Events of the day of Willie's death. Trying to wash blood out of a pair of pants.

WITNESS	SYNOPSIS OF TESTIMONY
28: Wright, John	Plumber friend of Willie's. Inspected elevator shaft. Impossible for hook to come loose.
29: Grandage Jr., Samuel	Lending money to the brothers. Events of Jan 16. Hyams brothers honorable men.
30: Lane, Richard	Lending money to the brothers.
31: McPherson, Dr. Duncan	Lending money to the brothers.
32: Leger, Ogilvie	Insuring of Martha. Ruled inadmissible.
33: King, Dr. Edmund	Being called to the scene of the death.
34: Smoke, Samuel	Financial dealings between Martha and Harry prior to marriage.
35: Richie, William	Purchased items from warehouse after Willie's death. Some of the items had blood on them.
36: Aylesworth, Ebeneezer W.H.	$6 to $7 worth of furniture sold from the warehouse after Willie's death.
37: Humphreys, Benjamin D.	Removal of body from the cellar. Condition of the body.

WITNESS	SYNOPSIS OF TESTIMONY
38: Grundy, George	Insuring Willie Wells.
39: McConkey, G.J.	Insuring Willie Wells.
40: Dart, William	Employee of N.Y. Life.
41: Hughson, Samuel W.	Employee of Covenant Mutual. Insuring of Willie Wells for $2,000. Abortive attempt to insure Harry.
42: Little, Thomas H.	Trying and failing to examine Harry for his Covenant Mutual insurance policy.
43: Deroché, Maximilian	N.Y. Life employee. Willie paying off note for first premium on the $30,000 policy with $500 given him by Harry.
44: Graham, David L.	Had warehouse before Hyamses. Never had any trouble with the elevator.
45: Imrie, John	Partner of David Graham. Confirmed his testimony.
46: Rankin, James	Employee of Imrie & Graham. Operated the elevator almost daily from 1886 to 1892 without any problems.
47: Lee, Charles	Repaired elevator.

WITNESS	SYNOPSIS OF TESTIMONY
48: Thompson, John	Put new hook on counterweight. Had to chisel the hole out to get the hook into the weight.
49: Fensom Jr., John	Employer of John Thompson. "I don't think the weight can come off the hook. I think it would be impossible for the weight to come off whether it were to catch either ascending or descending."
50: Wilson, Joseph	Sold the new hook to Fensom.
51: Kidd, Henry	Installed two gates on the elevator shaft at the first and second floors. Built a platform for the weight.
52: Fryer, Albert E.	Made repairs to elevator after tragedy.
53: Hackney, Charles	Made repairs to elevator after tragedy.
54: Aldridge, John	Made repairs to elevator in October of 1893 after Hyamses vacated the premises.
55: Craig, Donald	Elevator maker who experimented with the elevator & couldn't make the weight fall off.
56: Russell, John	Withdrawn by Crown after being called.

WITNESS	SYNOPSIS OF TESTIMONY
57: Galt, John	Weight could not accidentally come off.
58: Cuddy, Alfred	Harry said he didn't know how much insurance Willie had.
59: Caven, Dr. John	Performed autopsy. Two lines of force produced injuries to skull.
60: Johnson, Dr. Arthur Jukes	Attended autopsy. A least two, and possibly three, lines of force produced injuries to skull.
61: Richardson, Dr. James Henry	Two lines of force necessary to produce injuries.
62: Heidelberg, Charles	Criminal activity of Hyamses in New York City. Testimony suppressed.
63: Pearson, Robert	Criminal activity of Hyamses in New Jersey. Testimony suppressed.
64: Grassett, Dr. Frederick	Two lines of force necessary to produce injuries.
65: MacFarlane, Dr.	Corroborative of first four experts.
66: Sweetman, Dr. Lesslie M.	Corroborative of first four experts.

WITNESS	SYNOPSIS OF TESTIMONY
67: Stark, Insp. William	Weighed the counterweight. It weighed 200 pounds.
68: Mackenzie, Dr. Barton	Corroborative of first four experts.
69: Cotton, Dr. James M.	Corroborative of first four experts.
70: Primrose, Dr. Alex	Corroborative of first four experts.
71: Hackney, Charles	Clarification of previous testimony.
72: Galt, John	Corroboration of Hackney.
73: Peart, George	Identified photo of victim wearing glasses.
74: Aikins, Dr. William H.B.	It was an accident.
75: Teskey, Dr. Luke	Injuries consistent with defense theory.
76: Cameron, Dr. Irving H.	Evidence of only one blow, but more than one may have been struck.
77: Spencer, Dr. Bertram	All injuries appear to come from one blow.

WITNESS	SYNOPSIS OF TESTIMONY
78: Lind, Dr. Adam	All injuries may be caused by one blow.
79: Atherton, Dr. Alfred B.	All injuries may be caused by one blow.
80: Strange, Dr. Frederick W.	All injuries may be caused by one blow.
81: Powell, Dr. Newton A.	All injuries may be caused by one blow.
82: Preston, Robert	Willie demonstrated the elevator to him on 1/15. He experimented with the elevator on 1/18.
83: White, James A.	Saw Preston's experiments on 1/18.
84: Rice, Omer	Banker. Withdrawn as a witness.
85: Moyer, George	Made model of elevator and shaft.
86: Colley, David	Corroborates testimony of George Moyer.
87: Preston, Robert	Father of Robert Preston. Corroborates son's testimony.
88: McCarthy, Dalton F.	Heard the elevator crash from an adjoining basement.

WITNESS	SYNOPSIS OF TESTIMONY
89: Siddall, J.W.	Drew plans of the exterior and interior of the hoist.
90: Bragg, Thomas	Corroborated testimony of Dalton McCarthy.
91: Rosvear, James	Corroborated testimony of Dalton McCarthy.
92: McDermott, Duncan	Worked on the weight shaft after the Hyams brothers vacated the warehouse.
93: McMillan, Joseph	Operated the elevator for ten months prior to the Hyams brothers renting the place. The elevator was unsafe.
94: Maguire, Thompson M.	The weight might fall off.
95: Dryden, Thomas	The weight might fall off.
96: Price, William C.	The weight might fall off.
97: Leighton, H.A.	If the weight became detached, it would fall.
98: Burgess, Mary A.	Received a hand-delivered letter from the Hyams brothers sometime in January of 1893.

WITNESS	SYNOPSIS OF TESTIMONY
99: Rammage, Matthew	Saw Willie enter the warehouse at 8:40. Saw Harry enter the barbershop on Leader Lane at 8:45.
100: Langdon, James	Hyams brothers' warehouse business was legitimate.
101: Palin, Charles J.	Hyams brothers' warehouse business was legitimate.
102: Taylor, Joseph	Hyams brothers' warehouse business was legitimate.
103: White, Octavious	Painted sign on door to warehouse.
104: Neil, John	Saw Dallas Hyams at 11 King Street address between 8:30 and 9:00 on the morning of the tragedy.
105: Westcott, Rod	Gave Dallas Hyams a shave and a haircut commencing at 9:00 or 9:10. It took 52 minutes to give him the works.
106: Collins, Joseph R.	Saw Dallas at the 11 King Street office between 9:00 and 10:00 am.
107: Jessamini, Joseph	Spoke to Dallas at the 11 King Street office a little after 9:00.

WITNESS	SYNOPSIS OF TESTIMONY
108: Shepherd, Joseph	There was a hole between the two basements at the Colborne Street address.
109: Statham, William	There was a hole between the two basements at the Colborne Street address.
110: Brodie, Francis	Dallas made a phony entry in his passbook purporting to show a deposit of $7950 that was never made.
111: Miller, David	Traced money from Martha's insurance proceeds into Dallas' bank account
112: Fensom Jr., John	Willie couldn't pick up the 200 pound weight. Testimony disallowed.
113: Fenton, Edward	Character witness against Rammage. Testimony disallowed.

APPENDIX C: THE ARGUMENTS OF THE LAWYERS[1]

Ebenezer Forsythe Blackie Johnston spoke on behalf of Harry Hyams. Annie Hyams, sitting in the grand jury box, put her handkerchief to her face and burst into tears. She would cry several times during Johnston's three-and-one-half hour summation. Harry and Dallas, deathly pale, sat the entire afternoon with their eyes riveted on Johnston. As he spoke, the twins began to perk up, and by the time that Johnston had finished his speech, they were smiling broadly. The lawyer put his hands in his pockets and leaned toward the jury box. He began: "Thirty-eight years ago two infants were born; they grew to manhood together and have never been separated, and tomorrow you will decide whether these two lives shall go out together at the hands of the hangman." He then cautioned the jurors that their verdict must be grounded in the facts as presented at trial, not on questions of suspicion, and certainly not on what the newspapers may have said. Johnston continued:[2]

These American citizens, who by reason of the laws of this country must be represented by Canadian counsel, are perfectly safe in the hands of a Canadian jury," said Mr. Johnston. "I am assured that the same British justice and British fair play will be vouchsafed them as would be given our own people.

The Crown has had the lives of these prisoners open like a book before them. No stone had been left unturned to secure evidence. The greatest criminal

---

[1] May 22-23, 1895.

[2] Unless otherwise noted, the quotations from Johnston's argument are from "The Fate of the Twins May Be Known To-Night," *Toronto World*, May 23, 1895.

lawyer had been retained, a detective had been on the case for months, the books of the prisoners have been impounded and their daily dealings for months and years laid bare, even the sacred privacy of the letters which passed from Harry Hyams to Miss Wells, prior to the date of their marriage, had been invaded and read, the letters bearing witness to the intense love and affection that he bore for her, and yet the Crown had signally failed in establishing the guilt of these prisoners.

Johnston referred to the old saw that it was better that 99 guilty men go free than that one innocent should be convicted, and then he began to attack Aylesworth's character. "Aylesworth is the keystone of the arch upon which the structure of the Crown's case rests." And a weak keystone Aylesworth had proved to be. Johnston argued that he was "stained with a moral taint" because he kept an apartment separate from his house; he suspected the Hyams brothers of murder from the outset but did nothing; despite his suspicions he continued to work for the twins; he helped his sister-in-law fill out the claims forms for the insurance; he received $4750 "blood money" from the insurance proceeds; he allowed Martha to marry one of the suspected murderers; he went on a fruitless expedition searching for evidence of the Hyams brothers' guilt; he went to gambling houses and racetracks; he frequented pool rooms; he manipulated his wife and sister-in-law into testifying against the brothers; oh, he was a most despicable character!

Johnston then asked two questions: "Was it because Aylesworth did not get the $15,000 on behalf of his wife that he is so bitter against the prisoners? Would he have been In the box against them had he got the money?

"How came Mrs. Harry Hyams here to attempt to hang her husband—one of the most astonishing things in the history of criminal law? She lived with the Aylesworths. She Is a weak woman—need I say more?"[3]

Take away the testimony of Martha, Aylesworth, and his wife, and the Crown's case collapses. There may be evidence of a motive, but proof of motive is not proof of crime. "There must be something more than mere suspicion. There must be facts, hard facts. The Crown cannot point to the supposed motive on the one hand and then point to a supposed crime, and say the crime is the result of the motive. The motive only shows that the person is one likely to have committed the crime. The Crown must prove that there was a crime. If the facts only raise a suspicion of crime and not proof, then you cannot import the motive, and say, by the reason of the motive we will hang the man."

The Crown's theory of how the brothers committed the crime is not only unbelievably complex; if true, it must have been concocted and carried out by a criminal mastermind, with "every detail attended to and thought out and carried out in the most deliberate and wicked manner that was ever heard of and this by two men who, according to the evidence of the Crown, are stupid, ordinary businessmen and more than ordinarily stupid businessmen."

Then Johnston argued that the very facts in connection with the tragedy showed that the men must have deliberately manufactured suspicions against themselves if they were guilty. Why did not they leave the weight lying on the head of the man, thus destroying evidence against themselves, instead of removing it? Why did they leave

---

[3] "Pleaded for the Life of Hyams," New-York Herald, May 23, 1895.

word for Wells to get down early? Why did they send Aylesworth and Miss Latimer out of the way that morning? Why did they leave blood on their clothes and make no attempt to destroy their clothes?

Then Johnston returned to Aylesworth: "I do not wish to cast the slightest shred of suspicion on Mr. Aylesworth as connecting him with the crime, if crime there was." Then he did his dead level best to make Aylesworth look guilty of the murder.

Johnston finally turned to a discussion of the facts of the case: The Crown had tried to show that the $1000 due to Wells had to be paid on the day of the tragedy, and they killed him to avoid paying it. "We dissipated that by two Crown witnesses. Richard Lane swore that he had arranged to advance the Hyams $1000 on Monday, and Dr. McPherson testified that Lane had negotiated with him for $200 of that amount."

He argued that, if it was clear that the weight could not have come off, the brothers would never have given that as a reason for the accident. "Do you think they would give out what they knew in their heart and soul was untrue?" he asked. But the defense had shown that the weight could fall off.

Johnston observed that the Crown had laid a great deal of stress on the medical testimony. He then argued that the medical evidence proved nothing. "They present the skull in court and say there are two blows—one heavy blow on the side of the head, and one from fore to back; and they base this on a piece of bone one-quarter of an inch long and half an inch wide—a state of things which might have been caused by the side of the weight coming on the head, resting on a hard substance. And bear in mind that the

324

Crown doctors were looking for evidences of crime and not of innocence."

Johnston then dealt with the Crown's allegation that the warehouse business was a sham. "We have disposed of that completely; so that we have left on the part of the Crown at best a mere suspicion of murder; aided by the eloquence of the counsel and his ability to turn a joke at the expense of a witness." Johnston argued that the warehouse business was too hard and the Hyams brothers too stupid to make a go of it.

Returning to Aylesworth, Johnston argued that it was Aylesworth, not the Hyams brothers, who was the moving force behind the $30,000 insurance policy; and besides that, they had no hope of getting the insurance proceeds because Martha was the beneficiary.

If the Hyams brothers had taken Wells to the insurance office, and if the policy had been payable to themselves, you might then say there were grounds for grave suspicion. These men were somewhat cranks on the question of insurance. Long after the tragedy Dallas paid something like $4000 to carry the insurance on his own life, and before his arrest he was making efforts to reinsure. But what are the facts as to this insurance? The evidence of Grundy, untouched by the moral taint of the bias, the prejudice or the passion of Aylesworth shows that Wells insured his own life for $1000, and at the time promised more insurance. Then Grundy recommends to him the 20-year endowment plan. There is nothing to show that the Hyams, although acquainted with Grundy, had any involvement in the transaction. Take away Aylesworth's biased testimony, and "you will find it is an honest state of facts which may happen to you or to me any day of our existence."

Now, take this significant fact. If these two prisoners were in a conspiracy jointly to kill Wells after the insurance had been placed—and the evidence shows that Dallas was insuring his own life in the interests of his brother, knowing that this brother was a murderer at heart at that time—do you believe that he would have put his head on the executioner's block, because precisely the same opportunities might exist for murder in the one case as in the other?

At the time of the tragedy, the companies interested investigated the facts and satisfied themselves that this was a proper claim to pay, and they paid it, and the man prominent in getting the claim paid was Aylesworth, with the suspicions rankling in his mind that something was wrong.

How could Dallas have any interest in the insurance? He was a married man. Neither had Harry any interest unless he married Martha Wells. The Crown asks you to say that he took the risk; that if she got the money, she was independent of either of them for a home, and that she might not marry Harry.

Having those risks, having that doubt as to the possession of the money, not knowing that they could ever handle a dollar, the Crown asks you to believe they committed a murder, almost unparalleled in the history of Canada, a crime that must have been committed by a man farseeing, deliberate, cunning, crafty—a damnable man—on the mere chance of marrying a woman who was to benefit by the insurance. Is it reasonable that a man should do this? We are not speaking of a romance that we read at our fireside, which has been ingeniously woven together by the author. We are not speaking of a newspaper report, which has perhaps half of its facts in the writer's brain.

Remember, in this connection, there are many accidents that remain unexplained, many circumstances in our own history which time alone can reveal and make clear. There was no eyewitness of the deed. So far as the Crown case is concerned, no man could be called to show how this thing occurred. Therefore, you must exercise more than ordinary caution, more than ordinary care.

You must be satisfied beyond all reasonable doubts that the insurance had its inception in guilt and its execution in crime. Think of a man who has committed murder going straight to the sister of the man he has slain; think of him taking this sister to the altar and pledging his heart and soul; think of them living as man and wife for two years, with all the relationship that husband and wife must bring; think of the honeymoon. Then you must think—that no man, not a fiend incarnate, not lower than the lowest spirit in the depths of hell itself, could do and live as the Crown alleges Harry Hyams did.

Johnston turned his attention to Dallas Hyams. Johnston admitted that $19,000 gotten from Martha Wells had been paid on the same day to retire a chattel mortgage on the twins' household furniture, but he argued that was not proof that Dallas Hyams was guilty of murder. The fact that $19,000 was transferred from Montreal to Toronto did not show that it was Martha's insurance money. The twins were doing a large business, and besides, they had received $16,000 from their American relatives. They were sure of receiving $200 a month. It arrived as regularly as clockwork.

Then Johnston returned to the elevator. The brothers had repeatedly warned Wells it was dangerous. Someone had been engaged to put gates on the elevator, to place it in workable shape and to make it secure, and yet the Crown says that all this time the twins were planning a murder.

Next Johnston referred to the evidence of McCarthy, Preston, and Rammage, which he claimed was fully believable because they had not been shaken by the Crown. The Crown had insinuated that the men were being paid. Certainly, they were paid. They left their jobs and came from a foreign country. Shouldn't they get compensation equal to what they lost? Should that destroy the value of their evidence? "If you believe the evidence of McCarthy, that he heard the whistling, the falling of the weight and the call of 'Wells' or 'Willie' and the footsteps you will acquit."

Johnston next mentioned the alibi, which he claimed that the two barbers proved conclusively, and the testimony of others who said they saw the brothers on the morning of the tragedy. The fact that Dallas was sick and unable to eat told in his favor. Would a man who could scheme and carry out a tragedy of this kind be likely to be affected that way?

Mr. Lount would deal more fully with the contradictory statements made by Harry, but it was reasonable for him to break the news of Willie's death to Martha and her sister as gently possible. "And if he did not tell the exact truth, even if he did tell a falsehood the Recording Angel, as he flew up to Heaven's chancery with such a falsehood as that, would drop a tear and blot it out."

In conclusion, Johnston said that even if the jurors said eleven one way and one the other, the man who was alone was entitled to the same consideration as the majority.

Then he mentioned the aged mother and the weeping wife, who asked for an acquittal, not only to prevent their aged mother from going down to her grave with the knowledge that her sons are murderers; but that an acquittal could reconcile the misguided wife who had testified against them and send her back to the wronged husband to ask his pardon for the harm she had done him. And with that last appeal to the sympathy of the jury, Johnston concluded his summation.

Court recessed, and the reporters swarmed the lawyers looking for comments. They were a tight-lipped group. Wellman refused to predict what the jury would do but said he was hopeful. "It rests with the jury now. The defense has been as strong as we could make It. We have been treated courteously here and we have no fear of injustice. We think we have made out a convincing case for the defense. As to that, the jury must decide." Osler said that in the case of an acquittal he would hold the prisoners in jail pending the resolution of the reserved case that Justice Street had given him.[4] Courtroom observers were predicting either an acquittal or a hung jury.[5]

There was one piece of drama the next day that went unnoticed at the time. It occurred in the robing room, where barristers put on their uniforms for court proceedings. Like English barristers, Canadian barristers wore robes; but they did not wear the horsehair wigs that adorned the heads of their English counterparts. Wellman went into the robing room to speak to Osler. Wellman described Osler as "a great bulk of a man, well over six feet

---

[4] "Pleaded for the Life of Hyams," New-York Herald, May 23, 1895.
[5] "Hyams Trial Closes Today," Buffalo Evening News, May 23, 1895; "Trial of the Hyams Twins," Buffalo Commercial, May 23, 1895.

in height and over two hundred pounds in weight, his face and hands terribly scarred and disfigured" from rescuing his wife from their burning home. Wellman found Osler robed and pacing the floor. Wellman recalled, "He was walking at such a pace that his silk robe almost stood out at right angles. I had to trot to keep up with him." Wellman asked Osler if the Crown contemplated bringing any further charges against the twins. Wellman said that, in the event of an acquittal, he intended to charter a private train to rush the twins back to the U.S., but he would not do so if further charges were brought.

Osler stopped abruptly, wheeled about, and peered down at the much smaller Wellman. "Mr. Wellman," he said, "you have done all you possibly could do for these two clients of yours, but you need give yourself no further concern about them. We do things very differently her in Canada than you do in the States. Just three weeks from tonight these two young countrymen of yours will hang right outside this courtroom."

At 10:00 a.m. William Lount began his summation before a packed courtroom. Justice Street interrupted his summation to give the jury an hour's break for lunch, after which Lount spoke until 4:16 p.m., and it was universally acclaimed a wonderful speech. He opened his speech by saying:[6]

> I do not feel that I can cover all the ground. My memory is not capable of grasping all events, and where I fail, I pray you gentlemen to help me out, for the life of a man hangs upon your memories, depends upon your recollection. Help me out, for you yourselves are more

---

[6] Quotations from counsel's speeches are taken from "An Anxious Day for the Twins," *Toronto World*, May 24, 1895.

responsible than I. My learned friend who will follow me will do his duty as he always does for the Crown with hard, strong, and almost cruel strength to bring home conviction against these men. His Lordship also when he has delivered to you an impartial and proper charge will have only helped to guide you. But, at the last, you gentlemen have got to pass the fiat. You have got to say the word. Each of you individually, not collectively, as you shall answer your God, have got to say these men are guilty beyond all possible doubt. It is your word that sends them to the gallows, and yours alone. You have, therefore, much more than anyone else, the duty, the terrible responsibility, of pronouncing against them.

I think I might have said at the close of the case for the Crown that the case had failed. Indeed, at the close of the Crown case I had some doubt as to whether to proceed with the evidence for the defense. No doubt there were many suspicions, many circumstances that might lead you to the presumption that these persons may have been guilty. But it is only a presumption, only a suspicion. And suspicion cannot in this country be regarded as sufficient to convict a man of the smallest crime, let alone the highest. I repeat I might have asked at the close of the evidence for the Crown: Where is your case? Where is your evidence that these men should be marched from here and at some later day be hanged by the neck until they are dead? I might, as I have said, leave the case in your hands confident that you could not say in your inmost souls there was evidence to convict. Everything, it may be said, has not been made clear. But has not the guilt been lifted from the shoulders of these men?

Circumstantial evidence is a dangerous thing to convict upon. It may be done, it has been done, and after conviction proof, undeniable proof, has turned up that the man hanged was innocent.

Men have been caught almost red-handed in crime, have been arrested and hanged, although innocent. I want you to believe, gentlemen, that your own lives are no more secure than the lives of these two men.

No matter how powerfully my learned friend may argue, I ask you here to look and listen, to weigh what he says with great care. He has a reputation of freeing the guilty, and I might almost say of convicting the innocent. He has that power language, he has that force of expression, he has that terrible power of convincing, he has that strength of voice and that awful influence over jurors that sometimes may lead you astray. Don't let yourselves be swayed from the line of perfect truth. Don't let your minds be influenced by anything that I may say, by anything that he may say, that is not perfectly in the line of truth and evidence.

Lount then got down to the particulars of the case. He outlined the circumstances attending Willie's death and made a point that the warehouse was in a busy section of town, and that the basement and first floor windows were clearly visible to passersby, where a cry help would certainly have been heard. He then turned to the testimony of Dr. King and Coroner Aikins:

Two men sworn to do their duty arrive at the premises shortly after the occurrence, examine the dead body, examine all the surroundings, investigate to their fullest ability the circumstances surrounding the death. While the circumstances were fresh, while the proofs were plain, while nothing could be disguised, they came to the conclusion that death was due to accident and there was no cause for suspicion. The companies interested, who were bound to enquire as to whether it was accident or design, made the most careful scrutiny and concluded it was an accident. Then a suspicion was engendered, how, I may show you later, and Detective Cuddy and other detectives, keen, sharp, vigilant, investigated the facts and could find no suspicion of wrong doing.

So the affair passed by. The prisoners, not prisoners then, remained here. They did not fly. They were not bound to remain. They belong to another country. They received their support from a brother resident in another land. They were as free to come and go as the wind is to pass to and fro. But they stayed because they were innocent. Two years and a half slipped by. Then the public mind became aroused. The newspapers started a crusade against those who had insured and against those on whom the receipt of that insurance cast suspicion, After the witnesses had died or disappeared, after the opportunities for defense had been minimized, some person aroused the suspicion that because there was $30,000 insurance on young Wells' life he had been murdered. Then the case was dragged from the grave in which it was buried and lifted up to the public eye and proclaimed broadcast. A vile press, which cares, not whether it kills a mail or kills his character, aroused the public mind against these prisoners—pilloried them, blazoned them forth as criminals, characterized them as murderers, damned them as much as it could. In black headlines and strong words it wrote them down. You all know how public opinion can be aroused, and public opinion was prepared for the guilt of these men before they were placed on trial. You all know what influence a newspaper has upon the public mind, and you all know what was said of these men ever since their arrest. All men ought to have a fair trial. These men have not had a fair chance. And here, gentlemen, let me ask you to blot from your minds, if it ever got possession of them, everything that you have read.

Let us come to the evidence. The Crown starts out with the proposition that fraudulent insurance means murder. It is not a true nor proper doctrine. There may be many fraudulent insurances, but no murder. But if murder is first established, then you may invoke for the purpose of trying to find the person who committed the crime the fact that insurance was effected.

I have indicated to you that the cause of their arrest was by reason of some other insurance matters where crime was said to have been associated. After two long years had passed, after opportunities had passed away to prove their guiltiness, after chances had passed that they might have availed themselves of, after witnessed had wandered from the city. These circumstances call for more care on your part that we do not suffer unjustly by the long delay.

Was there ever in history, poetry or romance such a plot depicted? There is more scheming, planning, and villainy, according to the Crown in the maneuvering of these prisoners, than the most careful scheming villain ever yet perpetrated in the records of crime. There is enough material to write a romance that would dazzle the mind. I challenge anyone to believe in it. Yet my learned friend will endeavor to uphold this romance of his and ask you to believe that which the most imaginative mind scarcely could conceive, will ask you to believe that those two men, physically and mentally weak, could conceive such a crime. All their record in this city shows their incapability of committing crime or conducting business. They were failures in most things they undertook, twin-born in the old age of their mother, weaklings, you are asked to believe, that they plotted all this successfully and brought about the death of one for whom they both had a love. You can read this in the letters written by Harry to his fiancé when there was no idea of anything wrong, when there was no plotting and scheming.

There you read that Harry Hyams loved with a devoted love the woman who turned against him. I pray God never again in my life to see such a thing. Oh, it was pitiful—a wife who swore at the altar to love and honor her husband for the first time in the history of crime goes voluntarily to swear against him!

To refute the Crown's contention that the prisoners were pressed for money at the time they placed the insurance on Wells' life, Lount reminded the jury of the $200 per month allowance from relatives in the United States. The money may have been sent to the mother, but it was for the household expenses of the twins.

He then attacked the Crown's contention that the prisoners rented the Colborne Street warehouse for the purpose of perpetrating crime. He argued that Lane advised the prisoners to take premises, not because he thought they would succeed, but because he thought they could lose money slower there than anywhere else.

On and on he went, covering much the same ground as had Johnston, answering every point in favor of the Crown. Toward the end Lount again took aim at the trio of Osler, Aylesworth, and Martha. Referring to Osler, he said, "My learned friend is subtle almost as the old serpent. He can make black white, or white black. He can reason from one premise to another, and almost convince your judgment, but he cannot get over solid facts." Turning to Aylesworth, Lount said: "The man responsible for all the present troubles is Aylesworth, a man with the heart of a devil, and a scheming, subtle intellect, who by his own record is an unworthy, detestable, devilish man. ... Every word he utters appears a lie, and if not a lie at least tainted, polluted and foul. How can you put to your lips a, drop of such putrid water as flows from such a stream?"

As for Martha, Lount said: "I have no sympathy for that woman. Her tears while she was in that witness box may have affected you at the time. But I say that a woman who can stand there and assist in sending her husband to the gallows is a woman without heart or soul. A woman with such a character is entitled to no sympathy. There is no such hate as that of a woman who has once loved the object of her hate. There is no crime she won't do, no wrong she won't descend to do, for she knows not the limit of wrong." Of course, the answer to this argument was that Martha spoke up in self-defense after she discovered the insurance plot against her own life; but Justice Street had ruled that vital evidence inadmissible.

Lount closed his summation with an argument which the *Toronto World* described as an appeal *ad captandum*:

If you acquit these men, you say to that wife over there, with her little child waiting at home for her father; "Go, God bless you; your husband is free; his life is saved; take him back to your heart. We give him to you." Oh! gentlemen, give him to her. It is not asking a great deal; but it is asking a human life to a poor weeping wife, and the poor old mother who is waiting for word to come. Give her the life of her son Harry and her son Dallas. They were born to her years ago, in her old age, and she looked. upon them when they were young, babbling children, when life was before them, and she believed in their happy future. Do not destroy it by one fell word. Give her the life of her two boys, born in one day and hour. And, oh! gentlemen, give to that unhappy wife the chance in years to come, when perhaps time shall have obliterated her bitterness and taken out of her soul that foolish, inexplicable horror [she] has of her husband, of being able to say: "Thank God the jury acquitted you, and I have you my husband now." Give her that chance. It is in your power to confer it; I pray you do so.

This, of course, is an appeal to emotion regardless of the evidence. Aristotle wrote of this type argument: "It is not right to pervert the judge by moving him to anger or envy or pity—one might as well warp a carpenter's rule before using it."[7] Such an argument is fallacious, but it is powerful, especially when arguing to an audience which has limited intellectual firepower.

After speaking for a little more than five hours, Lount surrendered the floor to Britton Bath Osler, who immediately shredded Lount's *argumentum ad captandum*:

The easiest thing for us all, gentlemen of the jury, is to accede to the request of my learned friend. It is a

---

[7] *Rhetoric*, §1356a.

hard thing for us all to endanger the lives of the prisoners at the bar. The easiest thing for me to say is, "Give them back to their friends," and for you to do. But you and I have more serious work than that. You represent the community, selected to decide whether a crime has been committed or no. The safety of other lives is in your hands. The pure administration of justice is with you.

Mercy is not for you; sympathy is not for you. It is easy to raise emotions when lives are in danger and weeping friends are around, but emotion has no place here. Emotion is but a perverter of reason in the court of justice. Men who ask for sympathy with the fruits of their crime before them, because their friends are dragged down in their disgrace, should think of their friends before they commit the crime, and if they have no mercy on their friends, if they put the mother and the wife in trouble, in danger, they cannot ask you to do that which they have not done themselves.

Osler then dealt with the *argumentum ad hominem* of defense counsel against himself, the Aylesworths, and Martha.

Now, I have been pleased with the powerful address of my learned friends, I only complain of a little unnecessary abuse, first of myself—whom they abused with honey—and then of Aylesworth and his sister-in-law and wife—whom they abused with vitriol. I would have preferred my learned friends had said nothing with regard to myself; it is a matter of taste. I do not think anything should have been said. The only remark I have to make is this: In my experience of jury trials, The only success that a man has at the bar is in endeavoring to deal with the facts only. The counsel who distorts facts and does not place them fairly before the jury does not succeed in his case. The warning my learned friends gave you against me was intended to draw your minds from the facts and unload upon me that which they cannot meet in the evidence.

A special attack has been made upon Aylesworth, and it is suggested he keeps a room for gambling. Well, if you disbelieve all who gamble you will have a hard time getting through. There are gamblers in corner lots, in wheat, and on the Exchange; and there are those who get at it more directly by means of poker or prefer the horse. I do not distinguish much between them; and yet, who has not taken a drive at a corner lot, bet on a horse, or put up a little on a wheat margin? It does not affect their truth in the box. When you find a witness subject to abuse without counsel turning up what he has sworn to, beware of the counsel, he is afraid of his case, as made by that witness.

Osler then argued that Wells died by violence; his body was found in the possession of the Hyams brothers; these facts carried the Crown's burden of proof, and now it was incumbent on the defendants to prove the violence was accidental. This argument was something of a *non sequitur*; simply finding the defendant in possession of a dead body does not prove the defendant committed murder. The argument is also objectionable as "burden shifting." The burden of proof never shifts from the Crown to the defense.[8]

---

[8] *Regina v. S.K.*, 2003 CanLII 38448 (Ontario Ct.App., 2003).

Even though they were not required to do so, the defense had explained how the death could have occurred by accident. Osler attacked this theory:

Mr. Lount gave you the theory of the defense. He says the hook was left as Preston saw it left. The young man went to pull the cage down with the hook in the shape Preston had warned him of the afternoon before. Lowering the cage he hoisted the weight, and the weight caught, and he looked up. Gentlemen, the weight catches when the hook is in that position, before the weight is out of sight, as it reaches the end of the roof. The weight hangs out to the south, as you saw it, two or three inches, and when it caught, according to the theory of my learned friends, it was in sight, right before him.

There was no need to get under it to look up. But it may be said that, with the full knowledge of his danger, he tries to squeeze the weight up the chute, with a margin of from an eighth to a quarter of an inch. The chute is measured and a difference is found of an eighth of an inch between the Crown's and the defense's measurements. You are asked to believe that the young man, having guided the weight up into the shaft, knowing, as he must have known, that the hook was not caught, knowing that it was in a dangerous condition, stood there looking at it, pulling with the pull-rope, seeing if he could get it up, and then it falls upon his face, which was almost in a horizontal position on account of his wearing glasses, and according to the theory of the defense leaves not a mark behind.

Osler continued his argument, point by point demonstrating the theory of murder to be reasonable and the theory of accident to be unreasonable. The biggest obstacles to the theory of murder came from Dr. King, the Hyams brothers' physician, and Dr. Aikin, the coroner. Osler's method of dealing with this adverse testimony was much different from the way Johnston and Lount dealt with the testimony of Martha and the Aylesworths:

> Dr. King seemed to give his evidence frankly and freely. He was not, however, apparently unfriendly to the prisoners. He was their medical man, the guardian of their health, and brought into personal contact with them while attending them in illness.

> It is also to be remarked that the prisoners gave the alarm, to him, and not to any of the neighbors Who were within a few feet of them. This thing happened in a thickly populated district, but no word is passed to any of their neighbors; but, whatever hour it was, they can go up some little distance to Dr. King's office and bring him down.

> The coroner is here more or less justifying the fact that he did not hold an inquest. I do not think he should think so, but he evidently gave his evidence under the impression that he had to justify himself as coroner for refusing to hold, an enquiry. The reasonable position he should have taken is that he did not know the moral circumstances surrounding the matter. Being told it was an accident, he perhaps somewhat carelessly accepted the statement. I need not say anything more harsh against the gentlemen you saw here.

There is far less backfire potential in Osler's undermining the doctors than in the defense's *ad hominem* attack on Martha and the Aylesworths. If the jurors had any

341

sympathy at all for Martha, the defense attack could have potentially steered them toward a guilty verdict.

At 6:00, Justice Street halted Osler's argument and called a recess for the night. The *New-York Herald* waxed poetic in describing the day's events:

> When Mr. Lount, Q. C., said the last word on behalf of the prisoners this afternoon, after an eloquent address of more than five hours, the prospects of the Americans seemed hopeful Indeed. Within an hour, B. B. Osler, Q. C., for the Crown, with his speech not half finished, seemed to have dragged the twins back into the shadow of the gallows. His wonderful arrangement of the Crown's evidence, together with his striking personal magnetism, leaves their lives in the balance until Judge and jury have their say to-morrow. To-morrow Is the Queen's birthday, but so vital are the interests at stake that Mr. Justice Street has decided to hold court without regard to the holiday. In spite of the great confidence of the Crown's attorneys and the knowledge that Mr. Osler, most dangerous of all Queen's counsel, is making the effort of his life, public expectation leans toward a disagreement of the jury.

On the next day, the last day of the trial, a mob of would-be spectators descended on the courthouse. The streets were so crowded around the courthouse that Justice Street had difficulty fighting his way in. A posse of uniformed police officers came to his rescue, charging into the crowd and forming a phalanx around him. They then plowed through the crowd and escorted him safely to the door. After the judge was safely inside, the police barred all the doors to the courthouse, turning away hundreds of disappointed would-be spectators.[9]

This was a great day in the history of the British Empire, one which would not be repeated until February 6, 2002. It was the 76th birthday of Queen Victoria, and it was a holiday throughout the Empire. Wellman would later recall, "It was the Queen's birthday, and all the bells in the city were solemnly tolling in her honor. It was all in all the most impressive occasion I had ever witnessed in a courtroom and I had already seen a good many."[10]

When court convened at 10:00 a.m., the first order of business was for Osler to conclude his argument. He had spoken for an hour the day before, and he would speak for another two hours and fifteen minutes.[11] The *Toronto World* called his speech a "mighty marshalling of the facts." Osler began by pointing out that the $200 per month stipend sent by their American relatives had ceased several months before Willie's death because the mother had returned to the United States.

He next spoke of the day Willie died: "Do the facts both before and after point to guilt? No general alarm is given; no neighbors are called in; the premises are kept locked; the family doctor is sent for; Dallas leaves in a coupe, the driver of which tells us there were stains on his trousers below the knee. ... Dallas refuses to see anybody. He locks himself up in the house. Fox cannot see him. Aylesworth cannot see him. He does not come out until the funeral is over.

---

[9] "Unanimous as to Guilt," *Toronto World*, May 25, 1895.

[10] Wellman, *Luck and Opportunity*, 96.

[11] This part of Osler's argument, as well as the instructions which Justice Street gave the jury, comes from "Unanimous as to Guilt," *Toronto World*, May 25, 1895.

When Grandage comes to the door that morning to collect his long past due note, he tells you that blood could be seen on H. P. Hyams—blood splashes on the shirt front, on the cuff, on the collar. Some of those splashes are seen when he comes to the Aylesworth house, about 12.30. Small splashes of blood like that are very different to smears. A man handles a bloody object and receives smears of blood. A man at the killing with blood spurting would get these small splashes.

Osler then cataloged the brothers' many conflicting statements about Willie's death: "Let us consider the statements of the prisoners as to the event. Are they consistent? Are they proper? Do they fit in with the other evidence? If so, give the prisoners the benefit, but if they are not consistent, and do not fit in with the evidence, then, they are to be taken strictly against the prisoners. Here are the statements:

First, H.P. Hyams' statement to Aylesworth: "There has been an accident at the warehouse, and Willie was hurt pretty badly." Then he says when he went in, he found Dallas lying across Willie; that Dallas had fainted; he didn't know how it happened; the weight must have struck and killed him; Willie must have been fixing the weigh.

To Mrs. Aylesworth: "Willie has broken his collar bone; I went to the warehouse and found Dallas lying across Willie."

To Martha Wells: "The weight fell on him and broke his collar bone." That was the first explanation. Afterwards: "Mina. I assure you, I was not there; I went downstairs and found Dallas fainting across Willie."

To Fox: "We have had a fatal accident; Willie, is killed; the elevator weight broke loose; Willie and Dallas were doing something to the hoist, and the weight broke loose."

There is the statement of H. P. Hyams, telling as closely as possible how it happened; that Willie and Dallas were doing something with the hoist and the weight broke loose. Poor Willie is killed, the weight had killed him. Dallas or his brother was upstairs fixing the weight and it slipped down. He was not there at the time. When he came in his brother was running about like a crazy man, and he sent him home in a hack.

To John Wright, a friend of the dead man: Wright looked up the shaft and said: "I suppose he must have been looking up this way," and H. P. Hyams said: "Yes, I suppose so."

To Dr. King: "An accident had happened to the young man. For God's sake, hurry up, for we don't know whether he is killed or not. The hoist was out of order and the weight came down and struck him on the head."

To Humphrey, the undertaker: "The weight fell through three stories."

Now are these stories consistent? Are they probable or improbable? Are they statements of fact or are they not? I don't ask you to give any weight to the first stories told at the house, that his collar bone was broken. I quite conceive the reasonableness of the contention as to that. A statement of that sort, breaking the news to relatives, is as consistent with innocence as guilt.

Here are the statements of Dallas:

To Aylesworth: "I had gone to the office to write a letter; heard a crash and went to the cellar and saw the weight on Willie."

To Mrs. Aylesworth: "I would rather it was my own brother than Willie Wells. I had gone to write a letter and was drawing off my coat when I heard a crash. I went to the cellar and found Willie pinned to the earth by the weight."

To Martha Wells: "I would rather it was my own brother. I went to write a letter to my wife. I heard a terrible crash; went to the cellar and found Willie. It turned me sick."

To Eliza Pengelly: "Had a terrible accident in the warehouse. Wells was killed."

Those are the statements made by Dallas, with the exception of the statement made to Fox, a year after, when he sent the message to Humphreys, the undertaker "Go to Humphrey and tell him to keep his mouth shut."

Consider these statements of Dallas in light of the evidence they have showing that he was on the premises at the time of the accident, which is true, and the evidence of the witnesses they have produced as to the time to try and make out that he was not there, or the statement that he gave within a day or two after.

Osler next described the numerous alterations to the elevator which made the "accident" possible; how Harry and Dallas fleeced Martha of almost the entire $30,000 proceeds of Willie's insurance policy. He then turned to a defense of the prosecution witnesses:

I will say a few words upon the principal witnesses we have had. First there is Aylesworth. I made some general remarks applicable to him. Why should he be disbelieved? Does his story fit in with the rest where he is speaking of facts other witnesses spoke of? Is there a disagreement or is there an agreement? Are not all the facts he speaks of confirmed and corroborated? My learned friends have spent a great deal of time in the abuse of Aylesworth, calling him "devil," and using also strong language in regard to him. But did they put their finger upon one single item of his evidence and show that it was wrong? I tell you that you can eliminate Aylesworth altogether from this case and the facts remain. Aylesworth's evidence is not necessary to the Crown's case. There is Mrs. Aylesworth: she gave a certain amount of evidence and got a certain amount of abuse.

Then there is the wife. What of her? How did she impress you? Did she impress you as a poor woman suffering under conflicting emotions, grieving for the death of her only brother; shaking like a leaf in the box; grieving over the terrible position she was in as the wife of one of the prisoners? Surely no one told a more pitiful tale in more truthful words. If the evidence of the eye and the ear is anything, surely you can judge of it. Do you believe her? Can you reject her? What are the words made use of by my learned friend, Mr. Lount, in regard to the poor woman? Are they true of her? "Lost to honor, pride and shame." These are the words the prisoners put into the mouth of their counsel. You are asked to say that this is a true description of that woman, coming from those men (pointing to the prisoners.) You are asked to find for the prisoners; to find against the wife. Yes, my learned friends say truly and with force, "What terrible event has happened, what terrible thing operated in the mind of that woman to bring her into the box to testify against her husband?" I ask the same question: what terrible thing has happened which compels that woman to go into the box? And do not fail to realize that her brother was the dead victim of these men, and that she was the living victim? Yes, something happened. But my learned friends do not dare to ask her what it was, although they could have done so. They content themselves by saying that she is "lost to honor, pride and shame," but they dare not ask why she was there. They content themselves with abuse. They ask you to reject that poor woman's oath and find that there was some reason why she went into the box. But the reason they have carefully avoided finding. Yes, something happened that has persuaded her mind that it was her duty to come forward and testify against the men whom she believes had committed this deed.

In this part of his speech Osler came dangerously close implying exactly why Martha had testified, but he could not outright say that she testified because they were planning to kill her, too. Justice Street had ruled that evidence inadmissible.

Osler then spent some time discrediting the defense witnesses, and he was finally ready for his concluding remarks, which dealt with circumstantial evidence and the many safeguards surrounding a capital murder prosecution:

Will you reject circumstantial evidence and say you won't act upon it? When you say that you deliver every man who commits a deliberate crime. All calculated

348

murders, all crimes that are not on the impulse of the moment are brought home by circumstantial evidence, and by it alone. The man who plots a murder so that there shall be no eyewitness would otherwise escape. And is the arm of the law so slack that he who in the heat of the moment strikes another and slays him with witnesses around him, unable to control his temper, is the only one to answer for his life? That is what happens if you reject circumstantial evidence. Then, gentlemen, my learned friends warn you of your individual responsibility in this matter. You have a grave responsibility. But look at the safeguards surrounding the lives of those in peril in the dock. The magistrate must first be satisfied that there is evidence to commit, then the grand jury must be satisfied that there is evidence of crime to be answered, then you have to be satisfied. Even if they are condemned to death the judge, who has also to be satisfied, has to report to the Minister of Justice; then the latter and the Governor in council have to take each line of the evidence ponder over it and consider it before lives are taken. Under the law, as it now stands, the Minister of Justice can order a new trial if not satisfied with the evidence; the Attorney-General can consent to a motion for a new trial if he is dissatisfied, or a judge can order a new trial. All these safeguards exist. Yours, withal, is the greater responsibility. Your words are of life or death. No sentiment, no emotion must be allowed to weigh. Bring your reason to bear upon the case and it alone. Judge as you would be judged, Give the benefit of all reasonable doubt to the prisoner. Having done that, if the conclusion you come to is that of guilt, do your duty like men.

Courtroom observers agreed that Osler's masterful speech had effectively cancelled out the lengthy speeches of counsel for the defense. The glum expressions on the twins' faces seemed to signal that they shared in that view. The lawyers had done their part and could do no more; but the jury would receive one other speech. Justice Street had the duty to "sum up" the evidence on both sides to help the jury arrive at their verdict. In modern courtrooms south of the Great Lakes, the judge has a very limited role in this "summing up." The judge can only instruct the jury on the law as it applies to the case and instruct them on general rules for weighing the evidence. The judge must never even hint to the jury which side of the case the judge prefers. Under the British system the judge could also discuss the evidence and make suggestions to the jury as to how they might evaluate these items of evidence. In Canada at that time the judge had great power to influence the jury toward one verdict or the other.

WORKS CONSULTED

About Us | St. Helen Catholic School (tcdsb.org), https://www.tcdsb.org/schools/sthelen/AboutUs/Pages/default.aspx

"Acquittal of the Hyams Twins Viewed with Alarm." *The Insurance Economist*. Vol. 19, No. 147. New York: January, 1896. Page 11.

Albany Law Journal. Vol. 51, No. 20. Albany NY: Albany Law Journal Company. May 18, 1895, page 310.

Birchall, Reginald. *Birchall: The Story of His Life, Trial and Imprisonment, as Told by Himself*. Toronto: The National Publishing Company, 1890.

Bostwick, Charles F., et al., eds. *The Brief of Phi Delta Phi*. Vol. II. Lancaster, PA: New Era Press Printing Company, Oct. 1899-June 1900.

Brode, Patrick. "Osler, Britton Bath." *Dictionary of Canadian Biography*, vol. 13, University of Toronto, http://www.biographi.ca/en/bio/osler_britton_bath_13E.html.

Brode, Patrick. *Death in the Queen City: Clara Ford on Trial, 1895*. Toronto: Natural Heritage Books, 2005.

Bryson, J. Kristin. "Johnston, Ebenezer Forsyth Blackie." *Dictionary of Canadian Biography*, vol. 14, University of Toronto, http://www.biographi.ca/en/bio/Johnston_ebenezer_forsyth_blackie_14E.html.

Canadian Criminal Law Digest, The. Toronto: Canada Law Book Company, 1920.

Charlesworth, Hector. *Candid Chronicles: Leaves from the Note Book of a Canadian Journalist.* Toronto: The Macmillan Company of Canada Ltd., 1925.

Charlesworth, Hector. Editor. *Cyclopædia of Canadian Biography, A.* Toronto: The Hunter-Rose Company, Limited, 1919.

Commemorative Biographical Record of the County of York, Ontario: Containing Biographical Sketches of Prominent and Representative Citizens and Many of the Early Settled Families. Toronto: J.H. Beers and Company, 1907.

Crankshaw, James. *The Criminal Code of Canada and the Canada Evidence Act, 1893.* Montreal: Whiteford and Theodoret, 1894.

Crankshaw, James. *The Criminal Code of Canada and the Canada Evidence Act.* 3rd ed. Toronto: The Carswell Company, Ltd., 1910.

"Crime in Insurance." *The Insurance Economist.* Vol. 18, No. 138. New York: April, 1895. Page 3.

Dedman, III, James M., and George R. Dekle Sr., *The Lindbergh Kidnapping Case: A Critical Analysis of the Trial of Bruno Richard Hauptmann.* Clark, NJ: Talbot Publishing, 2016.

Dekle Sr., George R. *The Last Murder: The Investigation, Prosecution, and Execution of Ted Bundy.* Santa Barbara, CA: Praeger, 2011.

Denison, George T. *Recollections of a Police Magistrate.* Toronto: The Musson Book Company Ltd. 1920.

Dictionary of Canadian Biography, http://www.biographi.ca/en/index.php.

Du Maurier, George. *Trilby.* 3 Vols. London: Osgood, McIlvaine and Company, 1894.

"Facts and Opinions." *The Weekly Underwriter.* Vol. 52, No. 7. Underwriter Printing and Publishing Company, February 15, 1895. Page 110.

"Facts and Opinions." *The Weekly Underwriter.* Vol. 54, No. 6. Underwriter Printing and Publishing Company, February 6, 1896. Page 84.

Guillet, Edwin C., *Insurance Murderers: A Study of the Evidence in The Queen versus Harry and Dallas Hyams for the Murder of William Chinook Wells 1892-1895.* Manuscript dated December 3, 1945. Clara Thomas Archives and Special Collections, York University, Call No. 1968-007/002(24)

Hassard, Albert R. "Great Canadian Orators: VII.—Britton Bath Osler." *The Canadian Magazine.* 54(4):353-360. Toronto: 1920.

Hassard, Albert R. *Famous Canadian Trials.* Toronto: The Carswell Company, 1924.

Hendershott, Len. *Beyond Doubt: The Murder of William Henry Hendershott.* 2nd ed. Research Triangle, NC: lulu.com, 2014.

"Hyams Case at Toronto, The." *The Insurance Times*. Vol. 28, No. 3. New York, Estate of Dr. P.T. Kemper, March, 1895, page 83.

"Hyams Twin Brothers, The." *The Insurance Economist*. Vol. 18, No. 139. New York: May, 1895. Page 11.

"Hyams Twins Acquitted, The." *The Insurance Economist*. Vol. 19, No. 146. New York: December, 1895. Page 11.

"Hyams Twins Released, The." *The Insurance Economist*. Vol. 19, No. 148. New York: February, 1896. Page 11.

"Insurance and Murder: Sequel to a Tragedy." *The Insurance Economist*. Vol. 18, No. 137. New York: March, 1895. Page 7, 8.

Johnson, J.K. *The Canadian Directory of Parliament, 1867-1967*. Ottawa: Public Archives of Canada, 1968.

Klinger, Leslie. Ed. *The New Annotated Sherlock Holmes*. 3 vols. New York: W.W. Norton and Company, 2005.

"Latest Sensation, The." *The Baltimore Underwriter*. Vol. 53, No. 4. Baltimore: Charles C. Bombaugh, Publisher, February 20, 1895. Page 85.

"Medical Evidence in the Hyams Trial." *The Canadian Practitioner: A Monthly Journal of Medicine and Surgery*. Vol. 20, No. 6. Pages 452-470. Toronto: The Bryant Press. June, 1895.

Morgan, Henry James. Editor. *Canadian Men and Women of the Time, The: A Hand-book of Canadian Biography*. Toronto: William Briggs, 1898.

"Mr. B.B. Osler, Q.C." *Canada Law Journal.* 35(9):289-291.

"Personal Sketch of the Late B. B. Osler, A." *The Canadian Law Review.* Vol. 1. Toronto: Canadian Law Review Company, 1901-1902. Pages 284, 285.

Report of the Superintendent of Insurance of the Dominion of Canada for the Year Ended 31st December 1895. Ottowa: S.E. Dawson, Printer to the Queen's Most Excellent Majesty, 1896, pages lii, liii.

Rhetorica ad Herennium, Harvard University Press: Cambridge MA, 1954.

Street, Justice William. *Bench Book*, Vols. 13, 14. Archives of Ontario. Reference Code RG 22-487-1-13-Container 2. Dates: May 9-25, 1895.

"They Rarely Succeed." *The Insurance Times*. Vol. 28, No. 3. New York, Estate of Dr. P.T. Kemper, March, 1895, page 77.

Toronto World, The, https://www.canadiana.ca/view/oocihm.N_00367

Tremeear, W.J. *The Criminal Code and the Law of Criminal Evidence in Canada.* 2nd ed. Toronto: Canada Law Book Company, 1908.

"Trial of the Hyams at Toronto." *The Insurance Economist.* Vol. 18, No. 140. New York: June, 1895. Page 8.

"Trial of the Hyams: Grand Jury Loses No Time in Returning Indictment." *The Insurance Economist*. Vol. 18, No. 139. New York: May, 1895. Page 13.

Wallace, W. Stewart. "The Hyams Twins Case." *Maclean's: Canada's National Magazine.* June 15, 1931. https://archive.macleans.ca/article/1931/6/15/the-hyams-twins-case.

Wellman, Francis L. *Gentlemen of the Jury: Reminiscences of Thirty Years at the Bar.* New York: The Macmillan Company, 1924.

Wellman, Francis L. *Luck and Opportunity: Recollections.* New York: The Macmillan Company, 1938.

Wellman, Francis L. *The Art of Cross-Examination.* 1st ed. New York: MacMillan and Company, 1904.

Wellman, Francis L. *The Art of Cross-Examination.* 4th ed. New York: Collier Books, 1970.

Wigmore, John Henry, *A Treatise on the Anglo-American System of Evidence in Trials at Common Law, Including the Statutes and Judicial Decisions of All Jurisdictions of the United States and Canada*, Vol 3. Boston: Little, Brown, and Company, 1923.

INDEX

www.ingramcontent.com/pod-product-compliance
Lightning Source LLC
Chambersburg PA
CBHW071029290526
45795CB00004B/1151